How to Build Max-Performance MOPAR BIG-BLOCKS

Andy Finkbeiner

CarTech®

CarTech®

CarTech®, Inc.
39966 Grand Avenue
North Branch, MN 55056
Phone: 651-277-1200 or 800-551-4754
Fax: 651-277-1203
www.cartechbooks.com

© 2009 by Andrew Finkbeiner

All rights reserved. No part of this publication may be reproduced or utilized in any form or by any means, electronic or mechanical, including photocopying, recording, or by any information storage and retrieval system, without prior permission from the Author. All text, photographs, and artwork are the property of the Author unless otherwise noted or credited.

The information in this work is true and complete to the best of our knowledge. However, all information is presented without any guarantee on the part of the Author or Publisher, who also disclaim any liability incurred in connection with the use of the information.

All trademarks, trade names, model names and numbers, and other product designations referred to herein are the property of their respective owners and are used solely for identification purposes. This work is a publication of CarTech, Inc., and has not been licensed, approved, sponsored, or endorsed by any other person or entity.

Edit by Paul Johnson
Layout by Tom Heffron

ISBN 978-1-61325-092-1
Item No. SA171P

Library of Congress Cataloging-in-Publication Data

Finkbeiner, Andrew.
  How to build max-performance Mopar big-blocks / by Andrew Finkbeiner.
    p. cm.
  Includes index.
  ISBN 978-1-934709-03-0
  1. Chrysler automobile—Performance. 2. Chrysler automobile—Motors—Modification. I. Title.

  TL215.C55F56 2009
  629.25—dc22

                    2009000790

Printed in USA

Back Cover Photos

Top Left:
The classic cross ram intake is common original equipment on many Max-Wedge engines. The long intake runners on the cross ram help improve airflow and throttle response.

Top Right:
This wedge 440 RB block is fitted with dry sump oil system for consistent high-volume oil delivery.

Middle Left:
This high-performance rotating assembly is destined for a low-deck 512 motor. It features a Callies crankshaft, big-block Chevy I-beam connecting rods, and custom-made Diamond Racing pistons with a large dish.

Middle Right:
The Victor heads require intake rocker arms with about 0.650 offset to clear the wide intake runners. The Harland Sharp rocker arms are mocked up on a Victor Max-Wedge head.

Bottom Left:
The solid roller cams is excellent choice for high-horsepower street engines and drag engines because it's important to match the compatible valvetrain components with the cam.

Bottom Right:
A belt-driven distributor is a perfect match for a crank trigger ignition because all the distributor needs to do is to pass the spark from the coil to the cylinders.

CONTENTS

Acknowledgments 5
About the Author 6
Preface 6
Introduction 7

Chapter 1: Planning the Engine Build 8
Budgeting Process 8
Power Goals 9
Formulas for Engine Design 9
Mopar-Specific Design Choices 10

Chapter 2: The Cylinder Block 13
Cylinder Block Selection 13
Thin Wall Controversy 14
Basic Block Dimensions 14
Fixes for the Factory Block 16
Aftermarket Blocks 17
Main Bearings 21
Cylinder Bore Preparation 22
Decking 22
Block Detailing 23
Valve Notches 24

Chapter 3: The Oil System 25
Oil Pump 25
Internal Oiling System 26
External Oiling System 27
Pump Cover 29
The Intermediate Shaft 30
Oil Pan 30
Oil Type and Operation Temperature 32
Oil Filter and Cooler .33
Dry Sump System 34
Top-End vs. Bottom-End Oiling 35
Extra Lubrication Requirements 36

Chapter 4: Crankshafts 37
Crankshaft Selection .37
The Funny Car Crankshaft 40
Crankshaft Preparation 40
Balancing 41
Harmonic Damper 42

Chapter 5: Connecting Rods 44
Connecting Rod Selection 44
Aluminum Rods 45
Connecting Rod Preparation 45
Rotating Assembly Balancing 46

Chapter 6: Pistons .47
Compression Ratio Considerations 48
Valve-to-Piston Clearance 48
Combustion Chamber Clearance 50
Piston-to-Head Clearance 50
Piston Rings 51
Gas Ports 51
Piston Pin Diameter .52
Vacuum Pump Considerations 52

Chapter 7: Cylinder Heads and Valves 53
Standard Port Cylinder Head 53
Max-Wedge-Port-Size Heads 56
Bigger Than Max-Wedge 60
Head Gaskets 61
Head Flow and Cam Lift 62
Valves 65
Porting 67

Chapter 8: The Valvetrain 69
Rocker Arm Geometry 70
Rocker Arm Ratio 72
Rocker Arm Material .74
Rocker Arm Types 76
Rocker Shafts and Supports 77
Rocker Arm Width and Length 78
Side Clearance and Alignment 80
Multiple Shaft Systems 81
Pushrods 81

Chapter 9: Camshafts and Lifters 83
Duration 83
Single Pattern vs. Dual Pattern 84
Lifters 85
Roller Lifters and Valvetrain Oiling 88
Rev Kits 89
Lifter Bore Bushings .90
Camshaft Bearings 90
Large-Diameter Cam Bearings 91
Roller Cam Bearings .91
Firing Order 92

CONTENTS

**Chapter 10: Camshaft Drives
and Valvesprings** 93
   Timing Chains 93
   Roller Cam Thrust .93
   Timing-Chain Covers 94
   Belt Drive 95
   Gear Drive 96
   Valvesprings 96

Chapter 11: Intake Manifolds 99
   Standard Port Intakes, B and RB 99
   Max-Wedge Port Intakes, B and RB 103
   B1 Intake Options 107
   EFI 108

Chapter 12: Carburetors 110
   Classic 4150 Double Pumper 110
   The 4500 Dominator 111
   Tuner-Friendly Carburetors 112
   Edelbrock and Carter Carburetors 113
   Carburetor Spacers 115

Chapter 13: Ignition Systems 117
   Electronic Ignitions 117
   Distributor 118
   Belt-Driven Distributor 120
   Crank Trigger 121
   Spark Plugs 122
   Indexing the Spark Plugs 122
   Spark Plug Wires .123

Chapter 14: Accessories 124
   Water Pumps, Electric and Belt-Driven 124
   Alternator Kits 125
   Engine Mounting Systems, Motor Plates
      and Elephant Ears 125
   High-Performance Hoses and Fittings 126

Chapter 15: Exhaust Systems 128
   Cast Manifolds 129
   Headers 129
   Picking a Header Size 130
   Relocated Exhaust Ports 130
   Merged Collectors and 4-2-1 Headers 131
   Stepped Tubes 131

Chapter 16: Tuning 132
   Reading the Plugs 132
   Wide Band 132
   Dynamometer Testing 133
   Chassis Dyno Testing 135

**Chapter 17: The Fantastic 451 and
Other Engine Combinations** 136
   Fantastic 451/470 136
   Two Ways to 512 137
   Big Bad 572 137

Chapter 18: Recipes for Power 138
   600 HP 138
   700 HP 138
   800 HP 139
   900 HP 139

Engine Build Sheets 140

Source Guide 143

ACKNOWLEDGMENTS

This book is built on the backs of other books. I remember staying up late at night as a teenager, poring over *Mopar Performance* by Larry Schrieb and Larry Atherton. *Mopar Performance* hasn't been available for a few years but if you ever find a copy, by all means buy it and read it. After 30 years, that book is still a high-water point for Mopar performance information. I can also recall spending hours enthralled by *The Chevrolet Racing Engine* by Bill "Grumpy" Jenkins and Larry Schrieb. I'm not sure how anyone ever persuaded Grumpy to spend the time during his busy Pro Stock days to author a book, but that book is a masterpiece. I have no illusions of being in the same company as these gentlemen. But I do owe them a debt because I would not have become interested in these subjects to the extent that I did without the time they took to sit down and share their knowledge.

I need to thank several magazine editors who took a chance on me and provided guidance and opportunities for me over the years. Scott Parkhurst, formerly of *Popular Hot Rodding*, was the first to give me a shot at a magazine article. He took a long letter to the editor and asked me to re-write it into an article. From there I was fortunate to work with Rick Ehrenberg at *Mopar Action*, Randy Bolig at *Mopar Muscle*, and Johnny Hunkins at *Popular Hot Rodding*. These editors in turn introduced me to a number of contacts within the performance parts business, who further helped me by providing parts and information. Without this support and guidance, I would not have been able to pull together material of much worth.

I also owe a large debt to the current community of Mopar engine builders and enthusiasts. I've met many people over the last 10 years, while writing magazine articles and selling parts, and I am constantly learning new things from each engine builder I meet. One advantage that I have these days over what Larry and Grumpy had is access to the Internet. Thirty years ago those authors were limited to a much smaller circle of fellow engine builders with whom to share information. I was fortunate to be able to access hundreds of other Mopar enthusiasts at any time of the day or night on Web sites such as Moparts.com and BigBlockDart.com. I also learned a great from the fellow engine builders at the popular technical site of SpeedTalk.com. And of course, now that so many vendors have complete catalogs on the Internet, it is easier than ever to surf for parts and information directly from the manufacturers.

I also need to acknowledge the tremendous amount of help that this project received from those listed in the source guide. People from those companies were willing to answer questions, provide parts for testing, send pictures, and provide information. Without their help I would not have been able to cover this subject matter in nearly as much detail.

And of course, I could not have ever finished a major task like this without the support of my wife, Tami, and our two children, Joshua and Ally. A book requires a lot of time so I missed a few chores, baseball games, and soccer matches while I was busy writing.

ABOUT THE AUTHOR

Andy Finkbeiner bought his first Mopar, a 1965 Dodge Coronet, when he was in college. The original 426 wedge motor in that car became the subject of many big-block projects over the years. Currently Andy has a 512-inch stroker motor in the Coronet, along with a Doug Nash 5-speed transmission and a Dana 60 rear end.

Andy has a BSME from the University of Idaho, an MBA from the University of Portland, and a JD from Northwestern School of Law. He lives with his wife and two children in the Pacific Northwest. He owns AR Engineering, which is a company devoted to designing and manufacturing parts for muscle-car-era Mopars.

PREFACE

There is a lot of information to cover on the performance aspect of Mopar engines. So when writing this book, he decided to leave out some of the more general information. This book is written with the assumption that the reader has a decent understanding of basic engine terms—not necessarily a beginner, but less experienced than the experts. If not, there are some excellent engine rebuilding books on the market that can help illustrate the terms used in this book. For the new engine builder, a book such as *How to Rebuild Any Automotive Engine* by Barry Kluczyk would be a good place to start. A more advanced book for an engine builder interested in racing engines would be *Engine Blueprinting: Practical Methods for Racing and Rebuilding* by Rick Voegelin.

This book was written 30 years after Chrysler installed the last big-block into production vehicles. A lot has changed over 30 years and a lot more will change over the next 30 years. This book is a product of the time in which it was written, 2008–2009, and the industry will continue to evolve after this book is published. In a few years, some of the parts discussed in this book will be obsolete and will be replaced with newer and better parts. Hopefully, the core knowledge conveyed in the book will remain relevant for a long time because the basic concept of understanding an engine as a system should never become obsolete. But individual parts do become obsolete and vendors come and go, so don't limit yourself to parts mentioned in the book if newer or better ones have become available.

INTRODUCTION

The Mopar big-block engine has performance roots that stretch back to the Golden Lion engine used in the Chrysler letter cars during the late 1950s. A few years later, the legendary Max-Wedge motors roared down Woodward and solidified the growing reputation of the big Mopar wedge motor. During the muscle-car era there was a steady stream of ground-pounding Mopars that came out of Detroit powered by 440+6 motors, 440-hp motors and high-winding 383-hp motors. Many times these high-powered muscle cars were run down by equally high-powered Dodge and Plymouth police cars packing Mopar big-block power under the hood. As the saying goes, all good things must end, and this era came to an end in 1978 when the last of the Mopar big-blocks rolled down the production line.

However, the big-block didn't die out after being discontinued. Instead, it remained a favorite on the drag strip and with street cruiser builders. The Mopar big-block started to become even more popular during the 1980s and by the time the 1990s came around, the engine had become more popular than ever.

One spark that really ignited this explosion of interest was provided by the aging baby boomers who grew up with the muscle cars during the 1960s. As these baby boomers hit midlife they started to spend some of their accumulated wealth on restoring and racing the cars of their youth. The aftermarket responded to these demands for parts with an enthusiasm that was unknown during earlier years. Today—30 years after Chrysler stopped building the big-block—it is easier than ever to build a maximum-performance Mopar engine. Not only is it easier to build a big-block, but it is also quite easy to build one that makes twice as much power as the best ones that ever came down the assembly line in Detroit.

The title of this book refers to "max-performance Mopar big-block engines," so I need to define what that phrase means. My goal in this book is to focus on normally aspirated Mopar big-blocks that are capable of producing between 600 and 900 hp. Engines making less than 600 hp would be considered moderate- to high-performance rather than maximum performance, and that subject is best covered in a rebuild-type book. An excellent book that covers building milder-performance Mopar engines is *How to Build High Performance Chrysler Engines* by Frank Adkins.

On the other end of the scale, maximum output these days for a Mopar big-block wedge motor without power adders is around 1,300 or 1,400 hp. An engine capable of producing 1,400 hp could cost upwards of $100,000 to build and is very expensive to maintain. Super-high-output engines tend to require routine replacement of the valvesprings, rocker arms, and connecting rods. The resources in this book do not fully explore the construction of 1,000+ hp engines, so we will be focusing on the more-affordable engines in the 600- to 900-hp range.

Before we tear into the specifics of the big-block Mopar, we need to spend a moment clarifying exactly what your goals are and what your budget will support. One of the common errors that beginning engine builders make is to mismatch components. If you are a less-experienced builder, you might be vulnerable to fancy advertising and could purchase parts that you do not need. Other times, beginning builders try to save money by purchasing parts that are inexpensive, and find out later that the parts are too cheaply built for the application. Correctly matched components will provide the most power for the money spent. But you, along with every engine builder, need to have an overall plan in order to do this. So our first topic will be planning; and when we have an overall strategy, we will then move into the selection and evaluation of currently available parts.

CHAPTER 1

PLANNING THE ENGINE BUILD

The first item on the build plan for you, and all builders, to resolve is the available overall budget. A 600-hp big-block Mopar can be built for as little as $5,000 by using used parts and cutting corners, while a higher-end 900-hp engine can easily cost more than $20,000.

Budgeting Process

It is a good idea to create a list of currently available parts at the beginning of the project. Very few projects start with a clean sheet of paper because builders often start with an existing motor that they wish to upgrade for additional power. By starting with a list of parts on hand, you can start to develop a plan of action that is based in reality. Remember, though: you don't have to use all the parts just because you have them on hand. If your list included a 383-ci block, a set of B1 heads, and a Quadrajet carb, then you might be able to build a project around one or the other but probably not around the combination of

This parts list is from a motor designed for a customer in 2008. This motor made right at 750 hp when dyno tested.

Parts List for 750 HP Big-Block

Component	Description	Cost
Pistons	Diamond, 4.350 bore, 5 cc dome, 13.5 compression	$681.00
Crank	440Source, 4.250 stroke with 2.200 rod journals	$595.00
Rods	Scat, 454-6800-2200, H-beam, 6.800 long BB Chevy rods	$495.00
Camshaft	Comp Cams Street Roller XR292R	$299.00
Main bearings	MS1277HG H bearings, full groove	$105.00
Rod bearings	BB Chevy connecting rod bearings	$110.00
Cam bearings	SH-876S Mopar replacement bearings	$20.00
Rings	4.355 bore, file fit, 1/16, 1/6, 3/16	$125.00
Timing chain	Cloyes Hex-a-just 3125	$144.00
Timing chain cover	Mancini Racing MRE 9916	$325.00
Rear main seal kit	Mancini Racing MRE 223	$70.00
Small parts kit	Mopar Performance P5249259 kit	$95.00
Damper	ATI 917122E	$349.00
Main studs	ARP	$55.00
Custom valley plate	AR Engineering	$235.00
Heads	Indy EZ heads, CNC ported, Max-Wedge port size	$2,795.00
Head gasket	Cometic C5462-040	$159.00
Oil pan	Milodon Super Stock style, 31470	$365.00
Oil pump	Milodon Dual line system, 21190 remote filter, pump	$555.00
Oil pump driveshaft	Milodon intermediate length 21503	$89.00
Intake manifold	Edelbrock Super Victor	$360.00
Carb	Holley Dominator UltraHP 80672	$1,050.00
Ignition wires	MSD-31459	$70.00
Spark plugs	Champion C59CX	$28.00
Rocker arms	Hughes 1510S-16 rocker arm kit with 1.50 ratio	$460.00
Lifters	Comp Cams 829-16 roller lifters	$430.00
Valvesprings	Comp Cams, 26094 dual springs	$302.00
Retainers	Comp Cams, Ti, 732-16	$373.00
Valve locks	Comp Cams, 10 degree, 613-16	$25.00
Valve covers	Indy cast aluminum plain covers	$155.00
Block	440 core from pickup truck	$300.00
Machine work	Deck, bore, balance, file fit rings, fit bearings and pins, etc	$969.00
Head bolts	ARP	$65.00
Distributor	MSD 8546	$279.00
Pushrods	Smith Bros, 3/8 diameter with 0.080 wall thickness	$182.00
Water pump	Meziere electric pump WP106	$380.00
Total		$13,094.00

all those particular parts. The parts on the list that are not going to be used in the project can always be sold or traded for other parts. The key is to have a plan, know what you have on hand, and what you need. You can then be prepared when a good deal comes along.

Power Goals

After the budget has been selected and the existing part inventory list is created, the next step is to determine the total power desired and the RPM range where the engine needs to make peak power. You also need to decide what type of power curve the engine should have because you can then select components that will provide either a broad flat torque curve or a narrower, "peaky" torque curve.

For any motor that is going to see significant street use, you, as engine designer, should pay attention to the torque curve as low as 2,000 rpm because the typical street-driven engine spends a lot of time down there. For a drag race engine, you need to consider the finish line RPM based on the gear ratio and tire size, as well as the weight of the car, the type of transmission, and the desired elapsed time. A 500-ci big-block drag race engine in a lightweight vehicle with 4.88 rear end gears requires a different combination of parts than a 500-ci big-block used in a C-body street cruiser with 3.23:1 rear end gears.

After listing your existing parts and the power requirements, you can start to list the additional parts required to meet the desired power output. Using a spreadsheet, such as Excel, makes it very easy to add up the total cost of the parts and machine work. If the total cost of the parts exceeds the budget, then you need to either find some more money or scale back on the performance goals. After you settle on the desired performance output of the engine and the operating budget, the design can proceed.

A larger-displacement engine typically produces horsepower at a lower RPM than a smaller engine. Hence, a larger-displacement engine allows builders to achieve a specific power output goal, and do it more affordably. These tradeoffs are not all easy to make because the cost to build a large engine goes up significantly as the size gets bigger than is supported by common parts. Hopefully, this book will help you make the correct tradeoffs necessary for building a higher-powered big-block that doesn't break the bank.

Formulas for Engine Design

Engine displacement has a large impact on the amount of torque that is produced, while the size of the intake runner in the induction system determines the torque peak. Increasing the displacement without

Average Piston Speed in Ft/Min

RPM	Stroke (inches)						
	3.380	3.750	3.900	4.150	4.250	4.375	4.500
9000	5070	5625	5850	6225	6375	6563	6750
8500	4788	5313	5525	5879	6021	6198	6375
8000	4507	5000	5200	5533	5667	5833	6000
7500	4225	4688	4875	5188	5313	5469	5625
7000	3943	4375	4550	4842	4958	5104	5250
6500	3662	4063	4225	4496	4604	4740	4875

Up to 5000 ft/min is possible with good quality aftermarket parts
5000 ft/min or greater piston speed requires high quality parts
6000 ft/min and above requires Pro Stock quality parts

Longer strokes mean higher piston speeds, which in turn will require higher-quality engine parts.

Torque Peak Based on McFarland Formula

Displacement Cubic Inches	Std Port 2.88 sq inches	MW Port 3.65 sq inches	B1 Head 4.50 sq inches
	RPM	RPM	RPM
375	5419	6868	8467
400	5080	6439	7938
425	4781	6060	7471
450	4516	5723	7056
475	4278	5422	6685
500	4064	5151	6350
525	3871	4906	6048
550	3695	4683	5773
575	3534	4479	5522
600	3387	4292	5292

The cross section area of the cylinder head is a primary factor in determining the RPM where peak torque occurs.

changing the cylinder heads will typically raise the torque output of the motor but will not significantly increase the power output because the torque peak will be at a lower RPM. When more torque is produced at lower RPM, the total power output remains roughly constant. The opposite result is when cylinder heads with large ports are used on a smaller-displacement short-block. The resulting combination will not produce very high torque levels at lower speeds, but the motor will produce high horsepower at very high engine speeds. There are several key formulas that are good guides to the builder. The first is the relationship between torque, RPM, and horsepower. It is important to remember that:

Rotating Horsepower =
Torque x RPM / 5252

So the more torque your engine can carry up the RPM range, the more horsepower you'll have.

People sometimes bench race about the question of whether torque or horsepower is more important. But as the above formula shows, the question really doesn't make much sense. Any running engine is going to be producing power because it is producing rotating torque. The important questions when designing an engine are: how much torque will the engine produce, and where will the torque peak be?

A Mopar big-block engine that produces 500 ft-lbs of torque at 3,500 rpm makes a powerful street engine. The 500 ft-lbs at 3,500 rpm equates to 333 hp, which doesn't sound impressive, but this type of engine would provide very capable performance in the typical B- or E-body car. If that same big-block was designed to produce the same 500 ft-lbs of torque at 8,000 rpm, you would have a very-high-performance engine that was producing 762 hp. This type of engine would be typically found in a drag racing or circle track racing car rather than a passenger car. In either case, the same 500 ft-lbs of torque were produced; the only difference is the RPM where the torque peak occurred.

Another very important formula is the relationship between cylinder head cross-section area (CSA), RPM, and torque peak. The classic formula is:

RPM =
CSA x 88200 / Cylinder Volume

This formula is sometimes referred to as the McFarland formula after Jim McFarland, who was head of R&D at Edelbrock for many years. Jim used this formula in writings that include the classic article, "The Manifold Parts of Automotive Induction Systems." In that article, Jim traces the formula to work done in the past. He determined that peak torque occurs when the intake velocity is about 250 feet/sec. There may be cases in which this general rule doesn't apply, but it has proven to be fairly accurate at predicting the torque peak of an engine. Given these qualifications, one can say that the relationship of the cylinder head cross section to the displacement of the engine has a lot to do with predicting torque peak. Again, the higher the torque peak occurs in the RPM range, the more horsepower will be generated for the same amount of torque.

Mismatching components can reduce the actual max-torque RPM, but it is difficult to shift it up much from what the formula predicts. This is because the cross section of the induction system acts as a restriction, which cannot be exceeded, but additional restrictions can be placed elsewhere in the system to reduce the power of the engine.

We will use the McFarland formula throughout this book because it is a key to selecting the right parts during the engine-design phase of the project. And selecting the correct parts is 90 percent of the game when building performance engines.

A third formula can also help you predict the torque output of your motor before any components are purchased. This formula calculates peak torque as a function of BMEP (brake mean effective pressure) and displacement:

BMEP x CID / 150.8 = Peak Torque

The trick here is to predict what the BMEP will be for a particular engine design. Pro Stock engines have a BMEP near 225, while high-performance engines are in the range of 160. A well-designed performance engine with properly matched components should be able to achieve a BMEP of 190. That would equate to a peak torque of 630 ft-lbs for our assumed 500-ci big-block. Notice that this torque level does not depend on the CSA of the cylinder head, so either the standard port or the Max-Wedge head could produce this amount. The size of the cylinder head port controls the RPM where the torque peak will occur. So the cylinder head with the larger port size produces much more horsepower because the same torque output will occur at a higher RPM point.

Mopar-Specific Design Choices

It is one thing to design an engine on a spreadsheet; it is another

PLANNING THE ENGINE BUILD

to actually find fitting parts that are available at a reasonable cost. While there are a lot of individual parts available to build a big-block Mopar, most parts will not actually change the size or shape of the torque curve. The brand or design of the connecting rods, pistons, crankshafts, oil pump, etc., won't really make a substantial difference. However, both the size of the short-block and the cross-section area of the cylinder heads have a huge impact on the torque curve. Since most builders need to pick components that are affordable, the range of choices narrows down to just a few combinations that make sense.

The 500-inch Sweet Spot

Running a smaller displacement motor at higher speed effectively makes horsepower, but a larger engine operating at lower speed can achieve the same power levels with less expense. Because any performance engine is going to require an aftermarket rotating assembly, there is no significant cost difference between building a 440-ci motor and building a 500-ci motor. The 500-ci-engine size can be achieved in either the low-deck 400-ci block or the taller 440 block with parts that are currently quite affordable. The combination of popular bore sizes and popular crankshaft strokes leads to several short-block cubic-inch arrangements, such as the 496, 505, 512, etc. For the sake of simplicity, we'll refer to all of these combinations as a generic 500-ci short-block. While it is also possible to build combinations that are larger than 500 ci, the costs begin to increase and the torque peak location is pushed lower in the RPM range. Before deciding to build an engine that is larger than 500 ci, you should carefully study the charts to see where the torque peak will occur and what the piston speed will be. Remember, higher piston speeds require higher-quality, higher-cost short-block parts.

If an aftermarket block is in the budget, then the combination of a larger bore size and a shorter stroke can really pay big dividends. The

Common Big-Block Combinations

Bore Size (inches)	Stroke (inches)						
	3.380	3.750	3.900	4.150	4.250	4.375	4.500
4.250	384	426	443	471	482	497	511
4.320	396	440	457	487	498	513	528
4.350	402	446	464	493	505	520	535
4.375	406	451	469	499	511	526	541
4.390	409	454	472	503	515	530	545
4.440	419	464	483	514	526	542	557
4.500	430	477	496	528	541	557	573

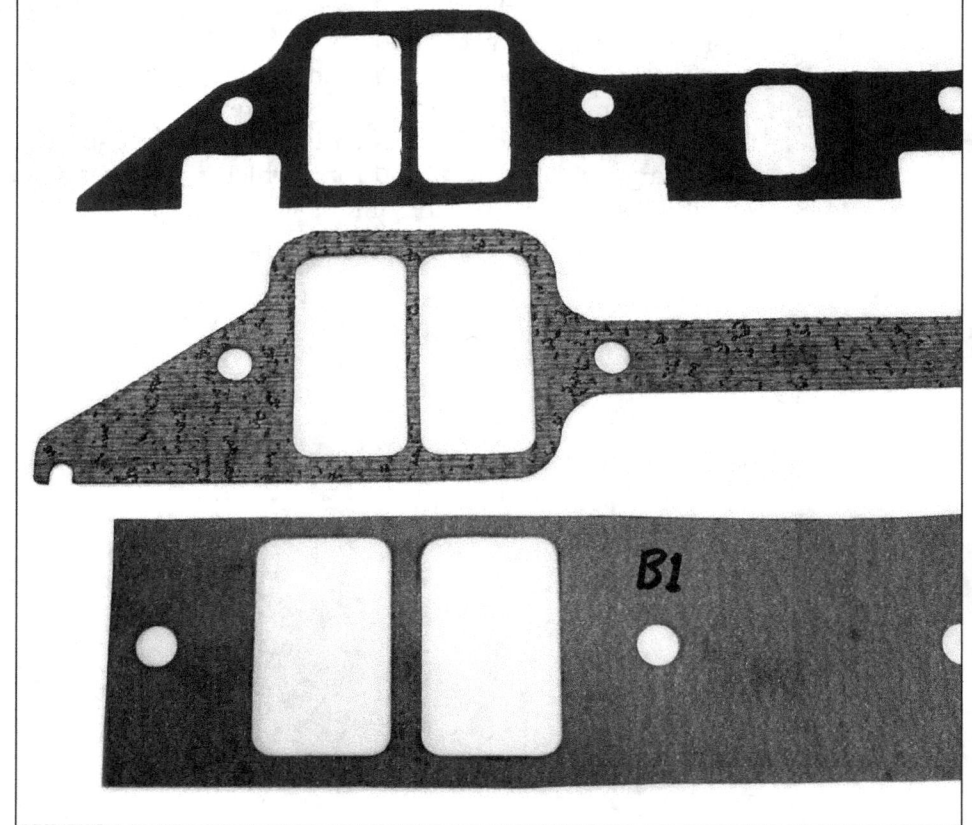

The cross-section area of the intake runners has a direct effect on where in the RPM range the engine will make peak power. For the big-block Mopar engine, there are three common intake runner sizes: the standard-production port size shown at the top, the Max-Wedge size in the middle, and the B1 on the bottom.

HOW TO BUILD MAX-PERFORMANCE MOPAR BIG-BLOCKS 11

larger bore size improves the breathing ability of the engine, while the shorter stroke will reduce the stress on the rotating assembly. For example, a 496-ci engine constructed from a 4.50-bore block and a 3.90-stroke crankshaft will offer significant performance improvement over an engine of similar size built with a 4.250 bore and 4.375 stroke.

Cross-Section Choices

In the Mopar world, there really are only two common choices for the cross-section size of the induction system: 2.88 square inches for the standard port, and 3.65 square inches for the Max-Wedge (MW) port. There are literally dozens of different intake manifolds and cylinder heads to pick from, but only two categories of parts that are available for a big-block-type engine design on a reasonable budget. A couple of other choices are available for the induction system if you choose something larger than the Max-Wedge-port size, and we'll discuss them later in the book. For now, we'll stick to just the standard port and the MW port.

Engine Design with Standard Ports

For a 500-ci short-block, the McFarland formula yields a predicted torque peak of 4,100 rpm for a standard port head. The actual point where peak horsepower is produced depends on how slowly the torque curve drops off. Generally speaking, though, you can expect to see the power curve peak at about 1,500 rpm after the torque peak occurs. A 500-inch big-block with standard port heads will usually torque peak near 4,100 rpm and horsepower peak near 5,600 rpm.

With properly ported cylinder heads and a correctly matched roller cam, the power peak of a 500-inch big-block with standard port-sized heads can be pushed up to the 6,000-rpm range. Also, a 500-ci short-block with properly ported standard heads can produce in the range of 600 ft-lbs of torque and 600 hp. An extremely well-designed combination could produce nearly 700 hp from these parts, but much more horsepower than that might bust the budget.

Engine Design with Max-Wedge Ports

If we use 3.65 square inches as the CSA of a Max-Wedge head, the torque peak for a 500-ci short-block will be at roughly 5,200 rpm, and peak horsepower will be in the 6,500- to 6,800-rpm range. A variety of cost-effective intake manifolds and cylinder heads is available in the Max-Wedge port size, and these parts will readily support the production of 750 to 800 hp when used on a 500-ci short-block. If the budget will support higher engine speeds and excellent port work, then the Max-Wedge-based engine can be pushed up past the 900-hp mark.

One can see that even with the larger Max-Wedge heads, a 500-ci Mopar big-block rarely needs to redline above 7,500 rpm. A drag race car will typically be shifted a few hundred RPM past the power peak, which makes it rare for that type of engine Max-Wedge to be spun much past 7,000 rpm. A 500-inch short-block that is constructed with a large-bore and short-stroke combination will have fairly low pistion speeds at 7,000 rpm, which should result in a long life span for the motor.

CHAPTER 2

THE CYLINDER BLOCK

The original big-block engine design dates back 50 years to the 1958 B block, which was available in either a 350- or a 361-ci displacement. The B engine was enlarged to 383 inches in 1960 and then finally expanded to 400 inches in 1972. While the older engines might have been fine performers in their day, the 400 is the only B engine that merits use as the foundation for a performance engine. Some will argue that the 383 B block could be considered a candidate, but you'd typically be better off finding a large-bore 400-ci block, rather than using a 383 block. The 400 block has a heavy-duty main web design, while the 383 has a small bore size and weaker main webs.

Cylinder Block Selection

The RB family consists of three modern blocks: the 413, 426, and 440. While the 413 and 426 engines both have impeccable performance histories dating back to the Max-Wedge motors in the early 1960s, neither of those blocks is now considered very suitable for a performance build. The smaller bore size used in the 413 and 426 blocks will reduce cylinder head flow and total displacement without providing any corresponding benefit. Most aftermarket parts such as cylinder heads, head gaskets, pistons, and piston rings are designed for the larger

Core engines are a little harder to find these days. Everything except the engine block will usually be thrown out, so don't worry if some exterior parts are missing.

When tearing apart a core engine, it pays to look closely for clues about its failure or its service life. Here we can see bearing material in the valley of the engine, which is a sure sign that the bottom end of the motor is heavily damaged. The block might not be useable if the damage to the bottom end is too severe.

440-bore size, so using a 413 or 426 block just starts your project off in the wrong direction. The 440 block makes an excellent starting point for a performance engine in the 600-hp range. But if you are going to push it much past that, then I highly recommend an aftermarket block. The bottom end of the 440 block wasn't designed to withstand the performance levels that modern cylinder heads can produce.

One of the ironies of Mopar engine building is that the very best production block comes from the 400 family. The 400 engine was widely considered to be a "smog" motor with no high-performance potential back in the 1970s, but for some reason the factory engineers designed that cylinder block with extra beef around the main caps. Koffel's Place, one of the premier Mopar engine builders during the last 20 years, developed their line of B1 head products with the 400 block in mind because it was the only production block that could handle the high power output of their heads. Koffel's Place used production 400 blocks to build many performance engines in the days before aftermarket blocks became available. The 400 block is still a suitable choice these days if the budget can't handle the price tag of an aftermarket block.

Thin Wall Controversy

Over the years, numerous Mopar Performance publications warned engine builders to not bore the post-1976 blocks more than .030-inch overbore because these blocks were "thin wall castings." However, as sonic testing has proven, we know that this information is more false than true. We do not know exactly what the Mopar Performance writers were trying to convey with their

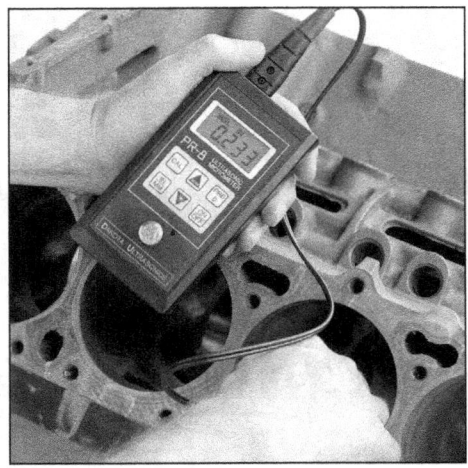

Sonic checking is the only way to tell if the cylinder walls are thick enough to handle the power output of a max-performance build. Only about one out of four production blocks are good enough to use as a foundation for a performance engine, so be prepared to sort through several blocks before you find a good one.

warning, but the late-model blocks are anything but thin. In fact, the later blocks tend to have thicker cylinder walls than the castings made in the 1960s.

What does seem to be true is that the quality control of the block castings decreased during the 1970s, and therefore these blocks are more prone to core shift than early blocks. It is possible that the Mopar Performance authors knew the quality control had decreased but were unable to publish that information. They might have used the thin wall story as a way to warn racers about the later blocks. Regardless, today we know that the blocks cast after 1976 are just as thick if not thicker than blocks cast before that date.

What did seem to change during the late 1970s was the cast-iron material. The block material used after 1976 is softer when tested with a hardness tester. I have no explanation for this change in hardness because factory sources have told us that the block material did not change during production. Some of these mysteries will likely never be solved, seeing how the original engine design is now more than 50 years old and most of the original engineers have passed on.

Basic Block Dimensions

Deck Height

The primary difference between the B and RB motors is the height of the block when measured between the center of the crankshaft and the top of the cylinder deck. This measurement, called the deck height, is 9.980 inches on the B motor and 10.725 on the RB motor. By comparison, the special tall Chevy truck block has a deck height of 10.200 inches while the standard big-block Chevy motor has a deck height of only 9.800 inches. This means that the RB motor is more than .500-inch taller than the special, tall truck Chevy motor and is almost 1-inch taller than the passenger car 454-ci block. The extra height in the RB block makes it very easy to add displacement because there is plenty of room for longer connecting rods and a longer crankshaft stroke.

Bore Centers

The center-to-center distance between cylinders on the production big-block Mopar is 4.80 inches. This bore-to-bore distance is commonly called the bore center dimension, and it is critical for determining how large the cylinder bores can be. The big-block Chevy engine has 4.840 bore centers, which is one reason why larger bore sizes are available in the Chevy motors. The muscle-car-era engine with the largest bore center dimension was the Ford 429/460 at 4.900. In the quest for more

THE CYLINDER BLOCK

The 400 block is a low-deck design, so the ID pad is located on the passenger's deck surface beneath the distributor. The only number that matters for a performance buildup is the displacement, because any production block can have cylinder walls thick enough to handle max-performance power.

The 440 block is a raised-block design, so the ID pad is located to the right of the distributor from front view. The engine builder has stamped 505 hp in this block. A production block would have a 440 stamp here as well as a letter or number for the model year.

This 400 block has been modified with aftermarket main caps that are cross bolted to the side of the block. This used to be a good option, but aftermarket blocks with this kind of bearing support are readily available so this type of extensive machine work is now unnecessary.

A bare cast-iron block will weigh about 225 lbs for a production block and up to 300 lbs for an aftermarket block. RB blocks do not always weigh more than B blocks.

displacement, several aftermarket vendors have started to produce engine blocks with wider bore centers. In fact, Mopar Performance sells a Pro Stock Hemi block with 4.900 bore centers in order to provide as much room as possible for large-diameter pistons. Of course, when using a block with wider-than-stock bore centers, nearly everything else in the motor also has to be lengthened, so this would be extremely expensive to build.

The maximum that the cylinders in a production big-block Mopar can be bored would be in the range of 4.400 inches, but only if a person was able to find a 440 or a 400 block with consistently thick cylinder walls. The World Products block, as well as some of the other aftermarket blocks, have "siamesed" cylinder walls that are capable of being bored out to the 4.600-bore-size range. The availability of larger-bore-size piston rings has started to improve recently as these engines have increased in popularity. JE, as well as other vendors, now have many piston ring choices available for the 4.500-, 4.530-, and 4.560-bore sizes. There is also a very large selection of piston rings available for the 4.600-bore size, although it might be difficult to find a head gasket that will live on a big-block Mopar with so little space between the cylinders.

Main Bearing Size

The production B block uses the smaller main bearing size of 2.625 inches while the RB uses a larger-size 2.750-inch-diameter main bearing. There are plenty of aftermarket crankshafts available for each main size and the smaller main size should not be a problem for a lower powered engine. You might want to think seriously before using a long-stroke crankshaft, such as the 4.250 in a B block, with the smaller 2.625-diameter main bearings though. The long stroke combined with the smaller main journals doesn't leave much overlap material available, reducing the strength of the crankshaft.

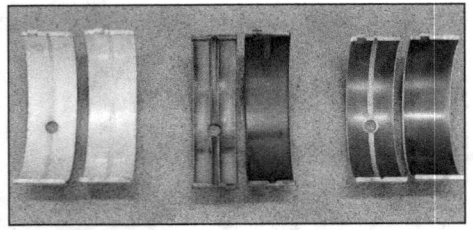

These bearings fit the larger 2.750-diameter mains in an RB block. From left to right are examples of full groove, three-quarter groove, and half groove.

Boring out a low-deck block to use the larger RB main bearings is an option that some builders recommend. The 2.750-inch main bearing size is much more popular with the bearing manufacturers, so there are many more bearings available and the crankshaft will be stronger with the larger-diameter main journals. Boring out the main bores in a production block from 2.625 to 2.750 is not an easy job. The boring bar must be very accurately located on the block to remove a lot of material. Also, the number-3 main cap needs to be remachined for the larger thrust bearing, which requires a special machining setup that most small machine shops will not have. Some of the aftermarket low-deck blocks can be ordered with the larger 2.750 main bearing size, and that is probably the best way to go for a higher-powered motor. For a B motor that will be making less than 600 hp, there is no reason to bore the mains out to the larger 2.750-diameter size. But if a B motor is going to produce more than 800 hp, then it is an item to discuss with your machine shop.

Fixes for the Factory Block

The weakest point on any of the production cylinder blocks appears to be the main web area. While some blocks might develop cracks in other

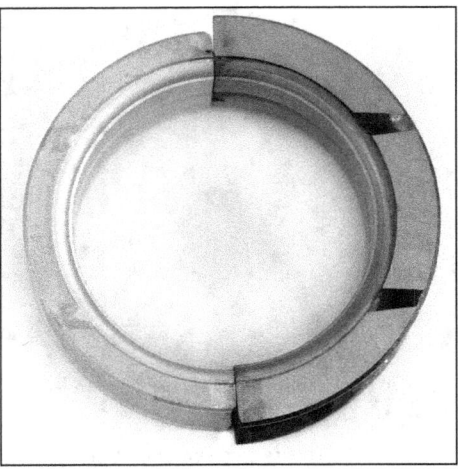

The later-model blocks use a larger diameter thrust surface on the number-3 main bearing. The bearing will not physically fit into the earlier blocks, so you need to know the year of your block before ordering the main bearings.

areas, the most typical failure for high-power motors is either broken main caps or cracked main webs. The very best of the production blocks are the thick web 400 blocks that were cast during the summer of 1971. These blocks are capable of handling about 800 hp before the main caps or main webs begin to fail.

For years, clever engine builders have developed "crutches" to beef-up the production blocks. These crutches include girdles, aluminum main caps, use of concrete or hard block, and cross-bolt conversions. One of the more popular fixes is the installation of aluminum main caps; the aluminum cap dampens some of the shock of the combustion process and protects the engine block from the stress. Detractors from the aluminum main cap modification point out that aluminum expands at a higher rate than cast iron and the main bore will be distorted at operating temperature. In any case, there are several premier Mopar builders who swear by the aluminum main cap modification for engines in the 800-hp range.

Another popular modification to the stock production block is to install aftermarket steel main caps in either the stock two-bolt style or to go ahead and install a complete four-bolt cross-bolted main cap. The two-bolt style is quite easy to install with just a standard align bore and hone performed on standard machine shop equipment. The cross-bolted conversion is significantly more difficult to install because the block must be precisely machined along the pan rail for the cross bolts. Everything needs to fit together properly or else, when all of the bolts are torqued into place, the main caps will shift and destroy the main bearings. A conversion of a standard wedge block to the cross-bolted mains seems to be more work than it is worth because of the considerable machining time required and the limited strength that is gained, but it does make sense in high-horsepower low-deck engines.

There are now several different girdle systems on the market for the Mopar big-block. The big-block casting is a Y-block design with material hanging down past the crankshaft

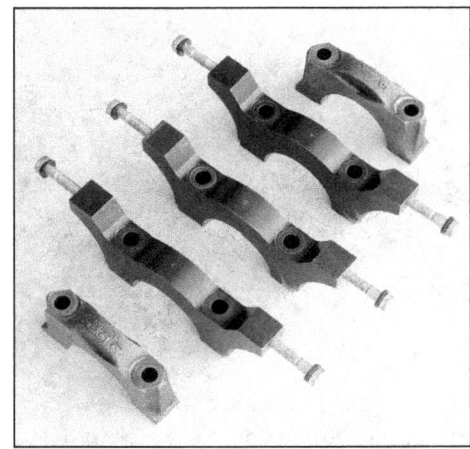

Special main caps are available to convert a production wedge block over to cross-bolted mains.

THE CYLINDER BLOCK

If you are going to use a production block as the basis for a performance build, you'll want to choose from a wide selection. Very few production blocks have thick enough cylinder walls to stand up to the power that can be created with modern cylinder heads.

centerline, so it is fairly easy to fabricate a girdle from a large plate of material. New main caps are machined with flats on them that connect to the girdle. Some of the girdle systems use aluminum main caps, while others use steel billet main caps. I don't have any direct experience with any of the girdle systems currently on the market, so I won't provide any recommendations. My advice is to talk with different engine builders to see what they recommend and then balance out the cost of the girdle and the installation cost against what it would cost to purchase an aftermarket block.

Partially filling the water jackets with a grout or epoxy-type of material is one very popular cylinder block modification for drag racing. The material used to fill the water jackets needs to have a coefficient of expansion somewhat close to cast iron, so it doesn't crack the block when the temperature changes. There are several types of filler on the market these days, and Hard Blok is a popular one. The filled water jackets make the block stronger by providing more support for the cylinder walls. The strength of the cylinders is highly dependent on the unsupported length of the cylinder, so adding in support at the bottom of the cylinder makes the cylinder stiffer. The filled water jackets will also insulate the water from the oil so the oil temperature will tend to run hotter in a filled block.

Aftermarket Blocks

The very best of the production blocks start to show signs of main cap fretting around the 600-hp level. Above 800 hp, the likelihood of a catastrophic failure increases drastically. As cylinder head technology improved during the 1980s and 1990s, there became a real need for a stronger cylinder block for the Mopar wedge motor. One obvious place to draw inspiration from was the Mopar Hemi cylinder block, which came from the factory with cross-bolted mains. The production Hemi blocks proved capable of making more than 1,000 hp when used in professional drag race classes such as Top Fuel and Funny Car. As the popularity of the Hemi motor in drag racing grew over the years, the aftermarket began to make heavy-duty aluminum Hemi blocks. Since the Hemi and the RB motor have a very similar design, it was fairly easy for some aftermarket vendors, such as Keith Black, to adapt their Hemi block tooling to the production of a wedge block.

The factory gave the wedge block some attention when Mopar Performance commissioned the Megablock in the 1980s. Around the same time, Indy Cylinder Heads

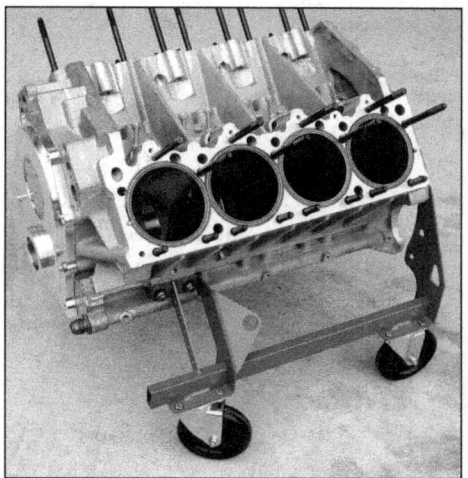

Before aftermarket wedge blocks were available, builders went to great lengths to fabricate what they needed. This older aluminum Hemi block has been modified into a wedge block by moving the upper head bolt locations. Fortunately, builders no longer need to perform this much work to get a good foundation for a performance big-block.

CHAPTER 2

The World Products block has cross-bolted main caps at all positions, except the rear main. Also visible is the blue-colored, billet rear main seal retainer.

A front view of the World Products block shows the extra material around the cam bore, which allows these blocks to be machined for a raised cam. Also notice the freeze plugs in the front water jackets. These freeze plugs quickly ID this block because the factory blocks never had plugs in this location.

began to cast aluminum and cast-iron wedge blocks, and Keith Black came out with a wedge version of their famous Hemi block. The Mopar Performance Megablock suffered through a number of quality and availability issues with the casting vendor and eventually a new block casting was developed with World Products for Mopar Performance in 2007. At the time of printing, there were no aftermarket cast-iron versions of the B block available, so the early 400 castings are still in high demand. The lack of aftermarket low-deck blocks will likely change at some point as the vendors see the potential size of the market for the B motor.

World Products

The World block has some new features that allow it to handle much larger displacements (up to 632 ci) than were previously available. The oil pickup tube boss in the production block has been replaced with a bolt-on adapter in the World block, which frees up some space in the block. Also, the adapter can be quickly changed in order to use a 1/2-inch NPT thread rather than the standard 3/8-inch NPT thread. This used to be a challenging machining operation in a production block; now it is just a five-minute job.

The World block has the front four main caps cross-bolted to the block, while the rear main cap remains a two-bolt design. There is an external oil pickup boss that accepts an AN-12 fitting, and the

A closeup of the front driver's side of the World block shows the tapped hole for an external line feeding the oil pump. Using this rather than the internal pickup will free up room in the crankcase for a larger-stroke crankshaft.

cam bearing bores can be machined to accept a 60-mm cam bearing. The World block is available with a 4.500-inch cylinder bore size, and they can be bored an additional .100 inch if the cylinder walls are thick enough. There will not be much space between the cylinders at that final bore size, so the head gasket

THE CYLINDER BLOCK

A rear view of the World block shows a slightly different arrangement for the oil ports. Notice the extra material in the bell housing area that allows this block to be drilled and tapped for a Chevy bolt pattern in case you want to run a PowerGlide transmission.

The new World Products blocks have an ID pad located on the front of the block near the timing chain cover. The ID pad has a serial number and part number stamped on it.

situation could be an issue. The block is machined to a standard deck height of 10.725, and the deck thickness is .600 inch for increased strength.

The race version of the World block can be ordered with a raised cam location. By moving the camshaft up in the block, there is more room for a longer-stroke crankshaft. Of course, moving the camshaft location means that a lot of other components have to move. This means that things such as the timing chain will have to be a different part, the location of the lifters will change, etc. These are modifications made on very dedicated racing motors, which are actually beyond the scope of what we'll cover in this book. One potential drawback to the World block is the extra weight. A bare 4.31-bore World block weighs a hefty 320 lbs, which is roughly 100 lbs heavier than a production 440 block. Some of that weight can be removed by machining away the unnecessary ribs and material, but that type of machine work requires large machine tools which are not common equipment at engine shops.

There are several different World Products blocks so you need to have some sort of plan of attack before ordering the block. The race versions of the World block are much more expensive than the street version, but they come with a dual bolt pattern on the bellhousing end for bolting on a Chevy transmission. Also, the race versions come with bushed lifter bores, which makes it easier to source roller lifters that are capable of pushrod oiling. World Products is also offering a CGI version of the cast-iron block, as well as an aluminum version. The CGI material is significantly stronger than regular cast iron, so that version of the block would be the one to use for extremely high-output motors. The aluminum block is quite expensive, as one can imagine, but the weight savings is significant.

Koleno Performance

A fairly new cylinder block on the market is the KP 440 block from Koleno Performance. The KP 440 block has all five main caps fully cross-bolted, rather than just the front four mains on the World block.

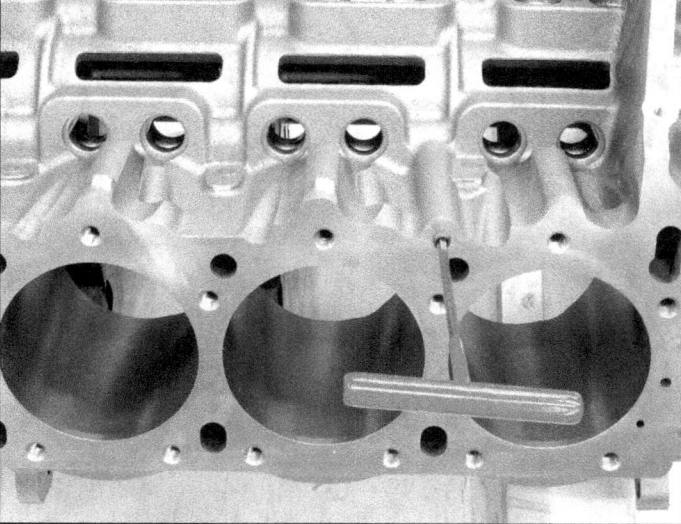

The World Products block sends oil to the valvetrain directly from the main gallery. Since the camshaft no longer restricts the oil flow to the top end, you must install restrictor plugs. The plugs are broached, so they can be removed with an Allen wrench.

CHAPTER 2

Koleno Performance is selling a heavy-duty RB block through their dealer channel. This KP 440 block has a revised lifter galley area that provides some extra freedom in moving lifter bore locations. (Photo courtesy of Koffel's Place)

This side view of the KP 440 shows cross-bolted mains at all five main positions as well as the screw-in freeze plugs. (Photo courtesy of Koffel's Place)

The KP 440 block also uses a priority mains oiling system rather than sharing the main oil gallery with the lifter bores. The KP 440 block can be bored to 4.600 inches and will accept up to a 5-inch stroke with machining. At time of publication, it wasn't known if Koleno was planning on introducing a low-deck version of this new cast-iron block.

Indy Cylinder Heads

Indy has been offering aftermarket wedge blocks for a number of years. The company used to produce a cast-iron version, but currently the Indy MAXX block is only offered in aluminum. Indy has a low-deck and an RB version of their aluminum block, so the racer has a choice.

Keith Black

The Keith Black brand is primarily associated with Hemi power, but it also offers a very nice version of their famous aluminum engine block with a wedge bolt pattern. The street version of the KB blocks come fully machined with full water jackets, dry cylinder sleeves, and cross-bolted main caps. The KB blocks are available in either the 9.980 deck height or the taller 10.725 RB deck. A few options are available, including drilling for hydraulic lifters and machining clearance for strokes greater than 4.500 inches. At publication time, I heard that Keith Black had closed its doors, and the blocks were no longer available. If that remains the

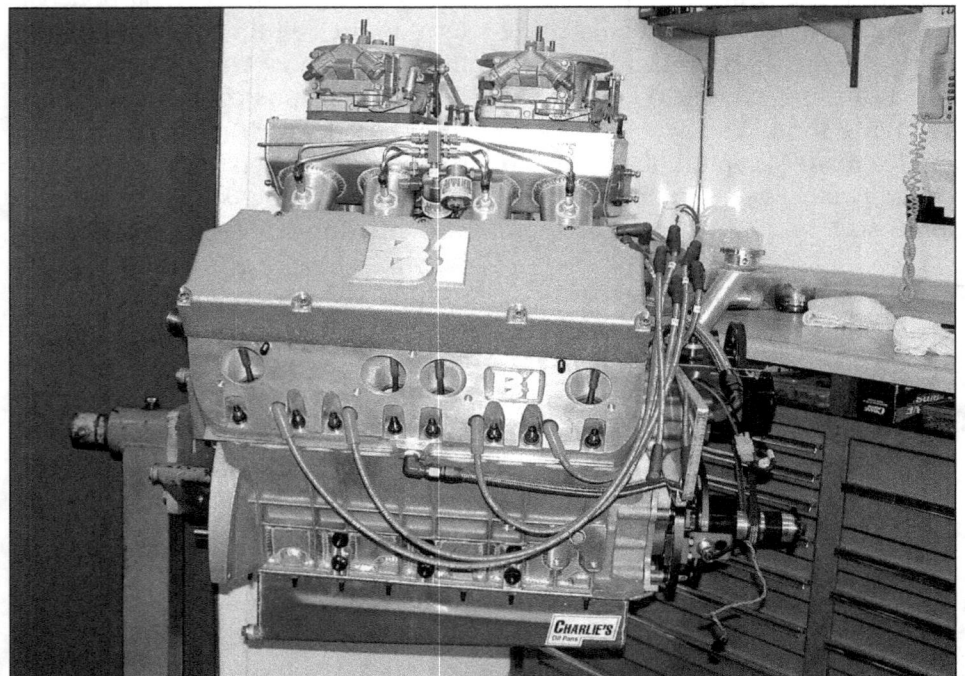

The Keith Black aluminum block has always been considered the premium block to use for super high-power combinations. The crankcase area on this KB block has been modified to clear a 5-inch-stroke crankshaft. (Photo courtesy of Koffel's Place)

HOW TO BUILD MAX-PERFORMANCE MOPAR BIG-BLOCKS

situation, Mopar racers will be unable to purchase what was one of the best new blocks on the market.

Main Bearings

Main bearings for the RB motor are available in three styles: full groove, half groove, or three-quarter groove. Each of these styles has its proponents and intended uses. There is also a decent selection of bearing types available for the Mopar big-block. For example, Clevite bearings are available in P-, V-, H-, or M-series for the big-block Mopar. The P-bearings are the most common because they have been around the longest. V-bearings are duplicates of the older Vandervell bearing, and they have a softer lead-indium overlay than that on the P-bearing. The H-series bearings are often used with stroker cranks because they come with enlarged chamfers that clear the larger-than-stock fillets used on many aftermarket crankshafts. The M-bearings are special-purpose bearings with a thick Babbitt layer for highly loaded engines, such as supercharged applications.

There are different applications for big-block main bearings because the B block uses a smaller crankshaft-journal diameter than the RB block. To make it even more confusing, the 1974 and newer blocks use a larger diameter thrust bearing than the earlier blocks. So, in total, there are four different main bearing applications: early B, late B, early RB, and late RB. Combine those four different applications with the choice of full groove, half groove or three-quarter groove, as well as the issue of standard size, undersize, etc., and you'll quickly get way too many choices for any one manufacturer to produce.

Depending on which block you have, you may not be able to find

The Clevite H-series main bearings are a good choice for most performance engines. They are chamfered to fit aftermarket crankshafts and are fully grooved. These H-series bearings fit the World Products block as well as late-model RB production blocks.

the desired bearing series, size, and groove combination because not all combinations are produced. The standard advice from Mopar Performance and other builders for years has been to use a full-groove, tri-metal bearing, and these are commonly available for both the B and the RB main size. The issue that some builders have with full-groove main bearings is that the groove in the lower side reduces the load capability of the bearing. The reduced load capacity doesn't seem to be a problem for performance engines up to 800 hp, but it is an area for you to keep an eye on in high-output engines.

Recently, the three-quarter-groove main bearings became available on a limited basis. The three-quarter-groove main bearing provides an oil groove for the rod bearings during three quarters of the crankshaft rotation but leaves a full-width bearing at the bottom of the main cap to withstand the heavy load during the combustion cycle. At this book's publication, at least one vendor was offering three-quarter-groove main bearings for both the B and the RB block, so these bearings could be an option to explore.

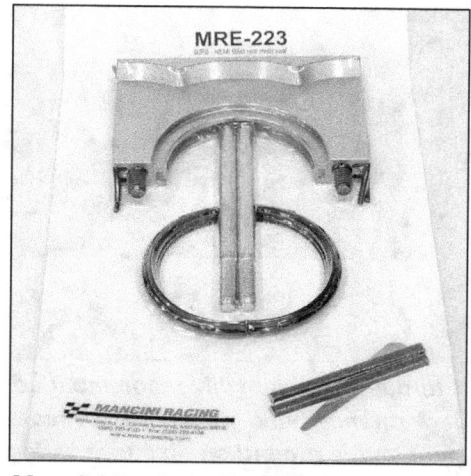

Mancini Racing offers a billet rear main seal holder that helps to eliminate oil leaks from the back of the block. This billet main seal block has grooves on each side for O-ring material to seal against the block.

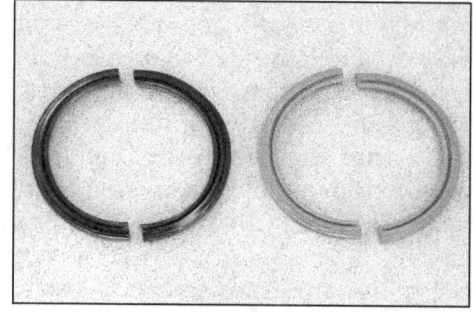

A standard rear main seal shown on the left is not as durable as the high-performance rear main seal from Fel-Pro shown on the right. The Fel-Pro seal is designed to operate with crankcase vacuum and to seal at higher engine speeds.

One of the more frustrating main bearing issues for the Mopar engine builder is the limited selection of bearings that are .001-inch-thinner than standard. You may want a little more clearance than what the standard bearings provide but there is no easy way to get that extra clearance. You can assemble a big-block Chevy motor and pick from a rather large selection of .001-inch-thinner as well as a few .002-inch-thinner main

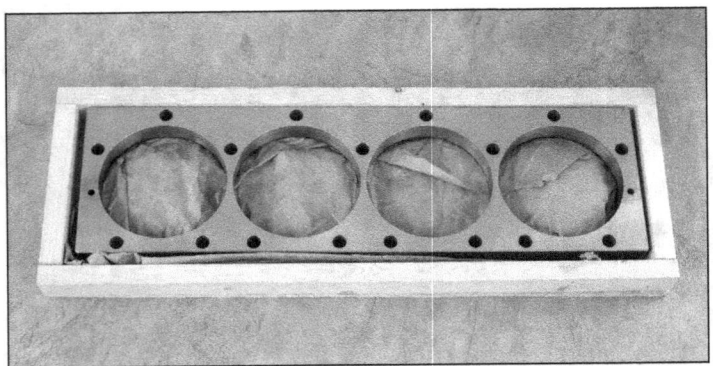
A torque plate is highly recommended for any max-performance build. This plate is made from 1-inch-thick steel and is ground on all surfaces for a precision fit.

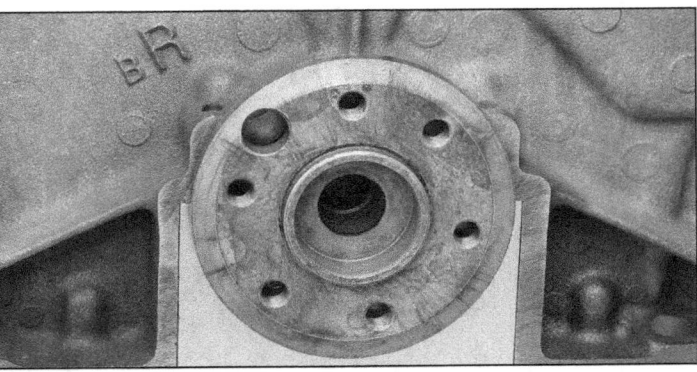
This motor has one of the Mancini Racing rear main seal holders installed. After a full season of racing, the back of the block is still dry and clean.

bearings, but so far the bearing vendors have not produced these same choices for the big-block Mopar. Chrysler used to have .001-inch-thinner bearings available over the counter but these were discontinued many years ago. Consequently you may need to either polish or grind the crank to gain the necessary clearance.

Main bearings should last for the entire life of the engine in a production vehicle but in an all-out racing engine, the main bearings will become a sacrificial part needing replacement on a regular basis. Builders who run big-block Mopar drag race engines making over 1,000 hp report that they need to change the main bearings after every 30 to 40 passes. A typical performance engine making 750 hp should be able to go an entire season of racing without having to inspect the bearings but as the power level goes up, so does the maintenance requirements.

Cylinder Bore Preparation

The proper finish on the cylinder walls is going to be a function of the rings used as well as the intended use of the engine. For better results follow the recommendations of the piston ring manufacturer. The piston ring vendors have spent a lot of time designing their rings to work properly with a certain bore finish, so they will be able to provide a specific honing process that works with their rings.

The blocks do distort a measurable amount when the head bolts are torqued, so it is important to use a torque plate when honing the cylinders of any production block. It might be a little difficult to find a machine shop in your local area that has a torque plate for a big-block Mopar, but that is the entry price for a performance engine. Many builders also recommend using the same type of head gasket when honing with a torque plate as will be used in the actual engine. MLS head gaskets have a different load pattern on the deck than composition gaskets, and this different loading can make a slight difference to the cylinder distortion.

You will find that most builders use a torque plate for high-performance engine work. You might even find some who also use a head gasket when torquing the plate to the block. However, you probably won't find many builders who bring the block up to temperature when performing the final honing process. These are all very slight improvements that can be made to the machining process, but the cost might not be worth the small improvement unless you are racing in a very competitive class.

Decking

The decks on the factory blocks were often machined slightly crooked for some unknown reason. It is possible that the fixtures at the factory weren't properly maintained or that the operators were not fully trained. Whatever the reason, it is common to find a factory original block with the deck height off by .010 inch from one end compared to the other. It is important to get the deck height corrected before you order the pistons, especially if the motor is going to be set up with tight quench. In the alternative, you can order the pistons with a little extra room at the top of the cylinder and then have the deck cut down to match the pistons. One problem with doing that is: if the deck height gets cut very much, then it becomes necessary to machine either the cylinder heads or the intake face in order to get the intake manifold to match up properly with the cylinder heads. It can be very annoying to have an engine with an odd deck height because every time a different

THE CYLINDER BLOCK

After the billet rear main seal holder is installed into the block, the O-rings need to be trimmed flush to the surface. Spreading a small amount of RTV into the joints between the cap and the block creates a leak-proof assembly.

Production engine blocks often need a little bit of cleanup work performed in the timing chain area as well as in the valley. Usually, the blocks can be cleaned up in 15 minutes with a good high-speed die grinder.

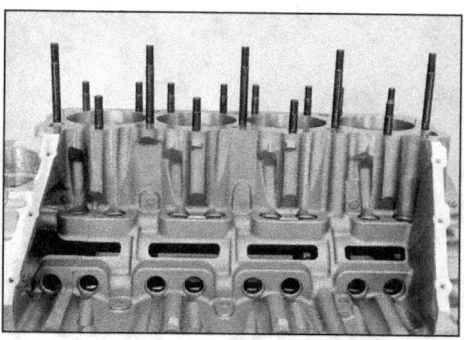

Cylinder head studs are an excellent choice for higher-compression engines, but they do require some extra attention during the assembly. ARP has stud kits for all of the popular big-block cylinder heads.

Some cylinder head studs are too long and will interfere with the header flange. The stud on the left in this picture is 2.750 long, a little too long for this application. The stud on the right is the same length but has extra threads so it can be installed deeper in the engine block, which provides extra clearance for the header flange.

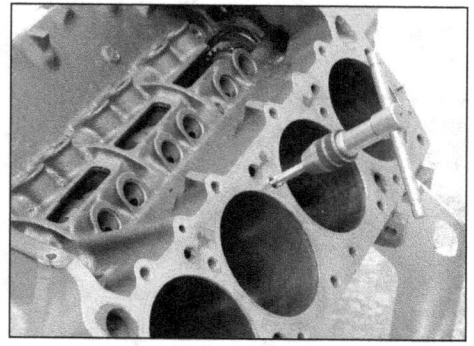

The threads for the head bolts need to be bottom tapped in order for longer head studs or head bolts to be used. If the threads are not bottom tapped, the studs will not fully engage thread into the block, and you might encounter other assembly issues. Do this operation before assembly begins.

intake manifold is purchased it must be machined to match. A little planning in this area can really make things simpler.

Do not overlook the walls at the end of the cam valley during the machining process. If the cylinder decks are machined down very much, the end walls also need to be machined down to match. This is especially important if a standard bathtub-type intake manifold gasket is used; the bathtub gasket only fits properly when the surfaces of the valley walls, cylinder head, and block deck meet at a point.

Block Detailing

A production Mopar block casting doesn't require much block detailing. Sometimes the factory casting is a little rough around the openings in the center gallery, but this can be fixed in a few moments with a die grinder. If you are going to be running a gear drive or a belt drive for the camshaft, those parts need to be trial-fitted to the block before final assembly because there is often some interference with the block casting. Often the oiling system needs some attention, but the attention depends on the type of valvetrain to be used.

On a production block, the first things to look at in the oiling system are the passages that feed oil from the main gallery down to the main bearings. Sometimes the factory drilling process wasn't very good and these holes are undersized or rough inside. A long drill or reamer can be run down these holes to open them up to 9/32 inch. Running a drill through these holes is quite risky because if the drill catches on an edge and breaks off inside the passage, the block will be ruined. The reamer is less likely to break, but it won't cut quite as well as a drill. One option is to have a grinding shop modify a long drill into a design that works for cast iron and then use this special drill only for this operation. If the valvetrain is going to be oiled via the number-4 cam journal, then it is usually a good idea to open up the oil passage from the main oil gallery to the number-4 main bearing to a full 5/16-inch diameter. The number-4

These B blocks are being prepared for race duty. The block on the left has been fully machined and is ready for assembly. Notice the bushings in the lifter bores as well as the clean and smooth surface finish on the cylinder walls and deck.

Mopar Performance sells a small parts kit that is very handy to have on hand when building a block. This small parts kit contains various plugs, keys, bushings, and pins that are required to service a bare block.

main bearing and the rod journals that it feeds tend to be the first ones to suffer damage from any sort of lubrication failure.

If you are going to run a solid flat-tappet cam or a solid roller cam without pushrod oiling, oil flow to the driver-side lifter gallery can be restricted significantly by driving a plug into the back of the driver-side gallery. Drive the plug in far enough to block off the oil feed coming from the crossover passage at the back of the block. Many builders drill a small hole into the plug before driving it into the gallery. The advantage is that oil will still flow into the gallery to lubricate the lifters, but the flow will be restricted if a valvetrain failure occurs on the driver's side of the engine. This restriction might provide just enough time to get the motor shut down without suffering extra harm. If the engine is going to use an internal oil pickup, then clean up and radius the passages between the inlet tube and the oil pump mount so that the oil will flow better to the pump. The old Mopar Performance engine bible shows the detail on doing this work. Also see Chapter 3 for more information on oiling systems.

Valve Notches

The tops of the cylinder bores can be notched, or flared, at the deck surface to improve the airflow similar to the way the factory Max-Wedge blocks were notched to provide clearance for the large exhaust valves. This bore-notching trick works with any block, but it isn't needed as much when using a large bore size. One way to properly locate the notches is to trace the outline of the head gasket on the block. Most head gaskets will not have a perfectly round bore shape but will instead have scallops for the intake and exhaust valve in the fire ring. First hold the head gasket against the cylinder head to double-check that it is actually a good template to use. If the head gasket represents the combustion chamber shape, then it can be used as a template to open up the top of the block. The chamfers, or notches, in the cylinder block cannot extend down into the cylinder bores very far because you do not want the top piston ring to extend over them. Typically that means the notches cannot extend more than .200 inch into the cylinder bores. When using large valve heads on a small-bore motor such as a 383, the notches may need to be fairly large. On a 4.375-bore motor the notches may be smaller. On an aftermarket block with 4.500-inch bores, there is probably no reason to notch the bores unless you are using an extremely large valve size.

This Indy Maxx aluminum block is machined for a Hemi, but a wedge version is also available. The Indy blocks feature fully-cross-bolted mains, siamesed dry sleeve construction, and weigh 133 lbs. (Photo courtesy of Indy Cylinder Heads)

CHAPTER 3

THE OIL SYSTEM

If oil is the lifeblood of an engine, then the oil pump is the heart, responsible for pumping the lubricating oil throughout the engine. On a big-block Mopar, the oil pump is conveniently located outside of the block, down low on the front corner of the driver's side. An intermediate shaft with a hex-shaped tip drives the oil pump at 50 percent of engine speed. This intermediate shaft, which also drives the distributor, is driven counter-clockwise by a helical gear on the camshaft.

Oil Pump

There were two versions of the oil pump from the factory. A standard pump was used on the majority of engines, and the high-volume pump was introduced for the higher-performance motors. The high-volume pump has both a taller gear set to pump more volume and a stiffer relief spring to increase the oil pressure in the main gallery at higher engine speeds. You can retrofit the stiffer relief spring to the standard volume pump as an easy way to increase oil pressure.

The question about which oil pump to use often comes up during bench race sessions. There are a few general rules to help make the decision. Most big-block Mopar engines are going to be happy with at least 20 psi of oil pressure at a hot idle and a maximum of 80 psi at wide-open throttle (WOT). If you have too much oil pressure, then an easy fix is to put a softer spring in the pressure relief valve, but a better solution

Oil-pump quality is not so great anymore, so builders need to carefully inspect new pumps before installation. The pump on the left shows how poor the inlet feed hole can be on a new pump. The pump on the right has had the inlet hole smoothed and blended out to the proper size.

The Ray Barton oil pump is a complex assembly carved out of billet aluminum parts. The key to this pump is the large-diameter rotor, which provides high-volume capacity in a low-profile design.

HOW TO BUILD MAX-PERFORMANCE MOPAR BIG-BLOCKS 25

CHAPTER 3

Comparing the Barton oil pump on the left and a stock pump on the right shows the large difference in rotor diameter.

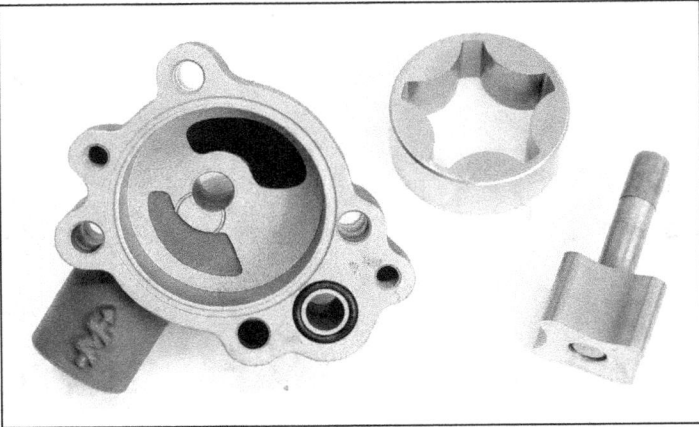

The Milodon PN 21815 oil pump is a longstanding favorite for Mopar big-block race engines. This pump uses a special tall gear set that is capable of producing 19 gpm (gallons per minute) of oil flow.

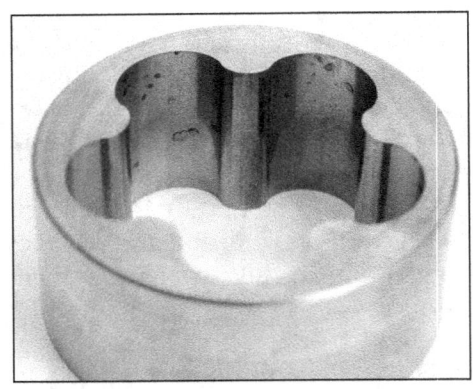

This high-volume oil pump rotor was ruined when some bearing trash was sucked into the pump. It only takes a few little particles like the ones shown in this picture to seize up the oil pump. If the pump is seized up, the engine will then quickly fail if it isn't shut down immediately.

would be to use a lower-volume oil pump. If the oil pump is providing more oil volume than the engine can use, the pressure relief valve just recycles the oil within the pump, which generates extra heat and consumes power. In the case of an engine with oil pressure that is too low, the easy fix is to use a high-pressure spring; but the better solution is to use a higher-volume oil pump. If excessive clearances within the motor are causing low oil pressure, the only cure is to rebuild the motor and fix the clearance issues. On a big-block Mopar, the standard oil pump typically works fine up to about 6,000 rpm, especially if half-grooved main bearings are being used. You would use the higher-volume pump when engine speeds are higher than 6,000 rpm or if using fully grooved main bearings.

In addition to the two factory-style oil pumps, there is a large selection of aftermarket oil pumps available for the big-block Mopar. Milodon is one of the original aftermarket vendors for oil pumps, and they still produce pumps that will fit any B, RB, or Hemi motor. Certain Milodon pumps are capable of pumping even higher volume than the high-volume pump, along with available options for the pump's inlet side. You will want to use a high-volume oil pump, such as the Milodon aluminum unit, if you build a racing-type engine using larger-than-stock bearing clearances and fully grooved main bearings. A high-volume oil pump matched with tight bearing clearances causes extremely high oil pressure, which can cause gasket failure or even failure of the oil filters.

If you are going to use a stock replacement type oil pump, you should disassemble the oil pump and carefully check it over before installation. The quality of replacement oil pumps has deteriorated over the years, and they should not be installed right out of the box. One common problem is that the casting flash can severely restrict the inlet side of the pump. This area should be opened up so that it matches the outlet hole in the cylinder block. The best way to do this is to install the bare oil pump housing onto the block and carefully inspect the inlet hole to see if it lines up with the hole in the block.

Internal Oiling System

The pickup for the oiling system in a stock big-block Mopar screws into the block near the number-1 main cap. Since the oil pump is located externally, the oil pickup has to pull the oil from the pan and send it out of the block to the pump before it is sent back into the block and into the main oil gallery. The big-block motor typically used a pickup

THE OIL SYSTEM

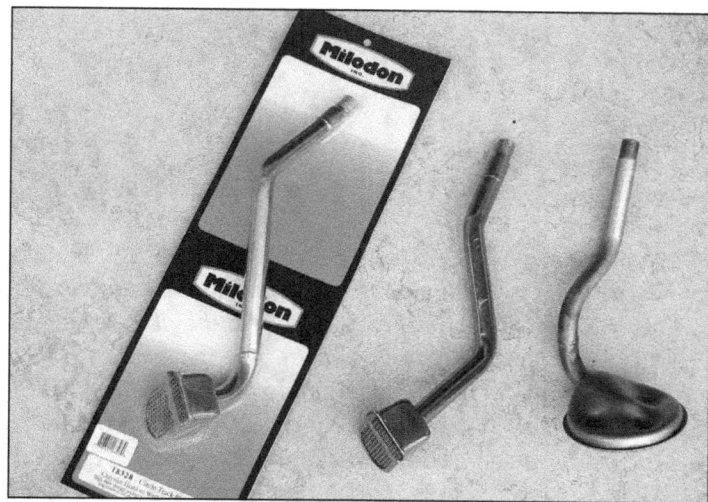

Different pickup assemblies are required for different oil pans. Many pickup tubes are available in either the standard 3/8-inch pipe thread or the larger 1/2-inch pipe thread that was used for Hemi blocks. Make sure the pan that you want to use has the pickup size that your block requires before you purchase it.

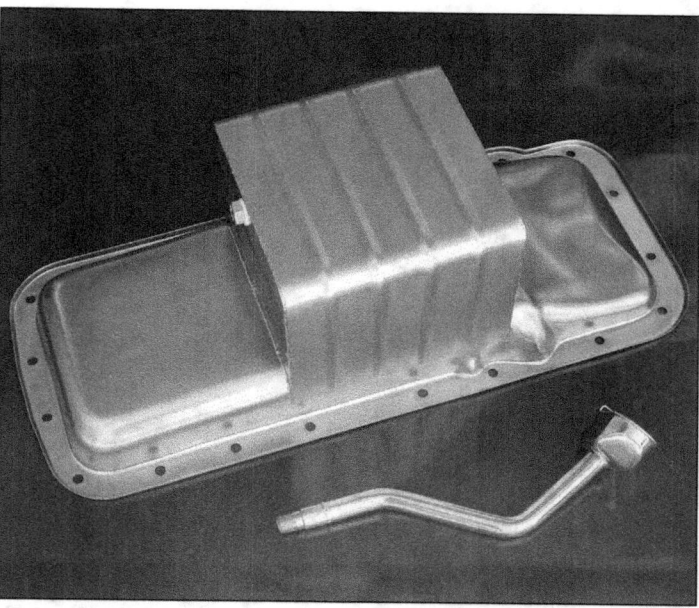

The deep center sump pan from Milodon with an extra-long 3/8-inch NPT pickup assembly is a good choice for many street/strip-type cars.

that screwed into a boss threaded for 3/8-inch NPT threads, while the Hemi motor used a larger-diameter pickup that had 1/2-inch NPT threads. Of course, many builders replaced the smaller wedge pickup with the larger pickup from the Hemi and re-drilled the block to accept the larger Hemi pickup tube. This is still a fairly standard operation today, but it is somewhat difficult to drill out the existing pickup threads in the block and to tap them to the larger 1/2-inch NPT size. The pickup hole is drilled into the block at a compound angle, which makes it tricky to set up on a milling machine. Caution: Re-drilling this hole by hand is very difficult and has led to smashed thumbs and even some cracked blocks when the drill caught in the hole and spun the drill motor.

The new cylinder block from World Products has a bolt-on oil-pump pickup adapter, which cleverly avoids the potential problems caused by trying to install an oversize pickup tube. The pickup adapter for the World Products block is available in 3/8-inch NPT and 1/2-inch NPT sizes, which allows you to quickly select the adapter size required and to bolt it in place. Some aftermarket blocks do not have a location for the internal pickup because most serious race applications will use either external pickups or dry sump oiling systems. If you order an aftermarket engine block, you will want to confirm that the block can support the type of oil pump and pickup that you intend to use.

External Oiling System

The externally located oil pump on a Mopar big-block is fairly easy to access and modify, making it a common builder alteration. One of the most frequent modifications is to block off the internal pickup and to feed the pump by pulling oil from the oil pan via external hoses. These external oil feed systems provide less restriction on the suction side of the pump, which is beneficial to its operation. Positive displacement pumps, such as the gerotor pump used on the Mopar engine, are much more effective pumping out the outlet than they are at sucking in the inlet. Therefore, reducing any restriction on the inlet side increases the oil flow. The external oil line systems are also a more flexible system design than the internal pickup setups because the sump on the oil pan can now be located anywhere that the lines can reach.

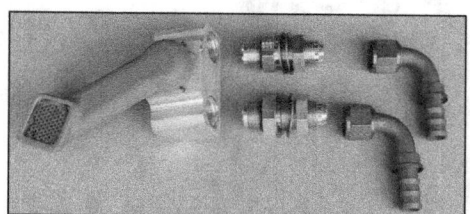

The dual-line swivel pickup is a key component for many big-block oiling systems. The swivel pickup travels back and forth in the oil pan to follow the oil during acceleration and deceleration. The dual number-12 AN lines provide a low-restriction supply path when plumbed to both sides of the oil pump.

CHAPTER 3

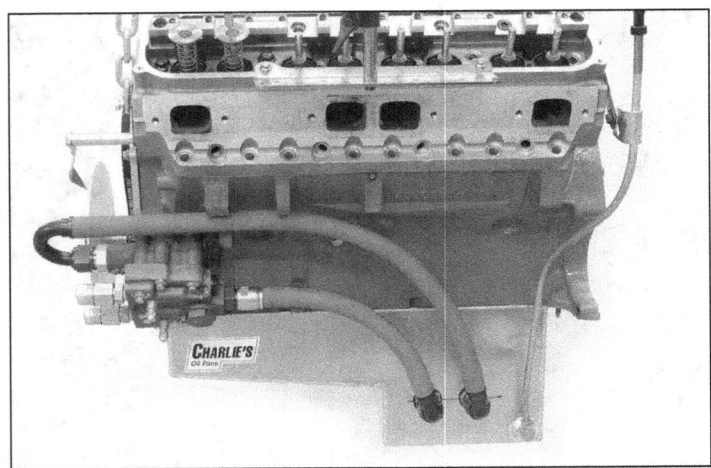

Here is an excellent view of an external dual-line system installed on an engine. This system uses a Milodon oil pump connected by number-12 AN hoses to a dual-line swivel-type pickup in the pan. The upper hose is looped over the oil pump to help keep the pump primed while the motor is shut off. This particular system works best with a motor plate, but a similar configuration could be fabricated that works with stock motor mounts.

This oil pan is a custom aluminum pan that was built in the classic Super Stock style with a deep rear sump, swivel dual-line pickup and the tube for the steering center link. The motor plate to the rear of the pan is required because the stock motor mounts must be removed to provide clearance for this particular oiling system.

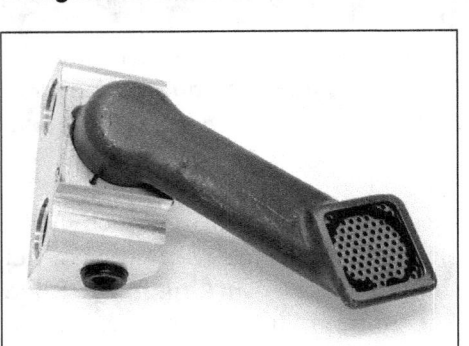
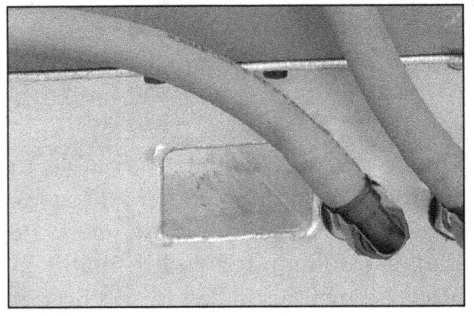
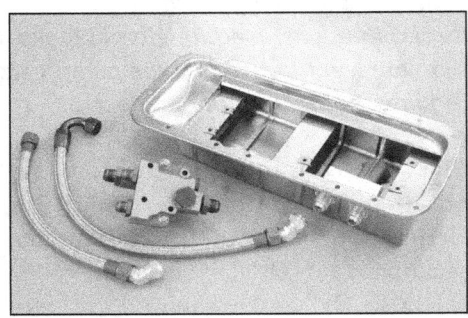

A dual-line pickup with a swinging inlet is used in many big-block oil systems. This combination is simple, effective, and proven to work.

This Super Stock-style oil pan has a window installed in it, so the tie rod can pass through the pan. These pans typically run a dual-line pickup as shown.

Milodon makes complete kits ready to bolt on. This kit uses a PN 31151 pan with a PN 21195 oil pump kit. The oil pump kit comes with the external lines and the dual-line pickup.

When using an external oiling system the internal system needs to be blocked off. This block was drilled and tapped for a plug at the oil pump mount but it is usually easier to thread a plug into the internal pickup in the crankcase.

This block is a casualty of trying to hand-drill and tap a block for 1/2-inch NPT threads. The internal pickup area was damaged during the process so this block had to be converted to external oiling.

The external pickup systems typically consist of either a single number-12 AN line or a dual number-12 AN line. The dual-number-12-AN-line system, sold by Milodon and others, is common and easily sourced from a variety of vendors. You do need to take care to route the external lines away from the headers, the K frame, or the steering box. Also take extra care to stop any air leaks or oil leaks at all of the multiple fittings.

World Products casts a cylinder block that has been drilled and tapped on the front face so it accepts an external oil line input. This port on the front of the block goes directly to the inlet side of the oil pump. When using this port, plug the internal pickup port located inside the crankcase to prevent an air leak. Using the built-in port for an external line gives you an easier way to construct a dual-feed oil pump while using a standard oil pump body.

Pump Cover

The production big-block oil pump has a separate cover with a cast mount for the oil filter. The stock cover works fine for lower performance applications but it will not accept an external feed line. To fix that issue, Muscle Motors recently introduced a cast cover that has an external line pickup but retains the stock-type oil filter mount. The Muscle Motors cover is perfect if you want to run an external feed line with the stock oil filter location.

For higher-performance oiling systems, builders will often want to run a remote oil filter to save space or as a way to use a special filter. Several available covers allow number-12 AN lines to be attached directly to the pump rather than using an adapter on the oil filter mount. Indy and Milodon both offer covers that are tapped for AN-12 fittings that can be used for routing the oil to external filters and coolers.

If you use an externally fed oil line system, there are a couple of different styles of pickups that can be placed into the oil pan. The fixed production, or static pickup, style can be effective if the oil pan sump is deep enough that it won't be uncovered during hard acceleration or deceleration. Milodon and other vendors have swinging pickups for situations where the g loads are high

This custom pump cover was built for an application where the builder needed to use an external oil filter. A similar cover made from cast iron was available for the Jensen Interceptor vehicles but the Jensen part is no longer available.

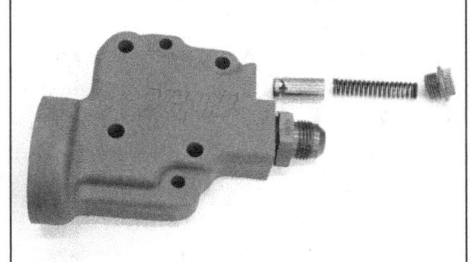

Muscle Motors offers a cast-aluminum pump cover with an integral oil filter mount and an external inlet. This is ideally suited for running a system with external pickups and it keeps the oil filter in the stock location.

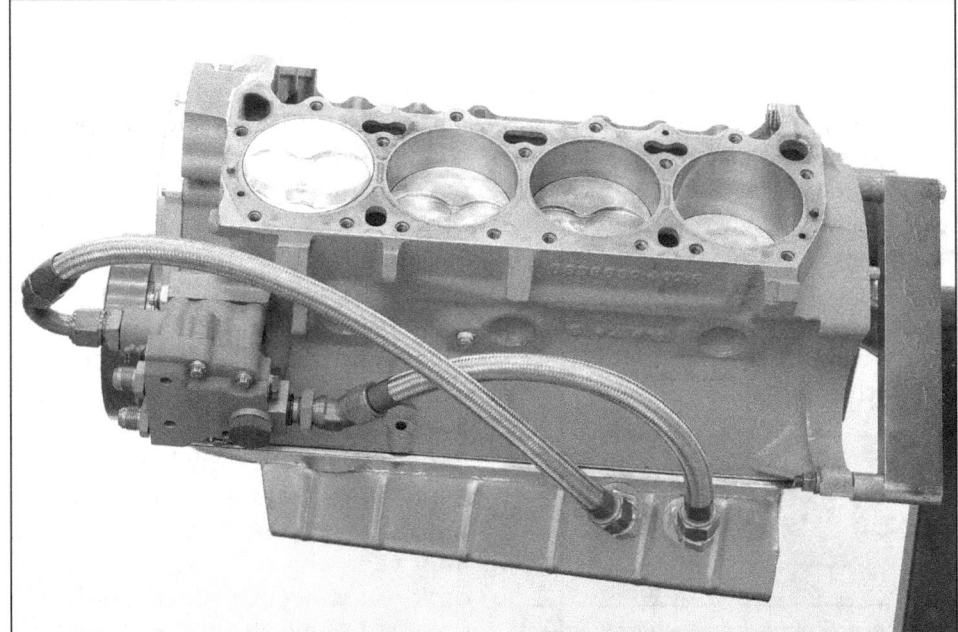

Dual external lines for this Milodon pan and pump were routed, so there will always be some oil trapped in the lines. This keeps the pump primed and eliminates dry starts.

enough that the oil in the pan might be forced away from a static pickup. The swinging pickup can be mounted so it swings forward and then rearward for a drag race car, or it can be mounted to swing right and left for a road race car. The model from Indy Cylinder Heads is physically larger than the Milodon unit, so if you are looking for the minimum inlet restriction, the Indy pickup might be worth a look.

The Intermediate Shaft

The shaft that drives the oil pump in a big-block Mopar is a straightforward part that seldom needs attention. However, there are a few situations where changes to other engine parts require a change in the intermediate shaft. For instance, the gear on the intermediate shaft needs to be made of a compatible material when using a steel-alloy roller camshaft rather than a cast material. For roller cam usage, the intermediate gear is typically made from a bronze-alloy material, which can be recognized by its golden color. These special intermediate shafts are available from Mopar Performance and Milodon.

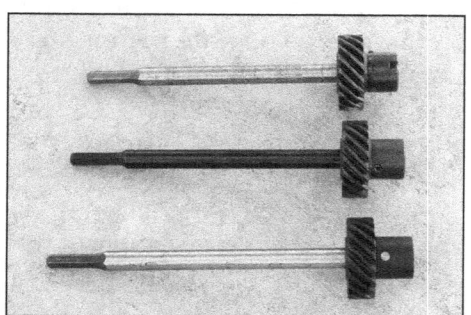
There are three different lengths available for the oil pump intermediate shaft. The correct length depends on which aftermarket oil pump you use. All three driveshafts are available with a bronze-alloy gear for use with roller camshafts.

The type of oil pump assembly determines the length of the intermediate shaft needed. There are currently three different shaft lengths available: 6.40, 6.60, and 7.0 inches. The factory replacement-type oil pumps use the standard length shaft, which is 6.40 inches long. The PN 21815 high-volume aluminum oil pump from Milodon requires the 6.60-inch-long shaft to fully engage the hex driveshaft. The 7.0-inch-long shaft is used for oil pump systems where a spacer is used to create the second inlet system. You need to carefully double-check and determine the required shaft length for the combination of parts you use in the engine because the wrong shaft length can lead to immediate engine failure.

Oil Pan

The Mopar big-block motor has a flat-rail design for the oil pan due to the extended crankcase design of the cylinder block. This makes it fairly easy to fabricate an oil pan because you can weld a box shape onto a flat rail to create the pan, so you have multiple choices in aftermarket oil pans. If the oil pan is going to be used in a typical A- or B-body car, select a pan that will fit the particular chassis. Another key item to consider is the depth of the pan. Deeper is usually better, but you obviously do not want the oil pan to make contact with the road.

If you are building a big-block, you should have this factory tool in your kit. It's used to install and burnish the distributor bushing in the block.

Aftermarket pans are available in steel for high-performance street driving and aluminum for all-out racing applications. Vendors, such as Milodon, Moroso, and others, have a large selection of drag race and circle track oil pans for the big-block Mopar. Pans are available for most of the popular body styles. Of course, if you're dropping a big-block into a Hudson, you might need to fabricate your own oil pan. Still, the odds favor starting with one of the aftermarket pans and modifying it for your specific needs rather than starting from scratch.

The factory often used a windage tray in the high-performance big-block motors. This windage tray is still available over the counter at any Dodge dealer and can easily be retrofitted to any oil pan by sandwiching it with two gaskets between the pan and the block. The original Mopar Performance manual claimed a 16-hp gain from the use of a windage tray with a stock-type oil pan. However, sandwich-style windage trays have fallen out of favor for the higher-powered engines, and been replaced with either screens or a tray that is mounted further down into a deep pan. The current theory (which changes often) is that the large flat windage tray mounted at the bottom of the block actually bounces oil back up into the crankshaft rather than stripping it off. So by moving the tray or screen further away from the crankshaft, less drag-inducing oil will bounce back into the rotating assembly.

A performance engine will definitely show a power increase if you can manage to fit a modern oil pan into your chassis. There are many options currently available for street/strip-type oil pans. A street/strip pan is usually 7- or 8-quart capacity and while it hangs down lower than a stock pan, it should still provide

THE OIL SYSTEM

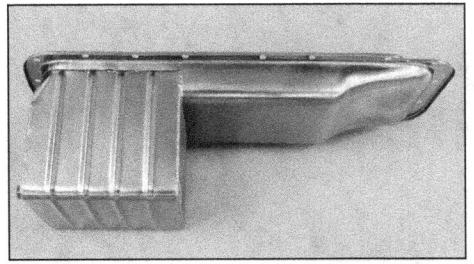

Milodon makes this deep rear sump big-block pan for pickup trucks or 4WD vehicles. This pan can also be useful for dyno testing because there is typically plenty of clearance on an engine dyno for a deep rear sump pan. This pan could also be used in some vehicles that have been converted to an aftermarket K-frame with front mounted rack and pinion steering.

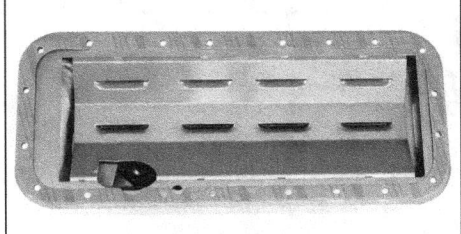

Fel-Pro oil pan gasket PN 1834 has a steel core with a rubber coating. Cometic has recently introduced a similar steel shim gasket so now builders have two good choices.

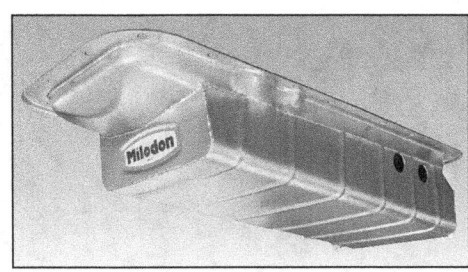

The 9-quart Milodon 31161 oil pan is designed to fit in a Mopar chassis with an aftermarket K-frame. This is a great performance pan if your chassis is set up for it. (Photo courtesy of Milodon)

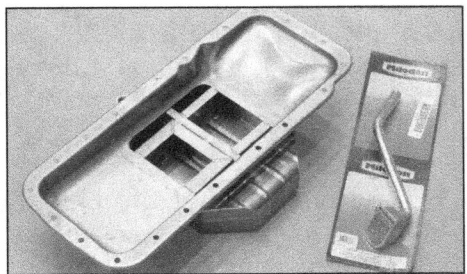

The 7-quart Milodon PN 31580 road race pan is only 5½ inches deep and has multiple baffles that keep the oil in the pan near the pickup during hard cornering. This is an excellent oil pan for high-performance street use, especially if your big-block car has an upgraded suspension capable of better handling.

A solid windage tray with louvers is the classic method for keeping the oil in the sump separated from the rotating assembly. A solid-type windage tray works well with stock oil pans but is not typically used with a deep racing pan.

enough clearance for ordinary street driving. As a teen, I once had to walk home more than 20 miles after tearing a hole in a deep sump pan on some railroad tracks, so this subject is near and dear to me. The standard street/strip pans might not show any performance improvement over a stock pan, but the extra capacity provides insurance. Some NHRA racers run a deep pan with only a few quarts of oil in it in an attempt to reduce windage and free up some power. I tried this trick once and ended up with a number of burned-up rod bearings and a ruined short-block, so be careful.

There are a number of vendors that sell Super Stock-type oil pans for several Mopar chassis types. These SS-style pans have kickouts on the passenger side to accumulate more oil. They often have deep sumps and built-in windage screens, and they sometimes have crank scrapers. The SS-style pans that are designed to

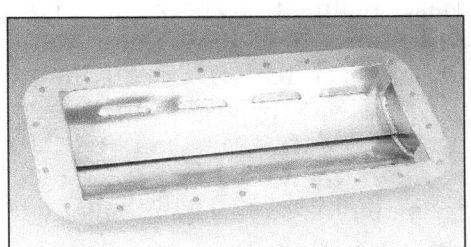

This Milodon aluminum windage tray is for an oil pan with a full-length sump. There isn't an access hole for an internal pickup because this tray is designed to work with an external pickup. (Photo courtesy of Milodon)

HOW TO BUILD MAX-PERFORMANCE MOPAR BIG-BLOCKS

CHAPTER 3

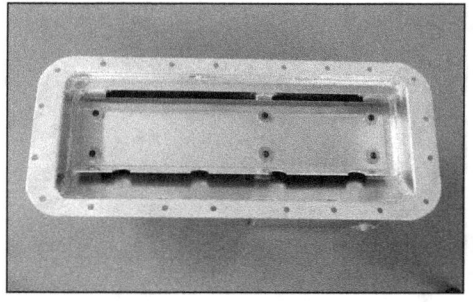

With a little fabrication a late-model pickup truck dipstick assembly can be adapted to the Milodon rear sump oil pan. Late-model dipsticks provide a better seal around the handle than the production units. A good seal in this area prevents dirt from getting into the crankcase when running a vacuum pump.

An inside view of a deep-sump racing pan shows that the windage tray is located quite a bit deeper in the pan than a stock-type windage tray. Also notice that it is notched for connecting rod clearance, and that it has openings on each side rather than louvers in the middle.

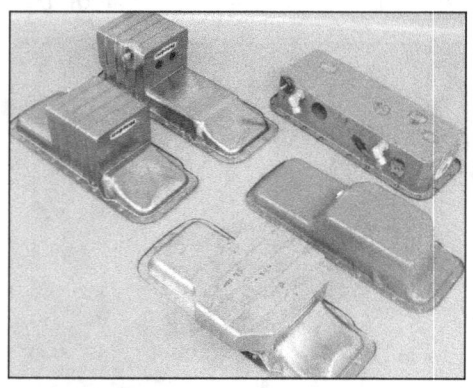

A small collection of big-block pans shows some vastly different sump designs. Starting at the front and moving clockwise is: the Milodon road race pan, a Milodon center sump design, the Milodon rear sump truck pan, a homemade box design, and a 6-quart reproduction Hemi pan.

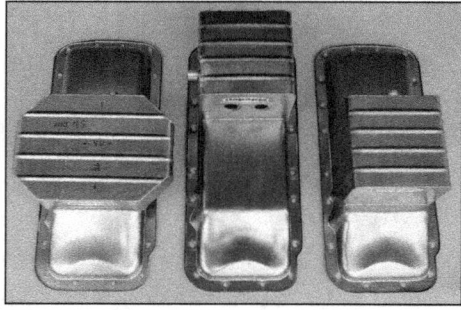

A closer shot of the three Milodon pans from the left: the road race pan, the rear sump truck pan, and the center sump design. The rear sump pan in this picture has been modified to accept a dual-line pickup.

work with a stock-type suspension will have a tube through the oil pan for the tie rod to run through. This makes pulling the pan or the engine a little more involved because the tie rod has to be removed before the oil pan. A well-designed oil pan can easily provide improvements of 20 hp or more when used on a high-RPM racing motor, so this is an important area to consider.

Oil Type and Operation Temperature

Motor oil has changed dramatically over the last 30 years, and no doubt it will continue to evolve in the future. The classic 10-30W and 20-50W mineral oil formulations were used when the big-block motors were in production and are still available today. However, the chemistry of the oil is significantly different than it was in 1978. Emission controls and economic factors have influenced the oil's components over the years, and the results aren't always for the better. As I will discuss in the camshaft chapter (Chapter 9), the biggest change has been the reduction of zinc in modern oils, which has caused lubrication issues with solid-lifter motors. However, despite big drawbacks, the improvement of oil blends and synthetic oils over the past 30 years permits more power production than ever. Several oil blends available today are designed specifically for use with flat-tappet camshafts. If you build a performance engine around a flat-tappet cam, you will definitely want to use that type of oil.

The availability of high-strength synthetic racing oils is one of the most important changes over the last decade. These specialty oils allow builders to use tighter bearing tolerances and to run the engines at cooler temperatures. Many professional race teams will now supercool their engines and push the cars to the line with the engine at only 100 degrees F. Racing a cold engine filled with conventional 20-50W oil would cause severe engine damage because the oil system would not be able to handle the power required to pump cold 50W oil. But new synthetic blends can safely operate at WOT even at cool temperatures. This technique frees up significant horsepower, but should only be used on constantly maintained race engines because low oil temperatures will trap moisture in the crankcase. There are also synthetic oils (designed for street/strip performance engines) that are worth the

THE OIL SYSTEM

Oil formulation has evolved for decades and will continue to be adapted. The current practice for many builders is to break in a new engine with specialized break-in oil and then switch to a high-performance synthetic for the racing season. Joe Gibbs and Royal Purple are two well-regarded brands offering specialized lubrication products.

extra cost because they handle high temperatures better than conventional oil.

Oil Filter and Cooler

The factory-type oil filter on a big-block seems to work fine for engines up to 600 hp. However, many racers don't like the horizontal filter because it can be awkward to work around. One common solution is to hang a remote oil filter from the inner fender or the motor plate and use large lines (such as number-12 AN) to plumb the external filter to the oil pump. An external oil filter offers flexibility; you can select a mount and filter that is not limited to the standard Mopar screw-on filter. There are many racing filters that use a larger thread size on the inlet; some inlet threads are as large as 1½ inches—twice as large as the stock Mopar threads. Another popular option is to use a remote mount that accepts the Chevy-style oil filter; there is a wider selection of oil filters for that mount. One popular oil filter is the two-quart-tall Chevy truck-style filter. This filter is 8 inches tall, so the remote mount has to be hung in a location that provides room to change the filter. A two-quart remote filter will provide tremendous capacity as well as extra cooling from the exposed surface area. You can simplify plumbing the external oil filter by equipping the oil pump with a cover that is threaded for number-12 AN fittings. Avoid using leak-causing extra adapters by threading the fittings directly into the oil pump cover.

For dyno testing, many builders use a screen-type oil filter that can be opened up for inspection and cleaning. As long as the filter stays clean during the dyno session, you know that the internals of the motor are in good shape. During the course of many dyno pulls, a pattern develops around what collects inside of the screen-type filter. Upon initial startup, the screen will often show lint from shop rags used during engine assembly. If the cylinder heads have had any porting work or other machine work, there will often be small pieces of aluminum in the

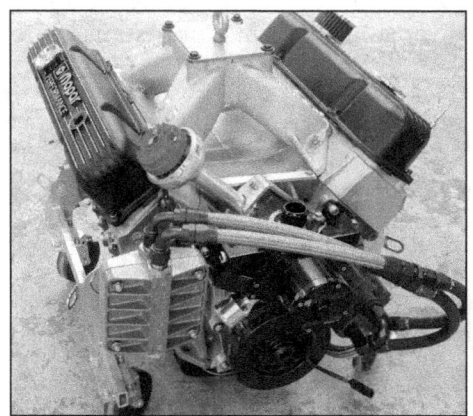

The gold-colored housing on the front of this race motor is a screen-type filter from Racor. The filter uses a fine mesh screen element that you can easily remove from the housing and clean.

oil. If you were too liberal with the RTV silicone during assembly, there will often be tiny chunks of that showing up in the screen. An engine that was assembled properly and kept clean during assembly will usually start to have clean screens after a few dyno pulls. If the screen stays clean after that, then the motor should be good to go into a car using a conventional canister-type filter. The screen-type filters often don't flow enough oil for use in a street-driven vehicle, but some drag racers do use them.

Oil coolers are rarely used on drag race cars but are a standard fixture on the road race circuit. If you feel the need to use an oil cooler with a big-block Mopar, then the same guidelines I covered for the remote oil filter would apply. The external, accessible oil pump on the big-block makes the Mopar easy to work with for external oil lines. For a street car, it is probably a good idea to consider a thermostat control for the oil

When the top cover of the Racor filter housing is removed, the filter screen can be quickly inspected for any trash. This engine has about 80 dyno pulls on it, and the screen is still very clean after each run. If there is any significant debris in the filter, the engine needs to be examined before further operation.

CHAPTER 3

cooler, so that the oil will come up to temperature fairly quickly. Keeping the oil temperatures above 200 degrees F best suits street-driven vehicles because any moisture in the oil is boiled off.

Dry Sump System

A dry sump system used to be considered fairly exotic technology, but a lot of hardcore engine parts are beginning to show up on the higher-powered bracket cars. A dry sump system has a number of advantages over a wet sump system, including less chance of dumping oil on the track if engine failure occurs. A properly designed and installed dry sump system will significantly improve power. Some builders claim a consistent 30- to 50-hp improvement with a dry sump. This is due to reduced windage losses in the pan as well as positive effects seen from running pan vacuum.

Dry sump systems are no longer much more expensive than wet systems. If you calculate the cost of a complete wet sump system, including oil pump and pickup, lines, external oil filters, a custom oil pan, and a vacuum pump system, the difference between a wet and dry system is small. A complete system might only cost 10 percent more than a complete wet sump system purchased brand-new.

One drawback to the dry sump system is the extra plumbing involved, as well as the space to accommodate the tank. Also, you will need fabricated brackets for the pump, block inlets, and other fittings. The dry sump systems are harder to install than wet sump systems, but race engine builders able to fabricate parts usually use them. I recently completed a dry sump installation on a big-block Mopar, and had to fabricate the drive system as well as the mounting system because I couldn't find anything currently on the market that would properly fit or work in our application. Using an ATI harmonic damper with a Chevy bolt pattern would have saved some time. If the Chevy crankshaft pulley bolt pattern is used, it is simple to mount any of the available Chevy drive systems that are currently on the market.

A dry sump system offers a great deal of flexibility. This allows more control of lubrication issues than in a wet sump system. For instance, the dry system is belt-driven, and you can quickly change the pulley ratio on the pump for a particular setup. This allows you to tune the oil pump output to match the needs of the engine and to minimize power consumption. Often, a dry sump oil pump is driven at 57 percent of engine speed by using a 16-tooth pulley on the crankshaft and a 28-tooth pulley on the pump. If the 57-percent ratio generates too much oil volume, then a 14-tooth pulley will provide a slightly slower 50-percent drive ratio. If neither of these ratios provides the correct oil volume to the engine, there are other choices for both the crankshaft pulley and the oil pump pulley from vendors such as Peterson and Moroso. A dry sump system can also be expanded from two scavenge sections to three or four scavenge sections. This allows you to place additional pickup lines into the valley of the engine, or at more locations on the oil pan, to ensure that less oil is whipping around inside the engine.

As stated earlier, the flat pan rail on the big-block makes it fairly easy

Mounting a dry sump pump on a big-block Mopar requires some fabrication because off-the-shelf parts are rare. A Moroso 63848 drive assembly and a custom-built pump mount are shown. The Moroso drive assembly is a good solution for those who do not have any fabrication capability, but it is fairly bulky.

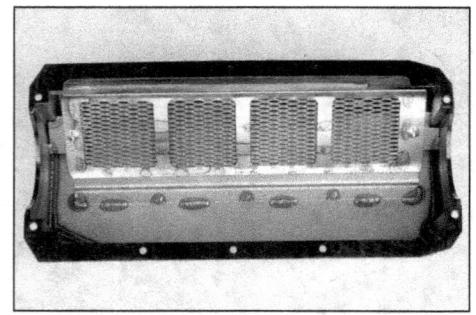

Here is an internal shot of a dry sump pan. This particular pan is for a small-block application, but the idea is the same for a big-block. The pickups for the scavenge lines are located beneath the screened area.

A dry sump system is the best choice for either road racing or drag racing. The cost is slightly higher than a conventional wet sump system, but there are significant benefits including more horsepower because of less windage in the pan. Not many parts are available, so be prepared to fabricate items to hang a dry sump onto a big-block Mopar.

This dry sump drive mechanism is lightweight and compact. The large hex on the nose of the drive can be used to rotate the engine with a wrench. This drive hub was fabricated to fit an MSD crank trigger wheel, but with minor modifications this design could be used with any damper.

This special spline drive adapter from Peterson bolts to the harmonic damper using the six crankshaft pulley bolts. In this application, a crank trigger wheel was also used, so the bolts needed to be slightly longer to reach through the trigger wheel.

This B1 motor is using a four-stage dry sump system with three scavenge pickups in the sump. Also pictured is the dry sump tank mounted on the motor plate as well as a special filter housing that mounts to the block in place of the oil pump. (Photo courtesy of Koffel's Place)

to fabricate different oil pans to see how they'll work in a particular chassis. Oil pans built for dry sump systems can be very similar to ones used in wet systems. However, the dry sump pans typically are shallower and have the pickups placed throughout the pan rather than located in a central sump area. It is also possible to convert a wet sump pan to a dry sump pan by adding the extra pickups into the sump. Converting a wet sump pan to a dry sump is a low-buck trick that you can use to test out a new system before investing in a dedicated dry sump pan.

If you decide to use a dry sump early in the engine design process, you can make other power-adding engine alterations. For example, a dry sump pump that is capable of pulling a vacuum in the crankcase can enhance the use of gas ported pistons and narrow piston rings. These factors will all work together to reduce losses from windage within the engine as well as to reduce ring flutter and improve ring seal.

As stated before, when taking aggressive steps to remove oil windage, it might also be necessary to provide extra clearance for items such as the piston pins, so they get sufficient lubrication. Another option: use parts such as the DLC-coated piston pins, to reduce their need for splash lubrication. Also, when designing an engine to operate with crankcase vacuum, you need to select gaskets and seals that keep the crankcase sealed.

Top-End vs. Bottom-End Oiling

The production-style big-block Mopar sends lubricating oil to the rocker arms through a passageway drilled in the number-4 journal of the camshaft. The passage in the camshaft only lines up with the oil hole in the bearing once every rotation of the cam, so the rocker arms get one squirt of oil for every two times the crankshaft rotates. This timed oil flow to the rocker arms seems like an odd design, but it works fine for moderate valvespring pressures at lower engine speed. However, engines operating at high speeds and/or using high-pressure valvesprings often develop problems with the rocker arms or pushrod tips due to a lack of lubrication.

One simple solution is to groove the number-4 camshaft journal, so there is a constant flow of oil to the rocker arms. But a groove in the cam journal usually provides too much oil, so oil passages in the cylinder block need to be drilled and tapped for a restrictor that corrects the amount of oil carried up to the rocker arms. A .060-inch-diameter restrictor seems to be a good starting point when using full time oiling. One problem with putting the restrictors in the block is that the cylinder head needs to be removed in order to change the size of the restrictor. So if you assemble an engine and find out that you have too much or not enough oil, then you can spend considerable repair time to fix the issue.

There's another issue that can be even more troublesome than inadequate oil for the top end. Any oil sent to the top end from the number-4 main bearing is not available for the number-6 and number-7 connecting rods, which are also fed from this bearing. If the number-4 cam journal is grooved in an attempt to send more oil to the rocker arms, there will be even less oil for the

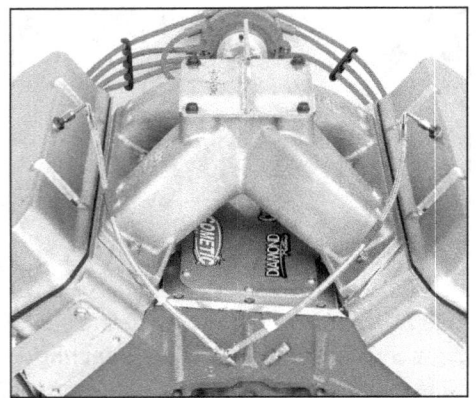

Valve cover oiling is an effective way to cool the valve springs and to provide extra lubrication to the rocker arms. The main oil gallery port at the back of the block uses lines to feed the spray bars inside the valve covers. The extra oil flowing to the valvetrain reduces oil pressure by about 5 psi.

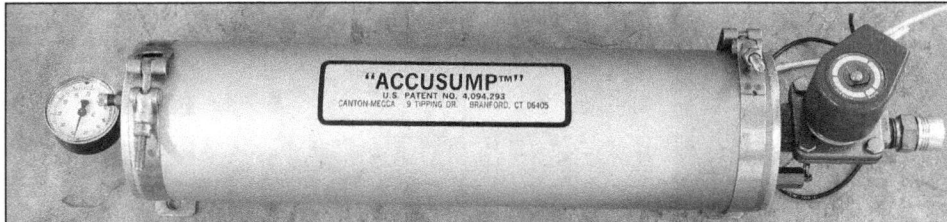

An accumulator provides excellent performance for any wet sump oil system. The accumulator stores oil under pressure that can be used either when starting the engine, or as a safety buffer if pickup is uncovered during high-g maneuvers.

number-4 main bearing. I once saw a big-block Mopar engine spin the number-6 and number-7 rod bearings during a dyno pull even though the dyno instruments showed a steady 70 psi of oil pressure at the back of the block. A failure like this is a significant clue that the oil volume diverted to the top end of the motor can have a detrimental effect on the life of the bottom end.

There are several possible solutions that will provide extra oil to the valvetrain without starving the number-4 main bearing. One possibility is to use external oil lines from the back of the block to the rocker shafts, such as Indy Cylinder Heads does with their 440-1 cylinder head package. With the Indy system, the cylinder head blocks off the internal oil passage from the number-4 cam journal so the number-4 main journal doesn't have to share oil with the top end. Another possible solution is to use a valvetrain that is oiled through the pushrods rather than through the block. Several of the higher-end rocker arm systems are designed for pushrod oiling, and we'll cover this method in more detail in the valvetrain chapter (Chapter 8). Oiling the rocker arms via the pushrods eliminates the issue with the number-4 main journal, but it does create another issue with how the pushrods get the correct amount of oil from the main gallery. One other possible solution is to connect the rocker arm oil passage directly to the main gallery rather than divert oil from the number-4 main. The new blocks from World Products are designed this way, with the rocker arm oil passages drilled into the lifter gallery rather than drilled over to the number-4 cam journal.

Extra Lubrication Requirements

As engine builders continue to push the specific output of the engines higher and higher, they continue to see new failure modes. Over the last several years, builders have seen more failures caused by excess heat in the pistons and the valvesprings. These failures typically show up in circle track use, but drag race motors will also see valvespring failure due to excessive heat. In both cases, the best solution is to use the oil system to provide cooling for the hot parts. Valve covers can be fitted with oil manifolds that spray a stream of oil onto each valvespring. This steady stream of oil will carry away heat from the valvespring.

The same concept is applied to circle track engines, and piston oilers are used to carry away piston heat. Piston oiling has been common for big diesel engines for years, but dedicated oilers are fairly new for V-8 race engines. The newest NASCAR-type engines have oiling systems with small nozzles that spray oil onto the bottom of each piston. None of the aftermarket Mopar blocks have this feature, but if you are designing an engine for extreme output, such as land speed record use or offshore powerboat racing, piston oilers might be something worth considering.

Remember that the pump needs to supply the additional oil volume for the valvesprings or the pistons. In a dry sump system, the pulley ratio can be easily changed to provide extra oil volume to the engine. For a standard wet sump system, you can either set the pressure relief higher or purchase a larger pump that has a higher volume rating. During some recent dyno testing, we saw a 5-psi decrease in oil pressure when valve cover oilers were installed. The addition of spray bar oilers in the valve covers required a small amount of oil and caused a small decline in oil pressure. In this case, we had plenty of oil pressure, even after adding the valve cover oilers, so there was no need to change pressure relief springs.

CHAPTER 4

CRANKSHAFTS

The factory crankshafts only came in two strokes, a 3.38-inch stroke used in the B motors and the 3.75-inch stroke used in the RB motors. All factory crankshafts were manufactured from forged steel until a gradual shift toward using less expensive cast-iron crankshafts occurred in the 1970s. There aren't many Mopar big-block motors in the wrecking yards anymore, but if you do find one, remember that a cast crank motor should have a stand-alone E stamped on the ID pad at the front of the motor. Also, the cast crank motors typically were externally balanced and the harmonic damper was physically larger with a built-in counterweight.

Crankshaft Selection

A cast crank is fine for up to 500-hp engines but, given the availability of forged crankshafts, there is no need to use a cast crank in a performance engine. The factory forged crankshafts were strong enough to be used in moderate-performance engines producing 600 hp, but tend to crack after continued use in higher-powered motors due to the rolled fillets on the main journals. If you design a maximum performance motor that is designed to make more than 600 hp, you should strongly consider an aftermarket crankshaft—any motor designed to make more than 750 hp should definitely use one. Besides the limitations of the stock crank in terms of durability, most performance engines built today use an aftermarket crankshaft to gain extra displacement.

It is easy to find an aftermarket crankshaft for the RB engine because vendors have long been building cranks for the Hemi motor. The Hemi crankshaft is very similar to the

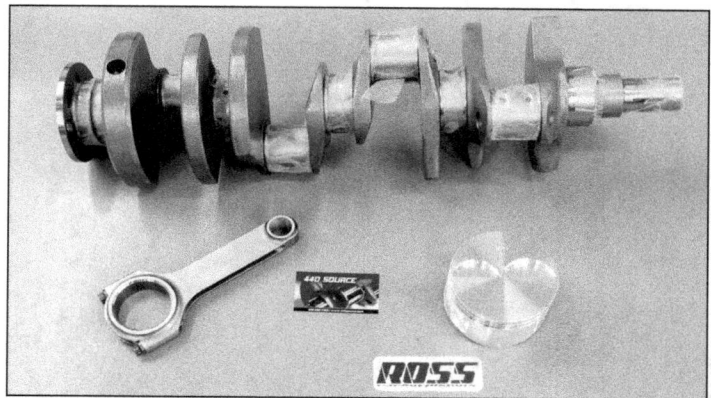

This brand-new rotating assembly still has the protective paper on the crankshaft journals. This 4.250-stroke crankshaft from 440Source has the popular 2.200 rod journals. The connecting rods are 6.700-long Chevy big-block rods with the 2.200 rod journals and .990 piston pins.

Here is a high-grade rotating assembly destined for a low-deck 512 motor. This is a Callies crankshaft with a 4.250 stroke and the 2.200 rod journals. The connecting rods are Crower big-block Chevy I-beam rods that are 6.535 long. The pistons are custom-made units from Diamond Racing with a large dish because this will be a street motor that runs on pump gas.

HOW TO BUILD MAX-PERFORMANCE MOPAR BIG-BLOCKS

wedge crankshaft and interchanges into the RB with only minor adjustments. However, aftermarket crankshafts were quite expensive until offshore-produced cranks started to show up. Several vendors, such as Eagle, 440 Source, and Ohio Crankshaft worked with suppliers around the world to bring low-cost, forged 4340 steel crankshafts to market. These crankshafts can sell for as little as $500 and they are available in a wide variety of strokes, bolt patterns, and bob weights.

For an economical performance engine, you will want to start with an off-the-shelf crankshaft, rather than have a crankshaft custom built. That would limit you to one of the five or six commonly available strokes, but this is not a problem because other major components will also only be available for the common strokes. As discussed in other sections of this book, the crankshaft stroke needs to be selected in conjunction with a decision on the cylinder head because these important subsystems need to work together.

Crankshaft strokes that are currently available include 3.75, 3.90, 4.15, 4.25, 4.375, and 4.500 inches.

The 4.500-stroke crankshaft fits best into the RB block because that length of stroke makes it difficult to fit everything into the shorter cylinder length of the B block. Not all of these crankshaft strokes are available off the shelf in both B and RB main bearing sizes, but some of the vendors will provide the B journal for an additional charge. Typically, the crankshafts with strokes longer than 4.250 will not be used with the smaller B block main size due to the lack of overlap between the main journal and the rod journal. This is especially true for the smaller 2.200-rod-journal

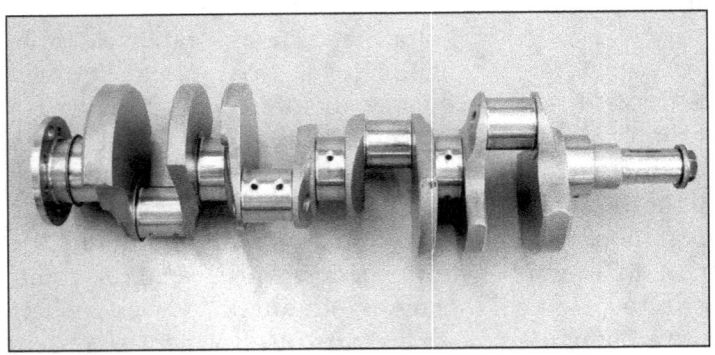

This is a 4.250-stroke crankshaft from 440 Source with 2.750 main journals and 2.200 rod journals. Even though this is a budget crankshaft, the oil holes are carefully chamfered and the counterweights are smoothly finished.

This is the bottom end of a 505 wedge with a 4.250-stroke crankshaft and 6.800-long SCAT rods. The SCAT rods are the H-beam style, which is a very economical design that is capable of around 800-hp maximum power.

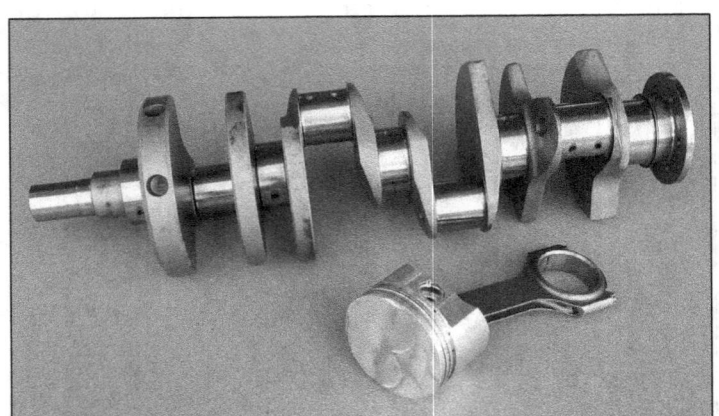

This rotating assembly is for a 505 Wedge motor. This is a 4.250-stroke crankshaft with SCAT 6.800 long connecting rods and custom Diamond Racing pistons. The small dome on these pistons generates a 13.5:1 compression ratio when used with Indy cylinder heads. These parts are all safe to operate up to about 850 hp.

Bottom view of a 431 stroker motor. This assembly uses a reworked RB crankshaft that was modified to fit into this 383 block. The use of a 3.750 stroke in a 383 block gives 426 ci at the standard 4.250 bore size and 431 ci when the block is bored to a .030-overbore size of 4.280.

CRANKSHAFTS

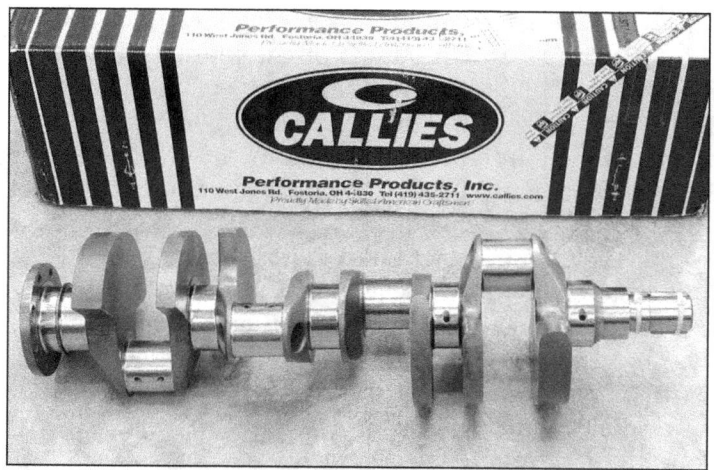

Callies offers their cost-effective Dragonslayer line of crankshafts for the big-block Mopar in several different stroke configurations. This crankshaft has a stroke of 4.150 inches and it uses the Chevy 2.200 rod journals. The Dragonslayer cranks come with an 8-bolt flywheel pattern and dual-crank keyways.

This crankshaft for a low-deck 470 motor was made by turning the mains on a 413 crankshaft down to 2.625 inches and offset-grinding the rod journals to a diameter of 2.200 inches on a 3.90 stroke. The 3.90 stroke works great with a 6.700-long connecting rod.

size because the cheek overlap is greatly diminished. As discussed in Chapter 2, the main bore in a B block can be bored out to the 2.750-main-bore size in order to run the larger RB-main size in the B block, but it is a lot of extra work.

After the crankshaft stroke is selected, you need to make a decision on the type of connecting rod to use. One of the major trends in engine building over the last decade has been the shift to smaller and smaller rod journals, with some NASCAR engines using very small rod journals from Honda or Mitsubishi engines. This trend has also been noticeable in the big-block Mopar world, with many builders switching over to the big-block Chevy connecting-rod journal size. This connecting rod uses a 2.200-inch-diameter rod journal instead of the larger Mopar 2.375 journal. Most of the crankshafts available can use the 2.200 journal, and within a few years the Mopar-size journal might be obsolete for all but the most powerful engines.

Another crankshaft option that tends to cause a little confusion is the number of flywheel bolts. The factory Hemi used an 8-bolt arrangement while the big-block wedge motors had a 6-bolt pattern. Not only did the Hemi get 8 bolts, but they were larger 1/2-inch diameter bolts rather than the smaller 7/16 bolts used on the wedge motors. There was no strength issue with the 6-bolt flywheels, so it is unclear why the Mopar engineers designed the 8-bolt arrangement. Was it the same sense of overkill that led them to use the big 2.375 rod journals and the heavy 1.094 piston pins? In any case, you need to decide which flywheel attachment bolt pattern to use. There are flywheels and flex plates available in both arrangements, so it might not matter too

This 431 stroker crankshaft was made from an original 413 forging. The main journals were turned down to 2.625, and the counterweights were cut down to clear the block. Also pictured is a 6.760-length I-beam rod from 440 Source as well as a shelf piston from Diamond Racing.

A deck bridge with a dial indicator is a good method for finding TDC. The piston should be wiggled back and forth to make sure it isn't cocked in the bore.

CHAPTER 4

Flywheel flange of a fuel crankshaft shows that there is no locating ring for the flywheel or torque converter. If you buy one of these crankshafts you won't have an easy way to properly locate the flywheel.

much. The 6-bolt parts are a little easier to find than the 8-bolt parts, so that would be the typical preference but it is possible that the only crankshaft that fits your need has an 8-bolt flange.

The Funny Car Crankshaft

There are many used questionable crankshafts for sale on eBay and other auction sites. Many of these come from professional race crews who replace the crankshafts on preventative maintenance schedules. Those crankshafts are very expensive new and if they can sell the used ones to offset some of the purchase price, then all the better for the budget. Some people think it's cool to have a Funny Car crankshaft in their street car, but it's a rude awakening when the crankshaft arrives in a box from their eBay seller and it won't work in their engine. The Funny Car crankshafts will bolt in because they typically use the same bearing size and length as a passenger car crankshaft, but the similarities stop there. These crankshafts often have a unique flange on the flywheel end for a slipper-style clutch, and sometimes the snout is also different in order to drive the huge superchargers that are used in the Funny Car motors. The other issue is that these crankshafts are often very heavy because they are used in Hemi-type motors with heavy pistons and heavy piston pins. With brand-new stroker crankshafts available for $500, why waste your time trying to get someone else's scrap parts to work in your engine?

Crankshaft Preparation

The subject of crankshaft preparation used to take a fair amount of space in books written in the past. Those authors would detail how to polish the crankshaft, remove excess weight, smooth the counterweights, and teardrop the oiling holes. Now, even the lowest-cost cranks have all of the basic machine work already finished. However, it's still important to closely inspect all of the crankshaft journals for proper dimensions. It is common for the lower-priced crankshafts to have excessive taper on either the rod or main journals. This might be due to lack of training of the machine operators who make the crankshafts or maybe a lack of investment by the lower-end companies in their production equipment. Sometimes the bargain crankshafts turn out to be not such a great bargain because you have to re-grind the journals undersize.

In addition to checking the journals for proper tolerance, the rear main seal area as well as the snout area should be checked for proper dimensions, so the damper will properly install on the crankshaft taper. For a super-high-power application, it is a good idea to check the roundness of the journals as well as the hardness of the crankshaft material. Nobody's quality control is 100-percent accurate and it is always better to double-check these critical parameters than it is to drive over your crankshaft at 150 mph.

Several of the higher-end crankshaft manufacturers can add features

It is always a good idea to check the runout on a new crankshaft to make sure it is straight. The crank should be supported by the number-2 and number-4 main bearings while it is slowly rotated to check for any machining errors or shipping damage.

Putting a 4.250-stroke crankshaft into a 400 block means a bit of grinding will be necessary around the oil pump pickup boss. The smaller 2.200 rod journals reduce the amount of grinding that is necessary.

CRANKSHAFTS

This is a close-up view of the oil pickup boss when using a 4.250-stroke crankshaft in an RB block. This crankshaft has the smaller 2.200 rod journal, which usually provides more space because the outer profile of the connecting rods can be made smaller.

A long travel dial indicator can be used to verify the crankshaft stroke. It is a good idea to check the stroke for each pair of cylinders to verify that the crankshaft has been properly machined.

Small notches needed to be ground into the bottom of the cylinder walls of this 383 block when a 3.750-inch-stroke crankshaft with stock-diameter Mopar rod journals were used. The amount removed may vary depending on which brand of connecting rods is used so if you plan to swap components in the future, you might want to grind the reliefs a little larger than necessary.

to the crankshafts, such as knife edging the counterweights to reduce windage. There are also features, such as pendulum weights, that move the heavy weight on the counterweight farther from the center of the crankshaft, so it has more leverage. A lighter weight rotating farther from the center is as effective as a heavy weight that is close to the center of the crankshaft. This approach allows the manufacturer to balance the crankshaft at a lighter total weight. Another way to save a few pounds from the crankshaft is to profile machine the flywheel flange or to gun drill the main journals. Also, the holes for the rod journals can be drilled out with either a straight hole or some manufacturers drill two holes in at an angle. All of these operations add time and expense to the manufacturing process, but the extra cost is often worth it if you are building a motor for competitive class racing.

Given all of these options, a crankshaft for a big-block Mopar can cost from $500 to $2,500 for basically identical specifications. Both will have the same stroke and bearing sizes and be made from an alloy such as 4340 chrome-moly steel. But obviously, there will be significant differences between the $500 crankshaft and the $2,500 crankshaft in terms of the material properties, heat treat, finish quality, extra features, etc. You do not necessarily need to spend $2,500 on the crankshaft in order to build a 750-hp motor, but you also might not want to use the least expensive crankshaft that you can find.

Balancing

The entire rotating assembly needs to be balanced before final assembly. To balance these components, the individual pistons, rods, bearings, and rings must be weighed, and then mounting bob weights are attached to the crankshaft to duplicate the weight of these parts. If the counterweights on the crankshaft are either too heavy or too light for the rest of the rotating assembly, the balancing process can become expensive. A crankshaft that is too light will need to have material added to it by welding on steel or pressing in Mallory metal. A crankshaft that is

The flange on this crankshaft has been scalloped out in an attempt to shave some weight off of the motor. Every little bit helps but this is a lot of work for just a few ounces.

too heavy will need to have material removed by drilling or turning on a lathe. You need to make a rough calculation of the piston and connecting rod weights before ordering the crankshaft. Most of the vendors will be able to provide a crankshaft that is rough balanced to a specific weight. This will save time and money at the machine shop.

Production-built 440 engines used heavy piston pins and heavier cast pistons, so the resulting bob weights were usually around 2,700 grams. Currently, a typical RB block with a 500-inch rotating assembly has lighter-weight forged pistons and pins than a stock motor, which means less counterweight. The total bob weight for a modern stroker assembly often is around 2,400 grams, which is significantly lighter than a stock motor. Since the rotating weight is lighter in modern stroker motors than factory engines, the aftermarket is producing crankshafts with lower bob weights.

Harmonic Damper

In any performance engine, a harmonic damper plays a crucial role by absorbing harmful crankshaft vibrations. If left unchecked, these internal vibrations inside the crankshaft can lead to catastrophic failure of the crank or the entire engine. There are many different harmonic dampers available, including units from ATI, BHJ, Romac, and Fluidampr.

ATI offers more than a dozen different dampers for the big-block Mopar engine, which gives them by far the largest selection to choose from. ATI's selection includes super-lightweight units with aluminum hubs, models that have extra clearance for gear drives, and dampers with the Chevy pulley bolt pattern.

The harmonic damper installation needs to achieve the proper amount of press fit onto the crankshaft. Follow the manufacturer specifications precisely; a loose fit will not work properly and there can be severe damage if it is too tight. A machine shop usually needs to hone

The front counterweight of this crankshaft had to be drilled multiple times to balance the rotating assembly. Many aftermarket cranks are manufactured heavier than they need to be because it is easier to remove weight than to add it. If you are using lightweight rotating parts, it might be better to turn the counterweights down on a lathe rather than drill a lot of holes like this.

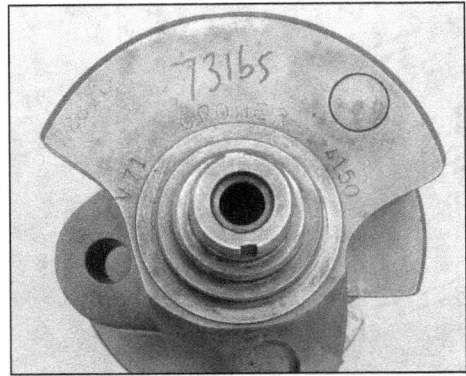

The front counterweight on this Crower funny car crankshaft shows a bob weight of 2821 grams, a stroke of 4.150 inches and a total weight of 73 lbs. This crankshaft is way too heavy for use in a wedge engine with modern pistons, so the counterweights would need to be cut down significantly before it would balance.

This crankshaft required some extra work to balance. Notice the slug of Mallory metal in the counterweight as well as the chunk of steel that was welded onto the end of the counterweight.

The rod pins are often drilled out to reduce the rotating weight on performance crankshafts. Some vendors drill the pins straight through as shown here, while others drill in on an angle.

There are a variety of dampers available for the big-block Mopar. Shown is a Romac damper on the left and a BHJ damper on the right. Both of these dampers have recessed faces that will mount the crankshaft pulley in the stock location.

CRANKSHAFTS

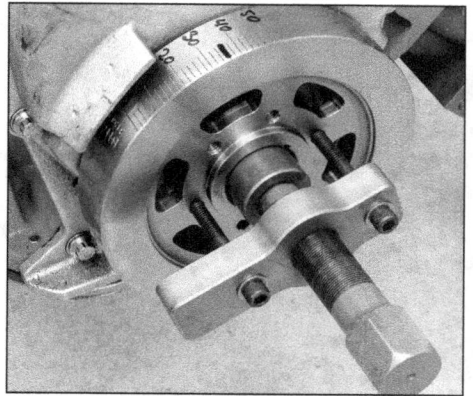

The damper should have a slight press fit in order to work correctly. The press fit requires quite a bit of force to overcome, so the correct tools must be used when installing and removing the damper. Here, a large threaded shaft is being used to remove the damper from the crankshaft.

The ATI damper has a flat face that is useful for mounting accessories. However, this flat face is not in the stock location, so a special pulley is required to line up with the water pump and alternator pulleys. The special 12-point crankshaft bolt visible in this picture is available from ARP.

The ATI damper makes a convenient mounting place for this crank trigger from MSD. Note also that the ATI damper has degree markings for the entire circumference.

This Fluidampr damper contains a special silicone fluid that absorbs the vibrations from the crankshaft. This damper has a recessed face for the pulley mounting that is in the stock location. Early Fluidamprs had a flat face, which required the use of a shorter Hemi-style crankshaft pulley.

ATI dampers are a modular design that allows them to be used in multiple applications. This picture illustrates two different hubs that fit the big-block Mopar engine. The longer hub is PN 916663 and it moves the damper farther out from the motor so that it can clear a gear drive or a Jesel belt drive. You need not buy a new damper if you upgrade to a Jesel belt drive; just order the longer hub.

the aftermarket dampers before they will fit properly. Sometimes the front snout of the lower-priced crankshafts will not meet the tight factory crankshaft specifications, so additional fitment work is required.

Keep in mind that many aftermarket dampers will not mount the pulley in the stock location. This can be a surprise if you are expecting to use your existing crankshaft pulley to drive the water pump and alternator. However, the accessories on a performance engine are often relocated, so sort out the pulley locations during the mock-up phase. For instance, if the engine is going to be mounted to the frame with a motor plate, then the water pump pulley will already be out of alignment with the crankshaft pulley. Also, many performance engines will use electric water pumps and do not require a crankshaft pulley. In any case, pulley alignment is one more area to consider when ordering an aftermarket damper.

CHAPTER 5

CONNECTING RODS

Unlike some of the other manufacturers, Mopar made connecting rods from beefy forgings. The B and RB connecting rods' primary drawback is that the rod journal and the piston pin were overbuilt. As much as it pains the traditional Mopar engine builder, it makes more sense to use a connecting rod with Chevy big-block pin sizes than to use those bigger and heavier Mopar sizes.

Connecting Rod Selection

Two big-block Mopar connecting rod lengths were available from the factory: a 6.358-inch for the low-deck motors and a 6.768-inch for the RB motors. Both factory connecting rods used a 2.375-inch rod journal and a 1.094-inch piston pin. By comparison, the Chevy big-block uses a connecting rod that is 6.135 inches long with a .990-inch-diameter piston pin and a 2.200-inch-diameter rod journal. While the stock length Chevy rod is a little short for a Mopar engine, the aftermarket offers a huge selection of connecting rods with the 2.200-/.990-inch pin sizes, so it is very easy to find an aftermarket connecting rod to fit almost any big-block build.

The Chevy connecting rod is a little narrower than the Mopar, but

Manley carries several different connecting rods for the big-block Mopar. Pictured here is an H-beam rod that is 6.965 inches long. This is a typical Hemi connecting rod length, but it can also be used in a wedge motor if the piston pin is moved up to compensate for the longer rod length. Manley also carries several professional quality connecting rods in an I-beam design.

One nice thing about using the 2.200 rod journal in a Mopar engine is that generic connecting rods are available at very low prices. These are Summit-branded rods, which are 6.700 inches long with the 2.200 and .990 pin sizes. A low-priced connecting rod like this should be fine at the 600-hp level but you would want a higher-quality part for much beyond that.

CONNECTING RODS

Crower has a nice selection of big-block Chevy rods, which can be used for Mopar wedge engines. This particular rod is 6.535 inches long, which fits well with a 4.250-stroke crankshaft in a 400 block. Also shown is a custom Diamond Racing piston that has a large dish in order to keep the compression ratio down to pump-gas range in a low-deck 512 motor.

the excess side clearance doesn't seem to cause any problems. The rod bearing width and clearance is what controls the amount of oil flow through the rod, not the side clearance. Most of the aftermarket Mopar crankshafts available with 2.200-inch rod journal pins are sized correctly for the narrower Chevy-style connecting rods.

440 Source offers several styles of connecting rods at very competitive prices. The rod pictured is a 6.760-inch-long I-beam rod forged from 4340 material. This rod combines the larger Mopar rod journal on the big end with the .990 pin size on the small end and would be a good choice for a stock-stroke 440.

Just for reference, the production Mopar rod journal pin is 2.375 x 2.050 inches while the Chevy big-block pin size is 2.200 x 2.009 inches. And the Chevy connecting rods are .991-inch wide, rather than the 1.015-inch width of the factory Mopar rod.

Rod length can be a controversial topic. Short rod "torque" motors and long rod "power" motors have respective proponents. Some builders simply claim that the correct rod length is whatever it takes to hook the crankshaft to the piston. Fortunately for us, the RB block has enough room for off-the-shelf rods that fit almost any situation.

A very common rod in a performance buildup is an aftermarket rod that is 6.800 inches long with the 2.200 rod journal size and the .990 piston pin size. When used with a 4.150- or 4.250-stroke crankshaft this rod provides a good rod-to-stroke-ratio, and it keeps the piston up in the cylinder bore and away from the crankshaft. The 6.800 rod is a little too long to fit into the shorter B block with a stroke bigger than 4.00 inches, but it works great in the RB block for most of the common stroke lengths. The slightly longer 7.100-inch rod with the Chevy pin sizes is another very popular rod length for the RB block. This longer rod works great with the longer-stroke motors with 4.375- or 4.500-inch-stroke crankshafts. The RB block fitted with a combination of a 4.50-stroke crankshaft with the 7.100-long connecting rod still provides enough room for the piston to have a common ring package deep valve pockets. I don't think the engineers who designed the original big-block back in 1958 had any idea that 50 years later people would be boring and stroking them to 600-ci monsters, but they would probably be proud to hear about it.

The 2.200 and .990 pin sizes are available in very large selection and competitive prices for these rods. On the other hand, fewer connecting rods are made in the Mopar sizes, so options for these are fewer and prices are higher. After you decide on rod length, it is easy to search the various vendors such as Manley, Crower, SCAT, and Oliver to find the possible rods to use. Connecting rods have become a commodity item over the years, so price is usually an indicator of quality. Any aftermarket rod with quality bolts is suitable for a 600-hp motor but if you are going to turn the wick up to 800 or 900 hp, then you should select parts from the higher-priced vendors.

Aluminum Rods

We have just focused on the steel connecting rods so far because that is the most logical choice for a 600- to 900-hp motor that is going to see some street miles. For a drag-race-only motor, aluminum connecting rods can be an excellent alternative. The aluminum rods are lighter weight and they provide some shock absorbing qualities, but they are also a little bulkier and are often more expensive. As with the steel rods, the most popular aluminum rods are going to come in the 2.200/.990-inch pin sizes and the lengths are typically going to be 6.700-, 6.800-, and 7.100-inch long. In the rare need for custom-length rods, aluminum would be easier to machine.

Connecting Rod Preparation

In the past, I would have written an entire section that covered the detailed procedures for re-working or blueprinting a set of stock LY rods for higher performance. This could involve honing, grinding the beams smooth, magnafluxing, shot peening,

CHAPTER 5

Various vendors offer bushings that can be used to float the pin in the small end of a stock connecting rod. Most aftermarket connecting rods on the market these days will already have bushings installed so there is no need to purchase them separately.

etc. But there really isn't any reason to use the factory rods anymore because they are more costly and of lesser quality than aftermarket alternatives, so...topic covered. Today, rod preparation should be limited to selecting the appropriate connecting rod for the build, and then giving those rods a very thorough inspection before installing them in the motor.

The vendor will likely recommend cycling the rod bolts several times before final torquing, and the bore must be checked for proper size and roundness. One problem with the lower-priced rods in the marketplace is that the big ends do not stay round after the bolts are pulled to the proper torque. So if you purchase the less-expensive rods, make sure you or your engine builder double-checks the big end for roundness after properly torquing the rod bolts.

Rotating Assembly Balancing

The big-block Mopar has a very heavy rotating assembly when assembled with factory parts. The average 440 motor will balance out around 2,700-grams bob weight using factory rods and pistons. The extra weight comes from the very tall cast pistons used in the factory block as well as the heavy 1.094-inch piston pin and the large 2.375-inch-diameter rod journal. The HP motors built during the 1970s were even heavier due to the large-beam connecting rod that was used. That might have been the "hot setup" in the 1970s, but today there is no reason for you to use such heavy components.

Over the years, higher-strength steel alloys have been developed for the manufacturing of engine components, resulting in today's stronger and lighter engines. A modern H-beam connecting rod that is 6.800 inches long with the 2.200 and .990 pin sizes is much lighter than a factory LY rod, yet it is capable of handling more than 800 hp. The piston and pin combination has also lost a lot of weight over the years. Modern high-performance forged pistons and .990-inch pins are much lighter than factory cast parts and the old TRW forged pistons. In the stroker motors, the piston can be even lighter because the longer stroke and longer connecting rod necessitates a shorter piston. Stock 440 pistons were as tall as 2.00 inches measured center-to-top, while stroker pistons used in a 505 motor with longer rods are usually about 1.50 inches.

The weight savings add up, and the net result is that the rotating assembly in a 505 motor can be up to

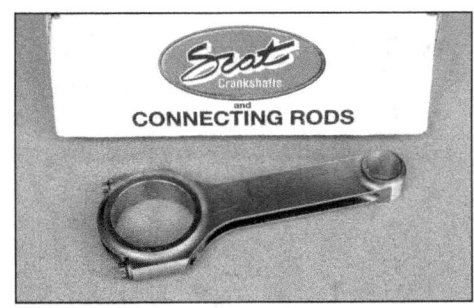

SCAT is an excellent place to purchase higher-quality connecting rods for motors in the 700- to 900-hp range. These SCAT H-beam rods are 6.800 inches long, which works really well with 4.150 or 4.250-stroke cranks in an RB block.

The Compstar line of products from Callies are known for their high quality and moderate prices. This is a 6.800-inch-long I-beam rod with the ARP 2000 rod bolt. Extra material around the big end bore on this rod distinguishes it from some of the other more generic connecting rods.

10 lbs lighter than the parts used in a factory stock 440. This is a 10-lb reduction in nose weight and crucial spinning weight. Another benefit of a lighter rotating assembly is reduced stresses on the cylinder block, crankshaft, and the connecting rods.

A modern 505 engine built with aftermarket connecting rods and high-quality forged pistons will typically have a bob weight in the range of 2,300 to 2,400 grams. This means that the crankshaft can be lighter and that the counterweights on the crankshaft can be smaller.

CHAPTER 6

PISTONS

There is a large selection of aftermarket pistons and piston vendors to choose from these days for building a performance big-block. Piston options have kept pace with the rapid increase in the number of stroker kits available in the catalogs. And if the exact piston isn't available, then it is often easy to have your favorite piston vendor make up a set of semi-custom pistons.

Most of the piston manufacturing companies today use the same material for their high-performance pistons. They are usually made from 4032 aluminum alloy with tighter fitting bores for moderate-performance applications and 2618 material with a looser fitting bore for the higher-horsepower applications. If you buy an aftermarket stock piston, it will

These pistons have a very small 5-cc dome on them, but that is all it takes to make 13.5:1 compression when using a 4.250-stroke crankshaft. The dome on these pistons is only .060 high, so it doesn't impede the flame travel too much.

Diamond Racing is an excellent source for big-block Mopar pistons. They have a large number of pistons listed in the catalog for various engine combinations, or they can quickly custom-build a set if nothing in the catalog fits the bill.

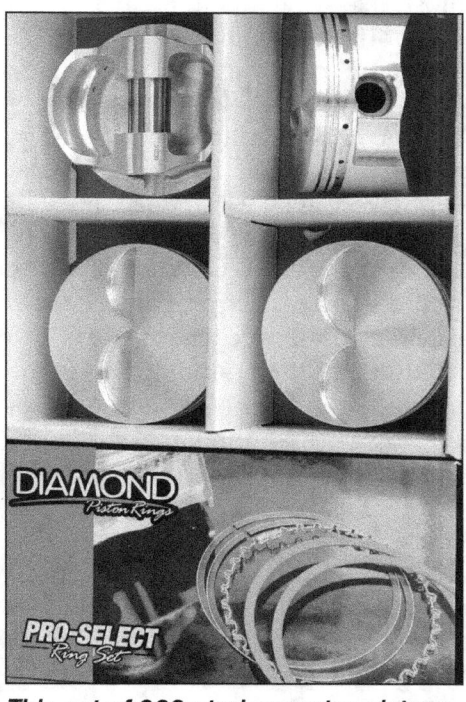

This set of 383 stroker motor pistons is designed to work with a 3.750-stroke crankshaft and stock length 440 connecting rods. The combination of the longer stroke and the longer connecting rods requires a piston that is much shorter than stock, but notice that there is still a small amount of space between the oil ring and the piston pin.

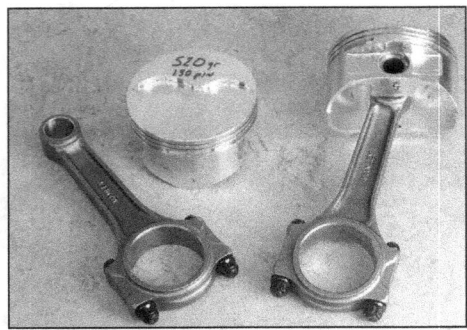
These stroker pistons are for a low-deck 470 motor. The combination of the 4.375 bore size and the longer 3.90 stroke in a 400 block makes for a compact and lightweight rotating assembly. These pistons weighed only 520 grams while the mating .990-diameter pins weighed 150 grams.

This piston is for a 514 motor with a 4.440 bore size and a 4.150 stroke. The intake valve relief is .260 deep because this motor will be fitted with a long duration roller cam.

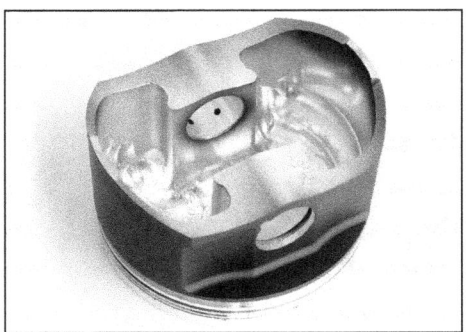
A view of the bottom of the 514 piston shows some of the extra machine work that was performed in order to reduce the weight of the piston. This customized piston is from Diamond Racing.

most likely be manufactured from one of these two alloys.

Many other aspects of engine design influence piston design, so a builder will usually specify piston requirements last. The valve pocket depth will depend on the camshaft lift and duration as well as the size of the valves and the valve angle in the cylinder head. The compression ratio is a key design element that also needs to be determined before the piston design can be finalized. Also, the bore size, the stroke length, and the length of the connecting rod all need to be selected before you chose the piston design. You also need to tell the piston manufacturer the style of ring, size of the piston pin, and the type of piston locks, so you get the product you need.

Compression Ratio Considerations

The compression ratio needs to be determined early in the engine design stage because heads, deck height, and so many other elements depend on it. In order to decide on a compression ratio, you need to initially decide on the use of the engine as well as the allowable operational costs. Building a high-compression engine that only drinks race gas can quickly take all the fun out of a daily driver street car, so stay on the conservative side.

If we assume that any performance big-block Mopar is going to be using an aluminum head with a closed chamber design, then we can draw a boundary of about 11:1 maximum compression ratio for a motor that is going to run on pump gas. A 10:1 ratio is probably a safer and wiser decision if you will be primarily driving it on the street because pump gas quality does vary. If it's a racing-only motor and you are willing to pay for race gas, the compression ratio can be increased significantly.

Most bracket-race-type motors will produce good power and have decent reliability if they have a final compression ratio between 13:1 and 15:1. You should discuss a suitable compression ratio with an expert and/or your engine builder. Be sure to take into account the fuel that is available at the local tracks and other such factors. But in general, the higher the compression the better the motor will run as long as the piston dome does not impede the flame travel. One nice thing about building up a 500-ci or larger Mopar is that compression is typically not a problem. A flat-top piston produces about 12:1 compression depending on the size of the combustion chamber in the head and it will only take a very small dome to push the compression up into the full-race category of 14:1 or 15:1.

Valve-to-Piston Clearance

For a moderate-level performance engine, you will likely be purchasing standard part number pistons that will come with predetermined valve pockets. These standard valve pockets work with the more popular cylinder heads and the more common valve sizes.

Any of the high-performance vendors, such as Diamond Racing, JE, Ross, Wiseco, etc., will have dimensions and specifications on file for the valve locations of the popular cylinder head choices. The shelf pistons will typically be designed for the most popular cylinder head, such as those from Edelbrock or Indy, and the valve pockets will be deep enough for a camshaft with about 270 degrees of duration at .050 lift. If you are going to build an engine with oversize valves or use a camshaft with really large duration, the standard valve pockets might not work and a custom piston should be ordered.

Most builders know the valve-to-piston clearance is critical; an error can quickly lead to engine failure. Besides checking the clearance, it is also important to make sure that the angle of the valve relief in the piston was machined at the actual installed angle of the valves. The valve angle for any big-block cylinder head will usually be 15 degrees so this is a standard dimension that the piston vendors have on file. If you are using a unique set of cylinder heads or have angle milled your cylinder heads, you will need custom valve reliefs in the pistons. Also check the radial clearance around the valve. As larger intake valves become popular, it is important to double-check that the valves have radial clearance in the piston because older pistons might not be compatible with the newer intake valve sizes.

The easiest way to check valve-to-piston clearance is with a pair of lightweight checking springs and a dial indicator. You can slowly rotate the crankshaft, depress the valves, and read the clearance off of the dial indicator. The valves will usually come closest to the piston at about 10 degrees before top dead center (BTDC) for the exhaust and 10 degrees after top dead center (ATDC) for the intake. These numbers vary according to how the cam is degreed in, so you need to sweep a wider range for critical applications. The lightweight spring method is okay for a moderate-performance engine buildup, but it will give you excessive clearance when you use stiff roller cam springs; the lightweight springs do not generate the same deflections in the valvetrain. Install the actual springs to check valve-to-piston clearance on any high-revving engine using a roller cam valvetrain.

Ideal valve-to-piston clearance is always a topic of debate. Typical recommendations for minimum clearances with steel connecting rods are about .100 inch for the intake and .125 inch for the exhaust, but professional builders will run the intake clearance as tight as .050 inch. However, you run the risk of damaging the engine if you need to run tighter clearances in order to maximize the compression ratio or the camshaft duration. The intake clearance can be reduced more than the exhaust

This close-up picture shows a high-compression piston in a 400 block. This engine needed the tall domes in order to achieve a 12:1 compression ratio since this is a stock-stroke 400 engine with 84-cc Edelbrock heads. A dome this large will impede flame travel a bit, but there isn't any other way to achieve the desired compression ratio.

The valve reliefs in this piston are deeper and located in slightly different locations in order to work with the valves in a B1 cylinder head. The piston vendor should have B1 valve reliefs on file.

CHAPTER 6

Valve drop is measured with the piston at TDC. The easiest way to measure valve drop is to remove the valve springs and install a dial indicator directly on the valve stem.

because the intake valve chases the piston down the hole on the intake stroke. However, if you set the intake clearance much tighter than .060 inch, you will likely start to see marks on the top of the piston, which tells you that the components are getting close. The exhaust valve clearance is rarely reduced to less than .120-inch clearance because the exhaust valve is moving in the opposite direction of the piston when the two are closest together. The quality of the drive system used for the camshaft will also influence how tight you can set valve-to-piston clearance. The higher-end motors can run tighter clearances because they will most likely be using belt- or gear-driven camshafts, which are more precise than chain drives.

Also verify the radial clearance around the valve during a pre-assembly parts check. Many of the aftermarket heads now come with valve sizes of 2.190, 2.200, or larger. These are much larger than previous-generation parts, so it is possible to end up with pistons that are too small for the valves on your new cylinder heads. Your pistons should have at least .050-inch radial clearance. This means if the intake valve is 2.200 inches in diameter, then the valve pocket in the piston needs to be at least 2.300 inches in diameter.

Combustion Chamber Clearance

If you use a custom piston with a dome, carefully check for possible interference between the dome and the combustion chamber. Piston manufacturers, such as Diamond Racing, offer piston domes for the cylinder heads from popular vendors, such as Indy and Edelbrock. If you are using a popular combination of parts, they should fit together but it is always a good idea to double-check. There are several ways to check for possible chamber/dome interference. You can perform an initial bench inspection by setting the piston into the combustion chamber and seeing if the quench area sits on the quench area of the cylinder head. Unless you are building a very-high-compression motor, the flat portion of the piston should be able to sit on the flat portion of the cylinder head. A typical .050-inch-thick head gasket would provide at least that much clearance between the dome and the combustion chamber. If the clearance appears to be very tight, then you can do a mock-up assembly of the short-block and then lay clay strips on the top of the domes. With the heads installed, turn the motor over by hand a few times to compress the clay strips. After the heads are removed, it should be obvious if there are areas that need to be relieved to provide operational clearance.

Piston-to-Head Clearance

Almost all modern cylinder heads currently available for the big-

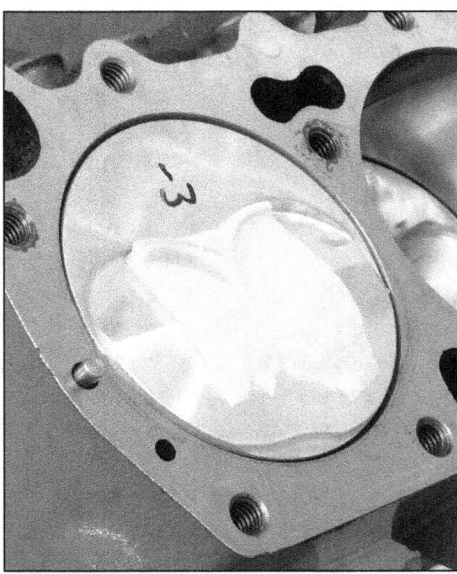

Old-fashioned clay is still a good way to visually tell you what the valve-to-piston clearance looks like. The clay method isn't very precise, but it does provide you with a clear illustration of the available clearance.

block Mopar are a closed-chamber design with a flat quench area on the intake side of the chamber. The distance between the top of the piston and the bottom of this quench area is called the quench height, and this dimension is an important part of the engine design. The tighter the quench height the better the combustion process, until you cross the line and the piston starts to hit the cylinder head. Quench height is usually set around .040 inch, but pay attention to the head gasket thickness because the head gasket can account for the entire quench height. Common practice is to machine the block deck so that the tops of the pistons are .005 inch down in the bores and then use a 0.039-inch compressed-head gasket. That gives a total quench height of 0.044 inch, which should be safe for most engine combinations. When using short pistons, the pistons might rock in the bores and, if this is

PISTONS

Mopar used to sell high-performance rings over the counter in various bore sizes. These rings would no longer be considered high-performance parts because the technology has improved dramatically over the last 30 years.

the case, the quench height should be increased slightly. If the engine is going to always use a thicker head gasket, then the pistons could be set up flush with the top of the deck or even protruding slightly. The piston-to-head clearance should be increased slightly for higher-speed engines and increased even more when using aluminum rods.

Piston Rings

A standard ring choice used today for a performance engine would be the 1/16–1/16–3/16 set from JE, Speed Pro, or other similar vendors. Ring choices greatly depend on the bore size. Some bore sizes have a very small selection of available rings while popular bore sizes such as 4.375 inches will offer many choices. The larger 4.500-inch bore size that is possible in the aftermarket blocks is also a popular size with multiple choices. The standard overbore sizes of 4.350 and 4.380 have more limited ring choices, so many builders use the 4.375-bore size.

Using a vacuum pump to pull a vacuum in the crankcase has become a lot more popular over the last several years. A vacuum pump and the correct ring stack have produced power increases of 20 to 50 hp. You would typically use the vacuum pump in conjunction with a thin ring such as a .043-wide top ring and a low-tension oil ring. This is another example of where you need to know the total plan for the engine before ordering parts. Adding a vacuum pump to a stock-type rebuilt engine isn't going to increase the power output significantly. On the other hand, building an engine with low-tension oil rings and then not using a vacuum pump could reduce performance by allowing extra oil into the combustion chamber.

Gas Ports

Gas porting is one area that used to be termed super trick, was downgraded to just "trick", and now it is somewhere between trick and routine. It takes about two decades for cutting-edge Pro Stock technology to emerge in the average bracket-race motor.

David Reher of Reher-Morrison fame has a tech bulletin on the Reher-Morrison Web site, where he explains the value of gas porting in the modern performance engine. According to Reher, gas ports can be worth as much as 50 hp on a large bracket-racing-type motor. Gas ports allow thinner rings and tighter ring grooves, which improves sealing and reduces ring flutter. Again, this is all about the system. An engine with gas ports needs to be designed with parts matched for maximum effect.

Gas-ported pistons typically use a thinner ring, such as a .043-inch top ring with a 3-mm oil ring. These thinner ring packages are only available in the more popular bore sizes, such as the 4.375-, 4.440-, and 4.500-inch diameters. Again, we get back to the

A side view of the 514 piston shows the lateral gas ports as well as the moly skirt coating. The top ring is a narrow .043 design, which works well with the lateral gas ports to provide a good seal and reduced drag.

CHAPTER 6

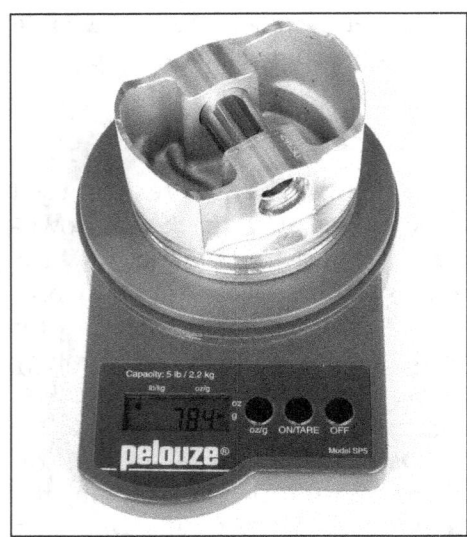

Modern pistons are a lot lighter than performance pistons from the muscle car era. These stroker pistons weigh 784 grams with the pin included. Factory piston and pin combinations often weighed about 1,100 grams.

issue of planning the motor and thinking of it as a system before buying parts. If you are going to run gas ported pistons for the extra power potential, then pay attention to the bore size implications as well as the need for either a vacuum pump or a dry sump system in order to help the rings do their job.

Piston Pin Diameter

The stock piston pin size for the big-block had a diameter of 1.094 inches. This is fairly heavy when compared to other piston pin designs and has been shown over time to be overbuilt for the average performance engine. The big-block Chevy size of .990-inch diameter is about standard for most big-blocks these days. Not only are the .990-inch pins smaller and lighter than the traditional Mopar pins, they are also less expensive because production volumes are higher. Given the popularity of the .990-inch pin, there is a tremendous availability of different wall thicknesses and lengths, which means a broad selection for builders.

It's important not to get too carried away with weight reduction when selecting a piston pin. One of the most common reasons for piston failure is that the builder selected a pin wall thickness that was insufficient for the load, causing the pins to deform during use. You would typically purchase the pins with the pistons, after discussing and determining the proper thickness with your vendor. At 600 hp, a standard .990-inch pin is usually strong enough, but if you're shooting for more than 800 hp, you should consider an upgrade to pins with thicker walls and/or a stronger material.

Vacuum Pump Considerations

There are currently some high-performance coatings, such as DLC (diamond-like carbon) that should be considered when building a performance engine, especially if you are going to run a vacuum pump. The vacuum pump can reduce the amount of oil vapor that is churning around inside the engine, which is good for increasing power, but it can be detrimental to parts that require lubrication. As builders began to experience part failures they looked for solutions that involved permanent low-friction coatings on the parts. Some part coatings have been considered "snake oil" for years but others are becoming required. Very-high-powered, high-speed engines such as NASCAR applications make extensive use of coatings.

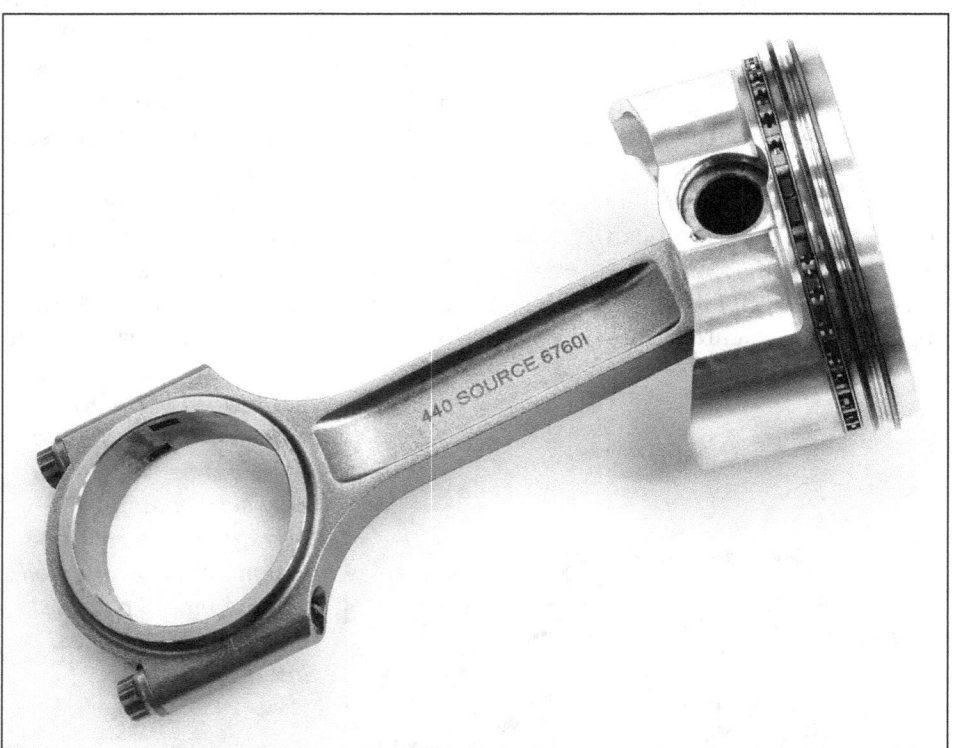

Here is another view of the 383 stroker piston, but this time with the connecting rod attached and the rings installed. These pistons weigh a little more than 540 grams, which really drops the weight of the total rotating assembly.

CHAPTER 7

CYLINDER HEADS AND VALVES

As discussed earlier in this book, cylinder head selection is probably the most critical choice to make when building a performance big-block. A cylinder head with standard port sizes will be less expensive and less complicated than a max-wedge port cylinder head, but the torque peak will be about 1,000 rpm lower. That might be exactly what you need for a strong street/strip-type of motor though, so do not fall into the trap of thinking that bigger is better.

The cross-section area of the cylinder head plays a primary role in determining the location of the torque peak. For a 500-ci motor, the standard head port will provide peak torque somewhere around 4,100 rpm while the larger Max-Wedge port increases that to about 5,200 rpm. There are several heads on the market, such as the B1, that have ports larger than the Max-Wedge port, so the torque peak can be pushed up even more, but then the cost of the related parts will also increase.

Most builders are going to use an aftermarket cylinder head, rather than try to rework original cast-iron heads. Original cast-iron heads can be made to work okay on a 500-ci motor, but it's fairly expensive due to the amount of work required and the resale value is low. Also, aluminum heads reduce 40 lbs from the nose of the car.

Standard Port Cylinder Head

In 2002, Edelbrock introduced the Performer RPM cylinder head, and it really shook things up for the

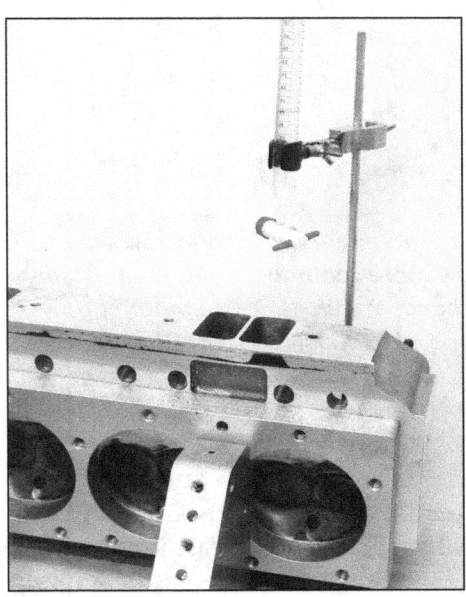

The volume of the intake runner can be quickly measured by using a burette to fill the runner with liquid. These Indy EZ runners measure 308 cc after being ported. You can only compare intake volumes between heads with the same runner length since longer runners will have more volume.

big-block Mopar builder. This was the first truly no-hassle, bolt-on aluminum cylinder head available for the Mopar big-block. Previously available cylinder heads were either full-race heads or heads that suffered from various quality issues. The Edelbrock Performer RPM cylinder heads quickly became very popular because they had excellent flow capability, yet they cost less than a set of fully ported cast-iron heads. Even today, the Performer RPM cylinder head is

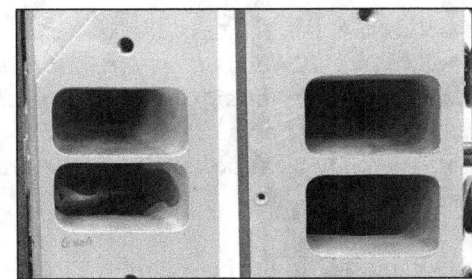

A comparison between the intake ports of the Indy EZ head on the left and the B1 heads on the right shows the huge difference in cross section. The B1 heads have gigantic intake runners when compared to most other big-block Mopar cylinder heads. The EZ heads shown in this picture made more than 800 hp on a 505 motor, so they are capable of serious power even though they appear small in this picture.

Most cast-iron heads had an open chamber as illustrated by the 906 head on the right. The Edelbrock head on the left of the picture shows how the left side of the chamber has been filled in so it is flush with the deck surface.

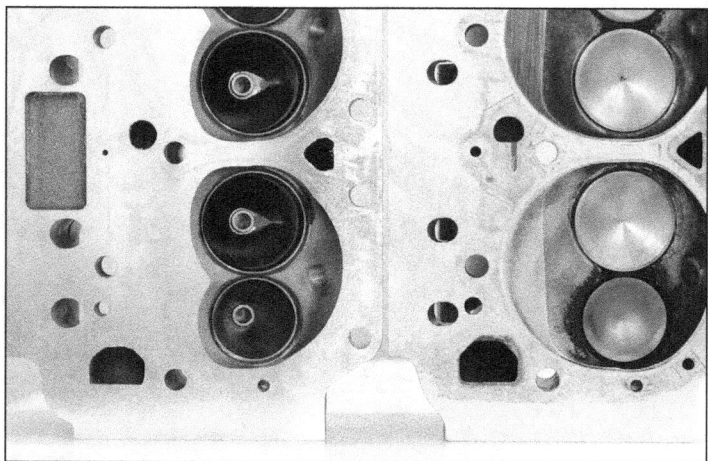

The Indy EZ head on the left has a heart shaped 75-cc combustion chamber while the Edelbrock RPM head on the right has a more traditional D-shaped 84-cc chamber.

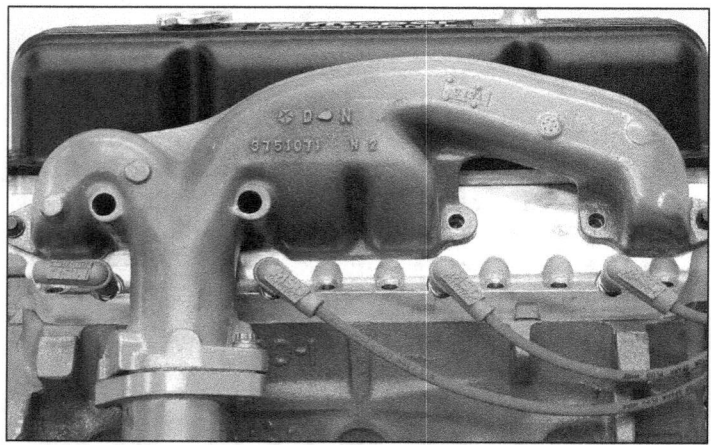

The Mopar 452 heads have straight rather than angled spark plugs. The straight spark plugs allow more room for the spark plug boots around these HP exhaust manifolds, and they may work better with some brands of exhaust headers.

The Mopar cylinder heads have the P5153524 part number engraved in the ends for easy identification. They also have a core plug in the end that the Edelbrock heads do not have.

still the most logical choice for a performance engine with an emphasis on lower-RPM torque rather than ultimate power. The RPM heads will easily provide 600 hp and 600 ft-lbs of torque on a 500-ci short-block, when combined with a suitable carb and camshaft.

The Performer RPM cylinder head has an 84-cc combustion chamber with a quench pad area that looks somewhat like the original 915 closed chamber head. The valve sizes on the RPM head have a diameter of 2.140 inches on the intake and 1.81 inches on the exhaust, so they are one step larger than a stock cast-iron head. A 500-ci engine will require a slightly dished piston in order to achieve a streetable 10.5:1 compression ratio with the Performer RPM cylinder heads. The exhaust ports in the RPM heads are in the stock location, but the heads do have angled spark plugs, which can cause some fitment issues with headers or factory-type exhaust manifolds. One nice feature: the exhaust bolt holes are dry rather than being open into the water jacket—so when you remove the exhaust bolts during a header swap, you won't get a coolant bath.

Another cylinder head available at the standard port size is the Mopar Performance P5153524. These "452" heads are basically an Edelbrock Performer RPM head with some slight machining differences and straight spark plugs. The straight spark plug

CYLINDER HEADS AND VALVES

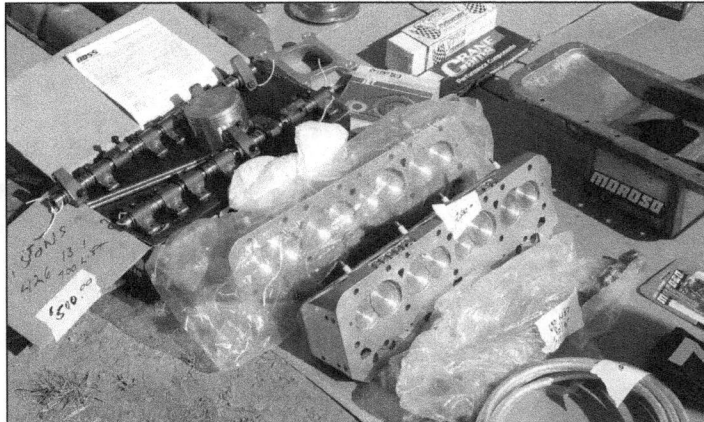

Here is a snapshot from a swap meet showing a set of B1-BS heads for sale. The B1-BS head is one of the best standard port heads available for the big-block Mopar, but they do require some special parts to fit properly due to the relocated exhaust ports and the small combustion chambers.

The Stealth heads from 440 Source are an economical choice for a moderate-performance engine. The straight spark plugs and the stock-looking exterior are two of the key design features on the Stealth heads.

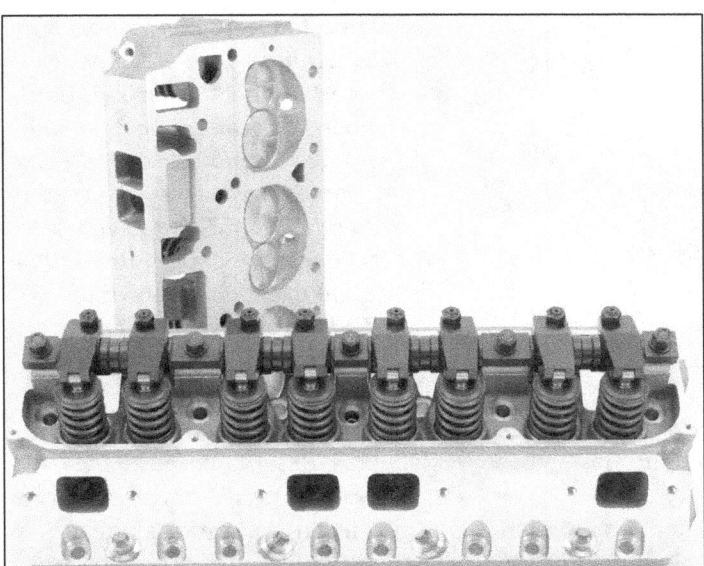

The Indy SR head uses rocker arms with standard offset and is available with a standard port size. (Photo courtesy of Indy Cylinder Heads)

These two head studs from ARP illustrate the difference between studs that will fit with stock exhaust ports and those that won't. The upper stud in the picture is the standard 2.750 head stud used in the ARP kits and it interferes with the header flanges on any cylinder head with a stock exhaust port. The lower stud is 2.725 long; but more importantly it has additional coarse threads so it can be screwed further in to the block. This 2.725 stud will fit header flanges on heads with stock exhaust ports.

design means that the 452 head will fit better with existing header designs as well as HP exhaust manifolds. Recently 440 Source introduced their own aluminum cylinder head, the Stealth, which appears to be an aluminum version of the factory 915 head. The Stealth head has similar flow characteristics to the Edelbrock RPM head but the exterior of the Stealth is cast to appear like an original cast-iron head.

Brodix offers a standard port cylinder head called the B1-BS. This head has been around for awhile but it never seemed to be as popular with most builders as the Edelbrock RPM head. The B1-BS head has a 2.200-inch-diameter intake valve and a 1.81-inch-diameter exhaust valve, and the combustion chamber is much smaller than a stock head at only 65 cc. A 500-ci engine requires a large dish in the piston in order to have a streetable 10.5:1 compression ratio. A flat top piston in a 500-ci motor with the small chambered B1-BS heads is a scorching 14:1 compression ratio. That's a great ratio for a drag race motor, but it would always need to run on race fuel.

The B1-BS head is available with a CNC-ported version that flows about 360 cfm at .700-inch lift. These types of flow numbers are excellent for a standard port head and dyno tests with the B1-BS heads back up the power potential of those flow numbers. The CNC-ported version of the head will also have a slightly larger combustion chamber size at around 75 cc. The exhaust ports have been raised and extended a significant amount on the B1-BS head. Consequently, some headers, designed to work with stock cast-iron heads, will not fit into a production chassis when using the B1-BS heads.

Mopar Performance has an aluminum Stage VI head with standard-sized ports that has a very clever design feature. The Stage VI head is a raised port design, but the engineers raised the ports just the right amount so that a RB intake manifold would line up with the ports when the Stage VI heads are used on a B block. An extra-wide intake manifold has to be used when the Stage VI heads are used on a RB block, so Mopar Performance tooled up several versions of these for those applications. The Stage VI heads have been around for many years now, but they never really became very popular. The original heads had quality issues because of poor castings, and the bad reputation from those early incidents stuck to the heads. In addition, the heads were quite expensive and didn't flow great right out of the box. Some builders had very good results with the Stage VI heads after the heads were ported, but the final cost was high enough that only a limited number of customers could afford these heads. There is a version of the Stage VI head that is CNC ported by Chapman. The Chapman heads have a special 77-cc chamber with 2.200 and 1.81 valves and a 260-cc intake runner. These Chapman heads are quite expensive to purchase, but they have extremely good flow numbers. If you are racing a smaller-displacement Mopar big-block motor, then the Chapman Stage VI heads mounted on a B block with an RB intake manifold would be a powerful combination.

The Edelbrock Victor is the most recent addition to the list of standard port heads. The Victor head has large 2.20/1.81 valves and a 75-cc dual quench-style combustion chamber. The Victor has raised intake runners and exhaust ports, so there can be fitment issues with some headers. A standard intake manifold does bolt onto the Victor heads, even with the raised port design, because the runners were lengthened enough to compensate for the additional height. A special valley pan is required with the Victor heads, and rocker arms with additional offset must be used because the casting around the intake port has been widened.

Max-Wedge-Port-Size Heads

The Max-Wedge-size port is about 25 percent larger in cross section than the standard port size, which moves the torque peak up significantly on smaller motors. But when the displacement is increased,

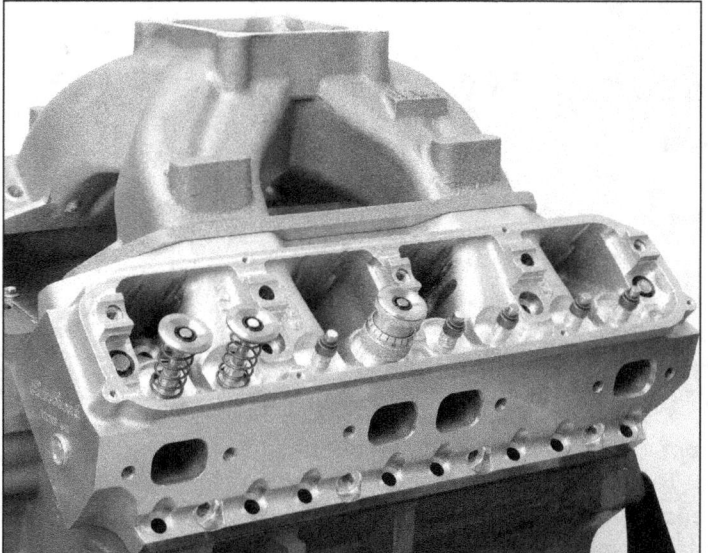

This mockup of the new Victor heads with an Indy 440-3X intake shows how tall the induction system becomes when you combine raised port heads with a tall intake manifold. Also notice the raised exhaust ports in the Victor heads and the angled spark plugs.

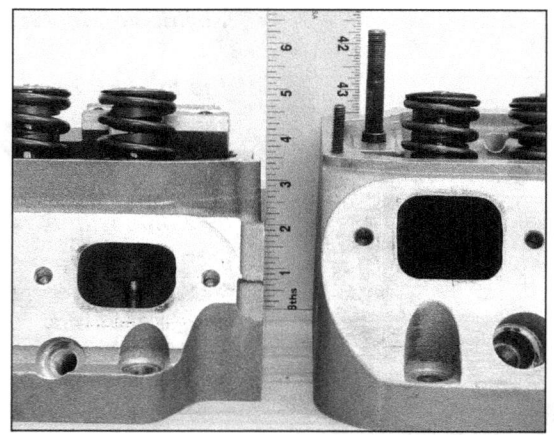

One more comparison between the EZ head on the left and the B1 on the right shows how high the exhaust ports have been raised in the B1 heads. These super-tall exhaust ports really improve the flow, but it can also cause some issues with header fitment. The EZ heads with the low ports are capable of 800 hp so the extra port flow of the B1 heads is only necessary at performance levels above that.

CYLINDER HEADS AND VALVES

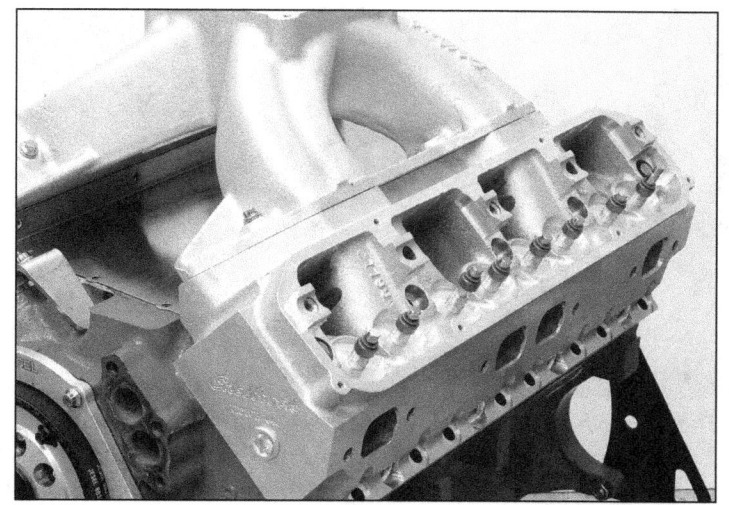

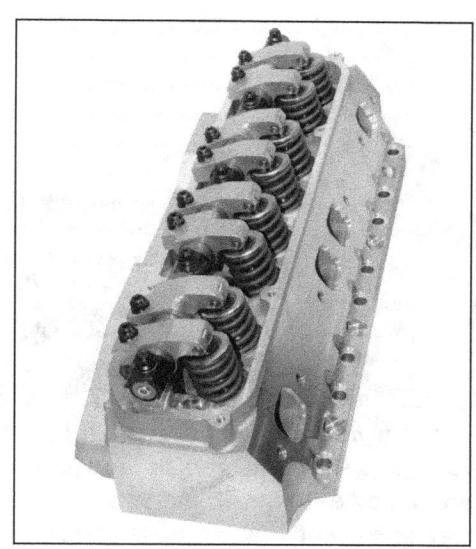

The Edelbrock Victor heads look very impressive when mated to the matching Edelbrock Super Victor intake manifold. This is a very-high-rise combination that has excellent flow capability.

Edelbrock Victor heads require special offset intake rocker arms such as this set, which is available from T&D. (Photo courtesy of T&D Machine Products)

A view from the side shows how the intake runners from the Super Victor intake flow smoothly into the intake ports in the Victor heads. This is a combination that can easily make 800 hp if the short block is up to the task.

These Moroso steel shim valve cover gaskets fit perfectly on other big-block heads but for some reason they do not quite line up with the rails on the Victor heads.

the increased port size keeps the torque curve in the same location. So while the Max-Wedge head was originally developed for racing performance on the older 413 and 426 motors, it's a good street performance head on a 505- or 512-type motor.

Indy Cylinder Head jump-started the shift to the Max-Wedge-size ports when they began offering heads as well as intake manifolds with the larger port size. Until that time, the lack of intake manifolds other than the factory cross ram really prevented widespread acceptance of the Max-Wedge-port-size heads.

After Indy broke that barrier and offered single four-barrel intakes that fit both the B and the RB block, there was a substantial shift toward the larger-port-size heads for performance engines. Indy Cylinder Head currently offers a number of different heads for the big-block Mopar, but the offerings that will interest you the most will be the EZ, SR, or 440-1 heads.

The EZ head is very close to being a bolt-on replacement for a stock Max-Wedge cylinder head. The EZ head accepts stock-type rocker arms and the exhaust ports are in the stock location, so most production-style headers will fit. The spark plugs are angled rather than straight, so it is possible that some header tubes will need to be clearanced for some of the spark plugs.

CHAPTER 7

The Indy head on the left has raised intake runners but, as you can see, the runners in the Victor head on the right are raised even more. The Victor heads move the intake manifold and the valve covers up quite a bit from where they are with stock heads so make sure you have the necessary clearance before switching to these heads.

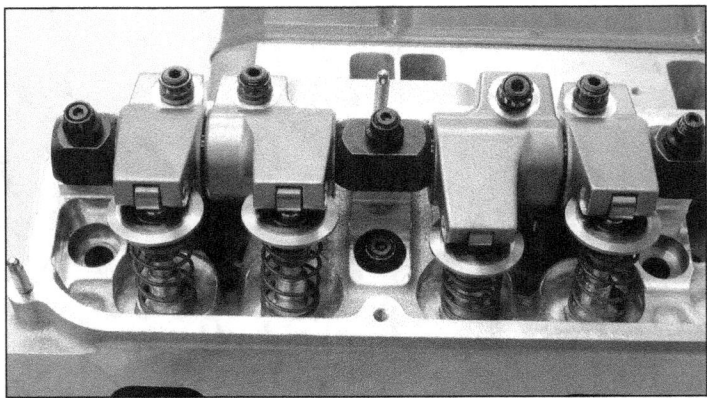

The Victor heads require intake rocker arms with about .650 offset to clear the wide intake runners. This picture shows a set of Harland Sharp rocker arms mocked up on a Victor Max-Wedge head. You might also need offset lifters on the intakes to keep the pushrods from rubbing with these Victor heads.

Indy Cylinder Heads sells a kit that include the correct head bolts, intake gaskets, and valley cover required to install their cylinder heads onto a big-block.

The EZ cylinder head oils the rocker shaft through the head just like a factory setup and these heads accept any standard Max-Wedge-type intake manifold. A special valley tray, is required because the EZ head, like all of the other Indy heads, has an extended intake runner that overhangs the lifter valley. The EZ head will flow upwards of 360 cfm on the intake side when properly ported and can easily support up to 800 hp on a 500-ci short-block, given the right cam and plenty of compression.

The Indy 440-1 head started the huge surge in the power output of big-block Mopar engines. Introduced in 1992 at the Mopar Nationals, the 440-1 cylinder head was a hit with big-block builders because it provided a relatively simple way to dramatically increase power output. The 440-1 heads have large Max-Wedge intake ports with raised runners and longer valves. The large ports are combined with a smaller 75-cc combustion chamber that has good quench properties and a raised-runner exhaust port. The 440-1 heads require offset intake

A production cast-iron head is shown on the left with an Edelbrock RPM head in the middle and an Indy EZ head on the right. While the Edelbrock head is very similar in size to the production head, the Indy head is noticeably taller.

CYLINDER HEADS AND VALVES

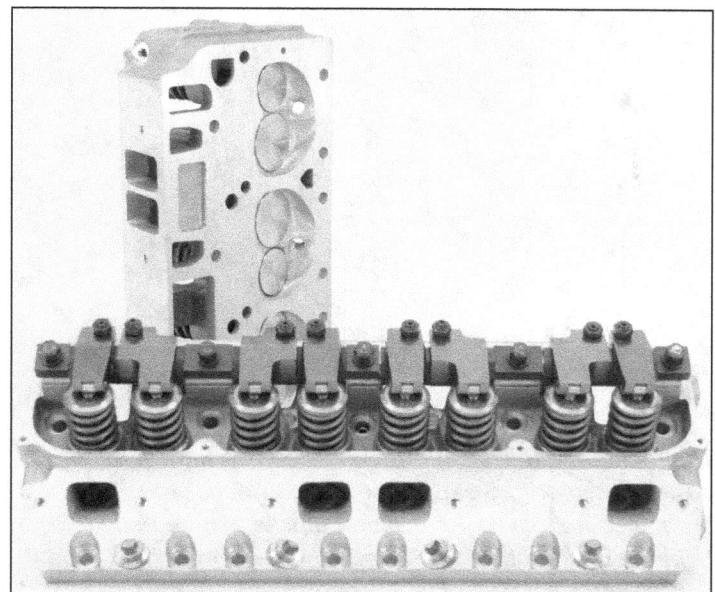

The Indy 440-1 cylinder head has Max-Wedge-sized ports and requires offset intake rocker arms. (Photo courtesy of Indy Cylinder Heads)

The 572-13 cylinder head from Indy is for larger motors. These heads have a 365- or 385-cc intake runner, require a 4.500 bore size, and come set up for Jesel rocker arms. (Photo courtesy of Indy Cylinder Heads)

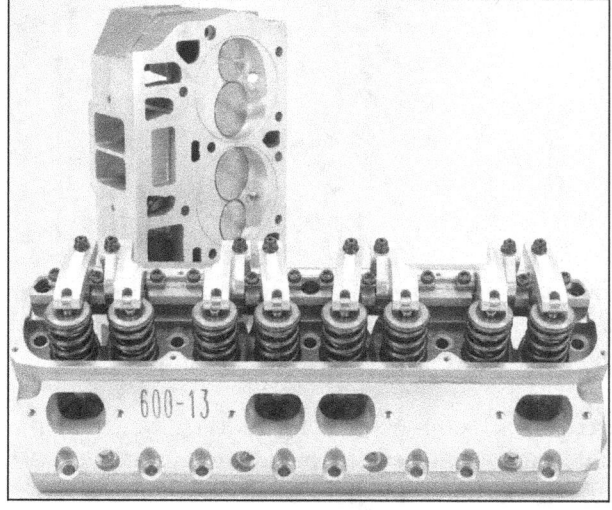

The 600-13 cylinder head from Indy is for King Kong-type motors. You'll need a big motor with a large bore size to effectively use these heads. (Photo courtesy of Indy Cylinder Heads)

rocker arms, external oil lines, and a special valley plate. Also the relocated exhaust ports might cause fitment issues with production-style headers. The intake runners on the 440-1 heads are substantially larger than production heads so the torque peak is moved to a much-higher-RPM level. The 440-1 heads are best used on engines with larger cylinder bores and short-blocks with at least 500 ci.

The Indy SR heads are very similar to the 440-1 heads, but they come with a smaller-volume intake runner and they work with stock-type rocker arms. The SR heads are available with a standard size port opening, but they are often opened up to the Max-Wedge size with some quick port match grinding.

Edelbrock recently introduced a Max-Wedge version of their Mopar big-block Victor cylinder heads. These large-port Victor heads flow a lot of air right out of the box and easily support 800 hp on a properly built 500-ci short-block. The Max-Wedge Victor heads share most of the specifications with the standard-port Victor heads, such as the chamber size, port location, etc. The Victor heads do require special high-offset intake rocker arms, and the relocated exhaust ports preclude many existing headers from fitting properly, which adds expense.

The Stage VI heads from Chapman Racing are also available with a Max-Wedge port window. These large-port Stage VI heads have a 285-cc intake runner with a 74-cc combustion chamber. They use 2.250 and 1.81 valves, and peak flow on the intake side is a little over 380 cfm. These Stage VI heads easily produce more than 800 hp on a properly prepared 500-ci short-block, but they are more expensive than some of the other currently available cylinder heads.

CHAPTER 7

The original B1 head has exhaust ports that are raised significantly over a stock cylinder head. Also notice the deep pockets for the head studs and the spark plugs.

The rocker shaft system on a B1 head is a little like the system used on the early Max-Wedge heads. The pedestals are milled flat, so that machined blocks can be used to hold the rocker shaft. The double hold-down bolts for the center retainers make the B1 valvetrain assembly very rigid.

The original B1 heads have a double quench combustion chamber with a large intake valve and a smaller exhaust valve.

The combustion chamber in the B1 head is small enough that a Fel-Pro 1009 head gasket will fit without overhanging.

Bigger Than Max-Wedge

When we get to port sizes that are bigger than the Max-Wedge size, we're starting to get into the exotic head territory. The B1 head is a very popular large port head that has been around for about 20 years, and it is capable of producing large amounts of power when used on a 500-ci short-block. The port size on the B1 is about 4.50 square inches, which makes it almost 25 percent larger than the Max-Wedge. This large port size puts the torque peak somewhere around 6,400 rpm and the horsepower peak at about 8,000 rpm when used on a 500-ci short-block. The B1 head is definitely a race head on anything smaller than 500 ci, but if you build a big enough short-block, the B1 head will also work fine as a street/strip-type head. Given deep enough pockets, the combination of B1 heads and a 572-ci short-block would work out great for a street engine. A big engine like this could make upwards of 800 hp on pump gas and be quite drivable. Unfortunately, the cost would be out of reach for most people.

The B1 head requires many parts to be changed from stock, so the conversion process is quite expensive when compared to standard-port engines. The valve pockets in the pistons have to be moved to accommodate the different valve locations of the B1, special rocker arms need to be used, a special intake manifold is required, etc. Consider the B1 head only if your goal is to make more than 800 hp; there are less-expensive ways to meet lower power goals. The decision to use B1 heads needs to be made at the beginning of a project because of the special parts required.

The B1 head is not the end of the line by any means because there is

CYLINDER HEADS AND VALVES

A side-by-side comparison of the Indy EZ combustion chamber (left) and the B1 original (right) shows some significant differences. The B1 chamber is filled in more on the exhaust side giving it more quench area on that side.

The B1 heads require an external oil drain plumbed from each end of the heads back to the oil pan.

also a variation of the B1 head with moved valve centerlines. In addition, there is the very efficient B1 PSO head available from Best Machine. There is also the no-compromise B1-TS cylinder head, which is an all-out design with splayed valves and spread intake ports. Indy Cylinder Heads offers their 572-13 and 600-13 heads in these no-compromise categories. The 572-13 head requires a 4.500 bore size while the 600-13 requires both a 4.563 bore size as well as a Chevy-style 4.840 bore-center cylinder block.

If the biggest wedge heads available don't do the trick, then racers turn to the Predator heads available from Predator Performance Products. The Predator head is a canted valve head with symmetrical port spacing, so it doesn't look much like a production Mopar head. But the Mopar Wedge Head design with paired runners runs out of steam around 500 cfm; so if a person wants to push their Mopar block past 1,200 hp, then it becomes necessary to consider switching over to the canted valve arrangement.

Head Gaskets

The 17-head-bolt system that the original engineers designed provides solid clamping pressure, so keeping a cylinder head gasket on a Mopar big-block hasn't been a problem. But that doesn't mean that there aren't plenty of reasons for paying attention to the head gaskets. Besides sealing the head to the block, the head gasket influences the compression ratio and the quench height. It is important to know which head gasket is going to be used so you can select other components that make the quench and the CR correct. There are a number of head gaskets available for the big-block in different thicknesses ranging from the steel-shim-type gasket at .020 inch up to the composition gaskets that are .051-inch thick. If you are trying to keep the quench height right at .035 inch, then the gasket thickness needs to be factored into the equation.

Another very important item that needs to be decided on during the engine design stage is the type of head gasket that will be used. Cast-iron heads can be used with any type of head gasket including the simple steel-shim gaskets, but aluminum heads are much more particular. The best head gasket to use for a cast-iron block with aluminum heads is the newer MLS gasket technology, which is available from several vendors. The MLS head gaskets were designed to combat issues that the OEMs were seeing with their aluminum headed motors and this new technology really improved reliability. One potential issue with the MLS gaskets: they do require a smoother surface finish than the older composition-type gaskets, so make sure your machine shop can meet these specifications.

The last area to pay attention to when selecting a head gasket is the size of the cylinder bore. There are plenty of choices available for the classic bore sizes of 4.250, 4.350, etc., but there are fewer choices for the bigger-bore motors. For instance, there is no steel shim gasket available at the 4.500-inch-bore size since there isn't much demand for a cast-iron head on that size motor. There are composition gaskets available for the big-bore motors, but they are only available in the .051-inch compressed thickness, which means you need to

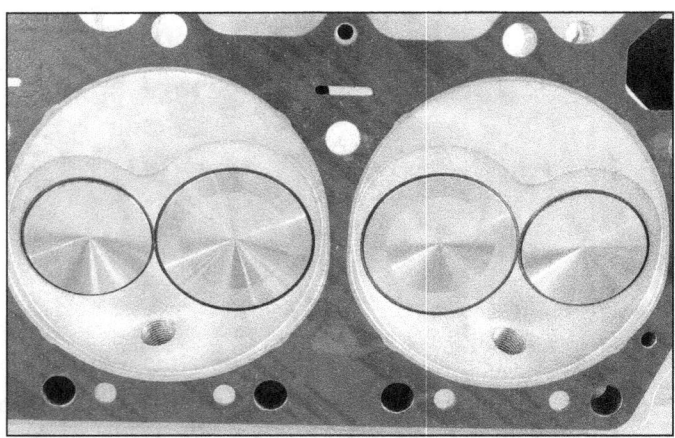

A Fel-Pro 1009 head gasket clears the fairly small chamber in the Edelbrock Victor head with room to spare. This gasket has a fairly small-bore size so that almost any head gasket should clear the small chambers in these as-cast Victor heads.

adjust the deck height of the piston in order to obtain a tight quench.

When selecting the proper gasket bore size, measure the chamber on the head as well as the block. Some combustion chambers are quite large around the intake valve, especially chambers that have been CNC machined. It is common to need a 4.500-inch-bore gasket in order to properly seal the cylinder head even though the bore size of the cylinder is less than that. Also check that the head gasket clears the chamfer at the top of the cylinder bore. Some production blocks have very large chamfers at the top of the cylinder bore, so even though the bore size might be only 4.350, you might need a gasket with a much larger bore size to prevent the gasket from overhanging into the cylinder bore. The head gasket must be clamped between the head and the block in order to seal properly.

Cometic Gasket Inc. started to provide a new solution several years ago with their custom head gasket program. Cometic can make head gaskets in a variety of thicknesses and they can make almost any bore size. A custom head gasket can help you avoid some tough choices by allowing you to use the head gasket thickness to tune in the exact amount of quench or compression that is necessary. Also, the ability to specify the bore size is a major advantage when dealing with oddball bore sizes. The Cometic head gaskets are the MLS type, which means that the deck surface needs to be machined to the proper specifications. Cometic is currently recommending a surface finish of 50 Ra or better for proper sealing with their MLS gaskets. Not all automotive machine shops have equipment that is capable of hitting this surface finish so double-check with your machinist before you make a decision on which head gasket you will be using.

Head Flow and Cam Lift

Simply multiplying the cylinder head airflow in cfm by a factor of 2 will give you an estimate of the horsepower output of a V-8 engine. For instance, if you have a set of cylinder heads that flow 350 cfm at 28 inches of depression, you can reasonably expect to see 700 hp from that engine on the dynamometer.

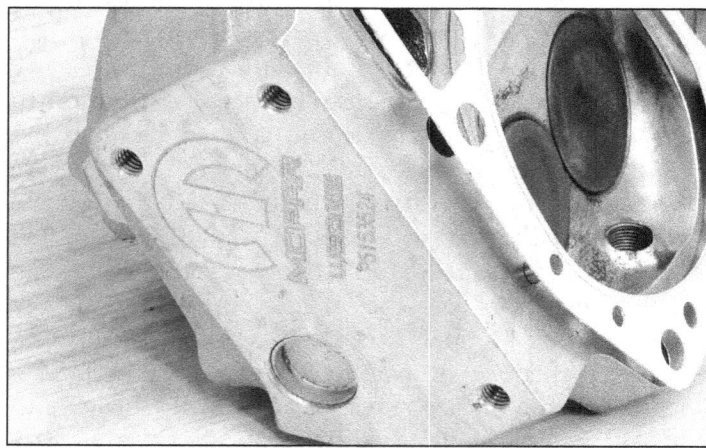

Some head gaskets do not fit properly, so be prepared to spend time fixing this issue. Pictured is an Edelbrock head gasket with locating holes that are too small to fit over the dowel pins. We have also seen this problem with other brands so pay attention during assembly.

An indentation from the fire ring in the head gaskets is visible in these cylinder heads after just a few dyno pulls of use. These are a composition gasket with a pre-flattened wire ring that are designed for use with aluminum heads, but they still cause enough damage that the heads needed to be re-surfaced.

CYLINDER HEADS AND VALVES

This is just a general rule of course, and it assumes that all other engine parts and systems are also capable of supporting 700 hp. This old rule is reliable as long as the engine is using conventional components that are properly matched for the intended use. You can also use this formula to estimate the power increase possible from porting a set of existing cylinder heads as long as everything else remains equal. For instance, if an engine made 600 hp with heads that had 300 cfm of flow, then it could be expected to make 650 hp if the head flow was increased to 325 cfm.

It is probably best to think of the cylinder head flow as an indicator of performance rather than a predictor; many other items come into play in determining the final output of the engine. Also, one should not confuse quantity of airflow with the quality of airflow. The velocity of the airflow as well as the quality will have a big impact on how much air and fuel actually makes it into the combustion chamber. It is quite possible to have two cylinder heads that flow identical amounts on the flow bench but are then very different in power when bolted to an engine.

The opposite case is also possible, in which a set of cylinder heads produce different power levels per cfm of flow when the heads are used in different situations. For example, a set of Indy EZ heads that I have used on various motors ranging from a fairly mild 431-ci motor to a 505-ci motor with high compression and a big roller cam. These EZ heads were not modified at all between the dyno tests, other than changing the valvesprings, but the 431 motor barely made 600 hp while the 505 motor made a little over 800 hp. The Indy EZ heads used during these tests only flowed 355 cfm at .650-inch lift on the flow bench, but these worked

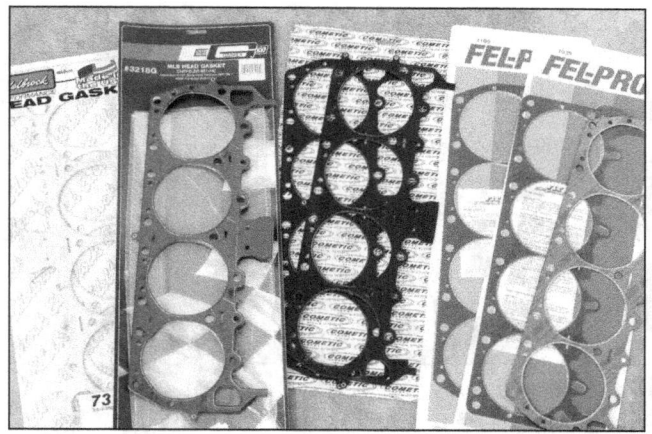

There are a lot of different head gaskets available for big-block Mopars, but only a few of them work well in performance engines. Purchase head gaskets with the correct bore size and thickness for your combination because the wrong parts can cause an engine failure.

well enough on the 505 motor with a .800-inch lift cam to make the 800 hp. If we consider the ratio of cfm to horsepower, we see that these EZ heads made 1.69-hp/cfm on the 431 motor and 2.25-hp/cfm on the larger, more radical 505. The 431 motor, besides being smaller, had a much milder camshaft and lower compression. When using the very exact cylinder heads, the engine size, camshaft specifications, and compression ratio all will have dramatic effects on the total power output of the motor.

The typical flow curve for a high-performance big-block Mopar head shows flow increasing up until about .700 lift, and then the flow plateaus or stalls. The point where the head flow stops increasing is a clue about the performance limitation of that cylinder head, but it does not mean

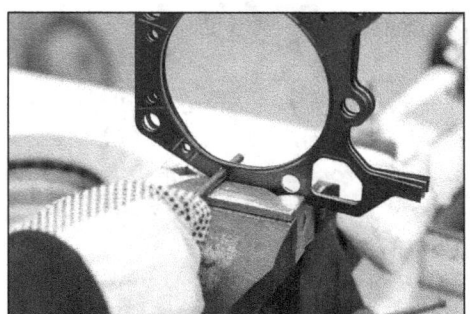

The MLS gaskets sometimes require some file work before they will fit over the dowel pins.

that valve lift in operation shouldn't be greater than the stall number. In fact, the engine can still make quite a bit of additional power by using a cam that lifts the valve well past the stall point on the head. This may or may not be an economical way to increase power, but it is an old racing trick and it does work.

There is also a definite sweet spot in terms of cylinder flow, valvetrain reliability, and total cost. A typical cylinder head with a Max-Wedge port will flow about 350 cfm at .650-inch lift, or maybe 360 cfm at .700-inch lift. This is enough airflow to support 700 to 750 hp when camshaft lift is in the .650- to .750-inch range. Most cylinder heads are designed with the installed height of the valvesprings to be 1.900 and can be set up at a 1.950 installed height by just changing the retainers or locks. Vendors offer many valvespring options that will provide reliable operation for a roller cam with a lift of .700 inch using a 1.950-inch installed height.

When you begin to move out of the common zone of .700-inch lift, then you will encounter more issues and exponentially increased costs. I converted a set of Indy EZ heads to a valvetrain that was capable of operating at .850-inch lift. The parts were all available off the shelf, but it did take considerable research to find which

CHAPTER 7

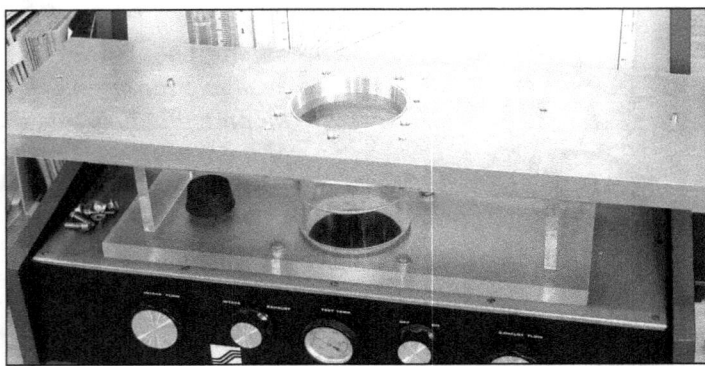

This flow bench has been updated with a fixture that is designed for use with big-block Mopar heads. Notice the holes for the five cylinder head bolts around the bore as well as the dowel pins that properly locate the head to the bore. If the cylinder head is not properly located on the bore, then the flow numbers will not represent what the engine will see.

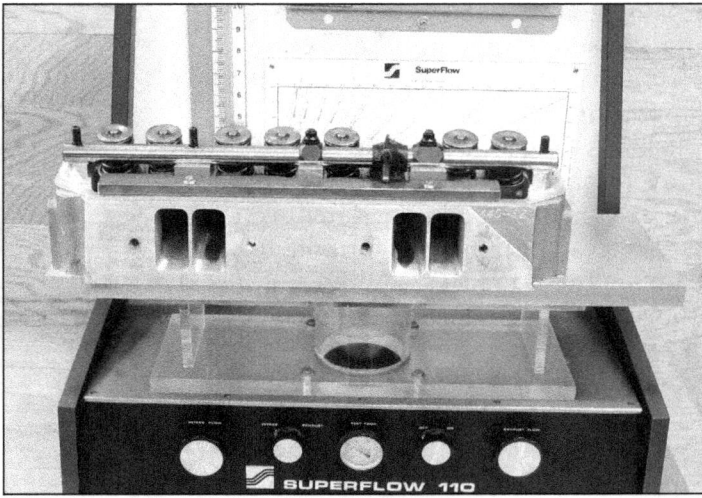

A CNC-ported Indy EZ cylinder head is mounted on the flow bench for testing. With the proper porting the EZ heads are capable of supporting up to 800 hp.

parts to use since there wasn't a recipe to follow. Multiple retainers, locks, and springs had to be purchased and trial fitted to the cylinder head to ensure that all of the parts would fit together and work because no one single vendor had a turnkey solution. The end result was worth 60 hp because the higher valve lift allowed the engine to continue to make more power than it had with less lift, but the cost for this particular conversion was several thousand dollars. Also, the maintenance intervals for a valvetrain with .850-inch lift are going to be much more frequent than if the valve lift was kept at .700.

There is a definite relationship between head flow and cylinder bore size because the larger cylinder bores facilitate more airflow. A larger bore size allows for the installation of larger valves, but, even if the valve size is kept the same, the cylinder flow increases with the larger bore size. If an aftermarket block is going to be used for the build, it makes sense to go ahead and go with a larger bore size such as a 4.440 or 4.500. Professional race engines that must fit into specific size classes are usually designed to have the largest bore because the larger bore allows better airflow. This trick gets very expensive at some point but you should be able to bore any of the aftermarket blocks to 4.500 inches without any problems. Any of the available cylinder heads will work better at 4.500 inches; so if you are buying an aftermarket block you might as well plan on using the large-bore size.

It isn't quite as common to test a combination of the intake manifold and the cylinder head on the flow bench, but it can be enlightening to do this work if a person is trying to optimize a particular combination of parts. The intake manifold will almost always (sometimes dramatically) reduce the total flow through the combined system. Dual-plane intake manifolds will often show a high variation from port to port when tested on the flow bench. This

With a CNC-ported Stealth head placed next to a factory 906 head one can see how similar the exterior shape is. The Stealth head when properly ported can flow over 300 cfm on the intakes, which is enough to support 650 hp.

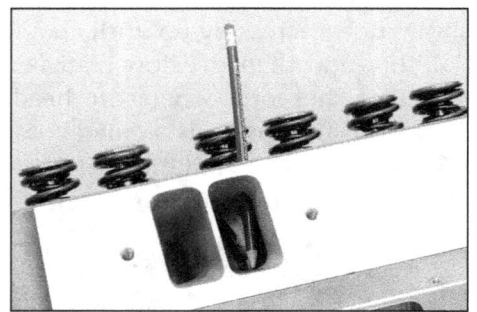

When the Indy heads are modified for Jesel rocker arms the bolts that hold down the rocker arm stands protrude into the intake runners. The pencil in this picture has been placed in the rocker stand hole showing how the bolt will intersect with the intake runner. Seal the bolt threads to prevent oil from the valve cover area from being sucked into the intake runner.

variation is one reason why the dual plane intakes usually make less power on the dyno than a good single plane. The biggest surprise I've seen in this area is how poor the classic Max-Wedge intake flow tested when attached to a set of Max-Wedge-ported cylinder heads. The total airflow through the Max-Wedge cross-ram intake was about 50 cfm less than a single-plane race intake manifold would typically flow. Subsequent dynamometer testing showed the single-plane intake to be worth an additional 100 hp in power output over the cross ram intake, which indicated that the flow bench numbers were in fact an appropriate predictor of power output in this case.

There are other situations though where the intake manifold with the best flow bench numbers makes the least amount of power on the dyno. This is possible because of other important factors—the taper of the intake runners, cross-section area, intake runners, and shape of the plenum. Again, raw flow numbers do not tell the entire story because we are trying to move a mixture of air and fuel into the combustion chamber from the carburetor. The fuel is much heavier than the air and it will fall out of suspension if the airflow has to make sudden changes in direction or velocity. The moral of the story is that intake manifolds that flow poorly will in fact produce low power numbers, but intake manifolds with high flow numbers do not necessarily translate into high power numbers.

Valves

In years past, there weren't nearly as many valve options. Today there is a much wider range of valve sizes, stem lengths, and materials. You need to select the valves according to the heads you're using, operating RPM, and performance goals. Stock valves are often suitable for low-revving, mildly modified stock engines, while larger titanium valves are ideal for high-revving race engines.

Valve Size

The valve size on a big-block production head was 2.08 inches for the intake and 1.78 inches for the exhaust. The Max-Wedge heads used larger 1.88 exhaust valves. Most of the currently available standard port heads use a slightly larger 2.14 intake and 1.81 exhaust valves. The cylinder heads with the Max-Wedge port size sometimes have larger intake valves. For example, the Edelbrock Victor heads come with 2.200 intake and 1.81 exhaust valves, while some of the Indy heads have an optional 2.250 intake with a 1.81 exhaust.

The B1 heads display a different design strategy by having an even larger 2.300 intake valve with a smaller 1.78 exhaust valve. This use of an oversize intake valve coupled with a smaller exhaust valve is often used on high-output racing engines as a way to maximize the power output. Since there is only so much space available in the combustion chamber, the exhaust valve must be reduced in size in order to provide room for a really large intake valve. One point of interest is the old Max-Wedge cylinder heads with their large 1.88 exhaust valves. The designers of the Max-Wedge head certainly had something in mind when they went with the extra-large exhaust valves, but whatever they were thinking, that type of design has fallen out of favor with designers of modern racing heads.

The general rule for valve sizes is to have the intake valve be roughly 50 percent of the bore size and then have the exhaust port flow 75 percent of the intake port. So for a 4.375-inch-bore motor, the intake valve would be 2.188 inches while a 4.500-inch bore could use a 2.250-inch intake valve. The exhaust valve needs to be 87 percent as large as the intake valve in order to have 75 percent of the flow area but the 87-percent rule isn't strictly followed because many other factors influence the airflow in the ports. If the exhaust port is very efficient, a smaller exhaust valve can be used and still achieve the 75-percent flow split between the exhaust and the intake.

The production valve stem was 3/8 (.372) inch in diameter, but the majority of the aftermarket cylinder

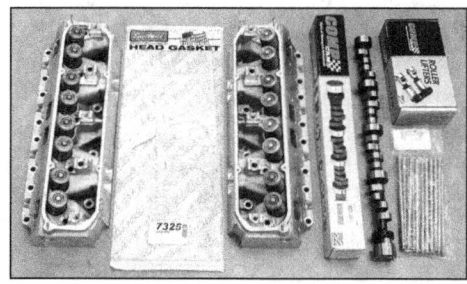

Here is a complete top-end package ready to install on a big-block Mopar. Shown is a set of CNC-ported Mopar Performance heads along with a street roller camshaft and the necessary lifters and pushrods. This set of parts made 680 hp on a 505-ci short block without breaking the bank.

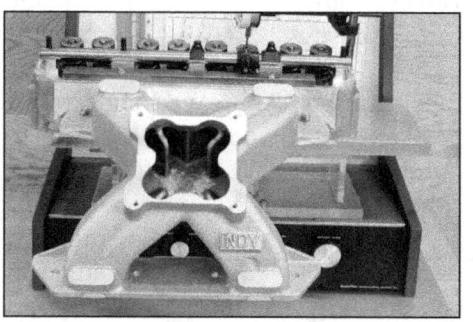

When testing cylinder heads on a flow bench it can be interesting to go ahead and bolt on the intake manifold to be used. Most modern intake manifolds show a slight decrease in airflow but some designs are very restrictive.

CHAPTER 7

The valves in the Indy and Edelbrock Victor heads are longer than stock valves. Both Indy and Edelbrock use an intake valve that is the same dimensionally as a +.100 big-block Chevy intake valve. You will also need longer pushrods when using these heads because the rocker arms shaft has been moved up to match the longer valves.

heads are now using valve stems that are 11/32 (.342) inch in diameter. You'll need to know the diameter of the valve stem when you order valve seals and locks so make sure you double-check the size before ordering parts. The higher-end racing engines are now using even-smaller-diameter stems in order to save additional weight from the valvetrain. Valves with 5/16-inch (.311) stems are now available for big-block heads, and some all-out professional-class race motors are starting to use 7-mm (.276) stems. These 7-mm valves look very spindly but they seem to work okay, and the lightweight design is easier for the valvesprings to control at high engine speeds.

The valves in production heads and many aftermarket heads are 4.90 inches long. Indy Cylinder Heads realized that the use of longer valves would allow a higher port location, which would improve airflow. Consequently, the Indy heads, such as the 440-1, use a 2.190-diameter intake valve that is 5.344 long. This 5.344-long valve is the same valve used by some big-block Chevy heads because it is a standard .100+ long Chevy intake valve. The Chevy big-block valves are available in a wide variety of lengths so a builder can easily order off-the-shelf valves and get more installed height when using high-lift cams. Of course, the longer valve will cause an issue with the rocker arm geometry, but such challenges are part of life as an engine builder tries to extract the last bit of power out of the engine.

The larger valves are a bit heavier since they are longer and have a larger head diameter. The typical weight for a 2.250 intake valve that is 5.344 long with a 11/32 stem is 142 grams. If you are willing to change the valve guides, then you can then use a big-block Chevy intake valve that is 2.250 in diameter, 5.344 long, and has the smaller .311 stem. Those valves with the smaller stem only weigh 125 grams, so that is a 12-percent weight reduction.

Titanium Valves

For the maximum reduction in weight, builders will use titanium valves rather than the more standard stainless steel. A 5.350-long intake valve for an Indy 440-1 cylinder head with a 2.250 head and .342 stem weighs only 90 grams when made from titanium. That same valve weighs 142 grams when made from stainless steel—a 37-percent weight savings. The total weight savings from a set of eight titanium intake valves would be 416 grams (almost 1 pound). When you consider the amount of power required to rapidly move 1 pound of material back and forth at high speeds you can see why titanium valves are an important element of professional race engines.

The large intake valves used in performance big-block Mopars are quite heavy when made from stainless steel. Stainless steel is relatively inexpensive, but the extra weight

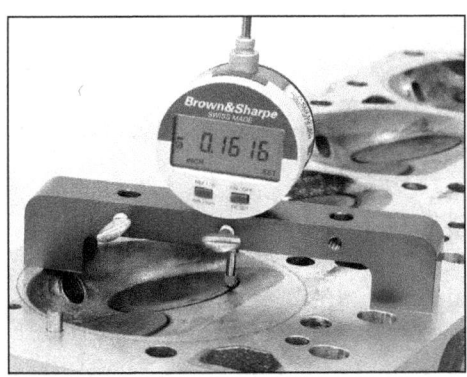

Measuring the depth of the intake valve from the head surface can be useful in determining what the valve to piston clearance will be. If you keep a record of these valve depths, then you will have a reference point that is useful for designing a new motor combination.

puts a strain on the valvesprings and the rocker arms when the engine speed begins to reach the 7,500-rpm range. At some point, it is more economical to use the expensive titanium valves than it is to constantly replace valvesprings. If you are intending to run engine speeds higher than 7,500, you should definitely consider the merits of switching to titanium intake valves. This is especially true if you are using a really large intake valve such as a 2.250-diameter or 2.300-diameter size used in the larger cylinder heads.

If you want to switch to titanium valves, you need to determine head compatibility. You should seek technical support from the head manufacturer or a reputable, professional builder. Often, the cylinder head vendors will use a different valve seat material for titanium valves than for stainless valves, but this is not a requirement in all cases. Some builders have the titanium valves coated so they will work with the standard seat material. On the valve-stem end of the valve, titanium valves typically use a hardened tip or else you can use a lash cap to protect the valve. Titanium valves are neither new technology nor exotic, but that doesn't mean that you can just heedlessly drop them in to replace the stainless valves.

Porting

Cylinder head porting is a very complex subject that would be difficult to cover in a book of its own, much less in a short summary within a book like this. The basic idea when porting a cylinder head is to improve the flow as much as possible while keeping the size of the port correctly matched to the needs of the motor. Anyone can make a huge port flow lots of air; the trick is to make a small port flow lots of air.

The cylinder head porter works with a variety of rules about the correct ratio of the throat diameter to the valve diameter, the correct valveseat angles, the shape of the combustion chamber, etc. These factors all change depending on the use of the cylinder head because a street/strip head will need more conservative valve work for durability than an all-out drag-race motor. Also, the head porter needs to consider the intended RPM range of the motor since they can trade off flow at low valve lift against flow at higher valve lift.

Remember: flow isn't the only thing to pay attention to, although it does seem to be the one specification that is usually advertised. The cross-section area is also important, as is the total volume of the port. The quality of the airflow is another very important consideration for power production. Quality of airflow is called swirl or tumble, but these characteristics can be extremely difficult to measure.

When evaluating the quality of the port work, you can reference some standard benchmark numbers that are widely used in the racing industry. One is the theoretical maximum flow of 146 cfm per square inch of cross-section area when measured at 28 inches of depression. The very best racing heads never reach 146 cfm per square inch but some professionally prepared heads will flow in the range of 130 to 138 cfm per square inch. The majority of ported Mopar cylinder heads on the market will have flow rates in the range of 100 to 120 cfm per square inch of minimum cross-section area, so there is definitely room for improvement if a person is willing to make the investment in a special porting program.

CNC Porting

Finding a cylinder head porter with the tools and experience to properly port a set of heads used to be very difficult and expensive. But times have changed for the better and high-quality porting work is readily attainable. Fortunately for us motorheads, the machine tool industry started to produce multi-axis machining centers at a cost that cylinder head porters could afford. These days, after a master head porter has developed a port that works very well in testing, the port can be digitized, and the machining center can be programmed to reproduce the port. This process is called CNC porting and it has dramatically reduced the cost of high-quality cylinder heads. What used to take 40 hours of physical labor by a highly skilled porting expert can now be done in a few hours on a machine. The cylinder head porter can focus on improving the porting work and developing new porting programs while the machine follows the program.

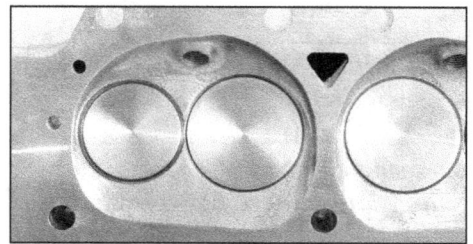

This is a close-up view of the combustion chamber on a set of Mopar Performance 452 cylinder heads that have been CNC ported. The CNC profile does not always cover the entire surface of the chambers due to casting variance.

Do not assume the term "CNC ported" means that the cylinder head will make huge amounts of power. The CNC machine does only what it is programmed to do. If the original design wasn't efficient or effective, the CNC duplication won't be any better. So the trick is still in finding a cylinder head porter whose design is correct for your needs and then purchasing the CNC porting from that shop. Also, this is only an option if someone has programmed a machining center to cut the ports that you need for your engine. Several different vendors will have CNC programs for popular heads, such as the Indy 440-1, but there might not be any programs available for either brand new or unpopular heads. Also you won't find CNC porting services available for highly competitive racing classes, such as Super Stock or Pro Stock. Those programs are trade secrets and will change constantly. So it is unlikely that you'll find a successful race team that is willing to share their current porting program, although they might sell you last year's heads.

Combustion Chamber Porting

Typically, the combustion chambers will also be ported during the CNC process. This chamber porting is beneficial because it will be very precise in equalizing the size and shape of the chambers. Also, the head

CHAPTER 7

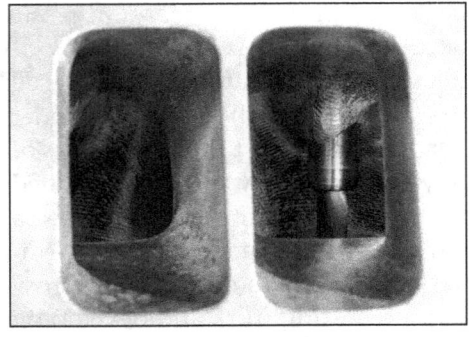

This is a view of the intake runners on the same Mopar Performance 452 heads. The ports in the Mopar heads are identical to those used in the Edelbrock RPM heads.

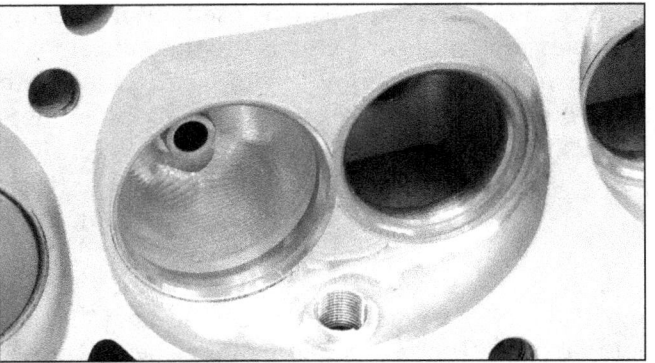

This is the combustion chamber on a Stealth head after it has been CNC ported. The chamber and runners are very similar to those used in the Edelbrock RPM head and performance is basically identical to the RPM head.

porter will usually set up the program so that it un-shrouds the intake valve as much as possible. The wall of the combustion chamber next to the valves can impede the flow of the air into the valve to the extent that these walls can be pulled away, or "laid back," the flow will improve.

There is a practical limit to how much the combustion chamber can be opened up. If the chamber size is larger than the cylinder bore, there will be a step that impedes airflow. Therefore, it should not be made larger than the bore size. Also, the head porter will usually want to keep the combustion chamber as small as possible in order to achieve a high compression ratio without using a domed piston. If you are buying CNC-ported heads, ask about the size of the combustion chamber and find out if the heads had to be surfaced in order to achieve that size. If they have, then find out if the surface finish is compatible with the head gaskets that you will be using. Remember: it only takes one error to ruin an engine and the error can appear anywhere in the build.

If you are planning a very-high-performance engine, tell the cylinder head porter what the final bore size will be, so the combustion chamber will match the engine. For lower-performance engines, you can just buy a CNC head package off the shelf that is designed to work with a common bore size such as 4.375. As long as you plan to use a common bore size, there shouldn't be a problem. But sometimes inexperienced builders purchase CNC heads designed for large-bore motors and try to run them on a small-bore 413 or a 383 motor. This could lead to an expensive learning experience.

It is very important, when inspecting a set of cylinder heads that have had any chamber work on them, to make sure the head gasket does not overhang the chamber. Also mount the cylinder head on a bare block and then scribe the outside diameter (OD) of the cylinder bore onto the cylinder head. This provides a quick visual reference when working on the heads and keeps anyone from grinding too far.

One last check: install a spark plug into the cylinder head, and then carefully inspect to see if any spark-plug-hole threads are exposed in the combustion chamber. The result of improper machining, those threads should be cleaned up before installing the heads in order to prevent detonation.

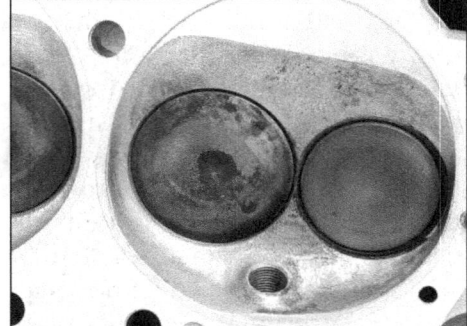

The head gasket fit must always be checked against the cylinder head chamber, especially when working with ported heads. These are CNC-ported Edelbrock heads and the only head gaskets that do not overhang the combustion chambers are ones with 4.500 or larger bore size. The Edelbrock head gaskets in the picture overhang around the intake valve and will not work with these ported heads.

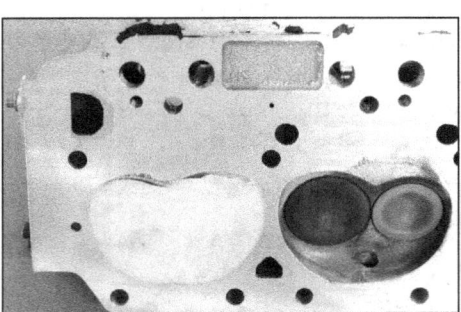

Modeling clay can be used to check for any interference between the piston dome and the combustion chamber. Any of the major piston vendors should have combustion chamber molds on hand for the more popular cylinder heads, so there should not be any interference issues as long as the heads have not been heavily modified.

CHAPTER 8

THE VALVETRAIN

Your valvetrain selection for any performance big-block is going to be heavily influenced by your choice of camshaft as well as the intended use of the engine. At the lower end of the power range, you could make 600 to 700 hp with a large-duration, solid flat-tappet camshaft or maybe even a hydraulic flat-tappet cam. When using a flat-tappet camshaft, the valvesprings' pressure doesn't need to be as high as on a roller cam, so there is much less stress on the rocker arms and pushrods. Consequently, you can use less expensive parts on a flat-tappet-cam motor than on a roller-cam motor.

You need to determine the actual operational speed of the engine when selecting valvetrain parts. The valvetrain items are some of the most highly stressed components in the entire engine and the loads increase significantly with speed. Therefore, an engine that is designed to produce maximum power at 6,500 rpm requires much less expensive parts in the valvetrain than one that must operate at 8,000 rpm to achieve maximum power. The typical 500-ci Mopar with Max-Wedge ports produces maximum torque at 5,200 rpm and maximum horsepower at 6,500 rpm, so you can usually get by with good-quality valvetrain parts without needing to step up to pro-grade parts.

In 1958 the original engine designers chose the excellent shaft-type rocker arm design. This system is fairly rigid and trouble free compared to some of the other methods for retaining rocker arms. This basic shaft system has evolved over years. Now there are thicker-wall shafts, higher-strength rocker arms, and rocker arms with different ratios than the original engines had, but the basic design has remained the same. The shaft-type rocker arm system works well until you get more than .750 inch of lift at the valve. If the valvelift gets above the .750-inch range, then the geometry of the stock rocker arm shaft starts to cause scrubbing and side loading issues on the valve stems. When the stock

There are several different rocker arms available for heads that use standard offset setups. Shown is a set of nodular iron rocker arms at the bottom, a set of Comp investment-cast rocker arms in the middle, and a set of extruded aluminum rocker arms at the top.

This picture shows a fairly wide selection of existing big-block rocker arms. Look closely and you'll see that some use needle bearings, others use bushings, and others are unbushed. Some require ball end pushrods while others need a cup-style pushrod.

HOW TO BUILD MAX-PERFORMANCE MOPAR BIG-BLOCKS

CHAPTER 8

This selection of Harland Sharp rocker arms shows the different amount of offset that is available for different cylinder heads. The Indy heads require up to .800 of offset while Victor heads need .650. Some of the MP heads work best with .450 offset while the stock offset is usually about .200.

shaft system can no longer support either the required valve lift or the spring forces required for high-speed operation, it must be replaced with a multiple-shaft system from Jesel or T&D.

Rocker Arm Geometry

Rocker arm geometry is an interesting subject to explore on a big-block Mopar because it is a combination of simple and complicated components. It's simple because the production big-block uses a fixed-shaft system. With the rocker arm shaft bolted solidly to the

One key to valvetrain reliability is to spend plenty of time mocking up the parts and checking for proper fit and function. This picture shows a set of Comp Cams steel rocker arms installed with a height gauge and checking springs in order to verify retainer clearance and rocker arm geometry.

Here is a basic evolutionary chart of big-block rocker arm systems starting with stamped non-adjustable rocker arms at the bottom and progressing upward to the split-shaft Jesel systems. There should be something here for every motor.

head, there isn't much room for the rocker arm geometry to change for the worse or the better. As long as the engine can develop the necessary power in the stock rocker shaft location, the issue of rocker arm geometry can remain unchanged. However, most performance engines require the valve lift to be .650 inch or higher, and at this point the rocker arm geometry becomes complicated. If valve lift is going to be greater than .750 inch of lift, then the factory geometry will most likely need to be completely re-worked.

The classic theory of rocker arm geometry is that the rocker arm should be at a 90-degree angle to the valve stem at mid-lift and that the tip of the rocker arm should stay centered on the valve tip. So for a .650-lift camshaft, the rocker arm shaft should be set up to put the rocker arm at a 90-degree angle to the valve stem at .325 lift. This is a problem on a big-block Mopar because the shaft is located right where the engineers put it back in 1958, and it isn't easy to move. So the geometry that was perfect for a .400-lift passenger car is going to

be a little off with a performance cam of .550 lift, and it is going to be off quite a bit if you put a big .700-lift cam in there.

There are a few techniques for changing the stock rocker arm geometry, and using longer rocker arms is one solution. Since the valve is going to open farther with high-lift cams, the valve tip will be pushed farther away from the rocker shaft at full lift due to the 15-degree valve angle. A longer rocker arm will help to keep the tip of the rocker arm on the valve at higher lift, but it might cause the opposite problem at low lift.

Another possible solution is to install longer valves when using high-lift cams. The longer valve changes the rocker arm geometry because it forces the rocker arm to start its travel at an earlier position in the arc. This means that the rocker arm ends up in the correct location at the end of the arc when the spring load is the greatest, but the rocker arm position might not be optimum early in the arc.

The use of longer valves can also solve a second problem, which is the need for a taller valvespring when using high-lift cams. However, longer

Jesel supplies a tool that is used to set the correct stand height for their rocker arm systems. The tip of the valve should be flush with the top of the tool when the stand is correctly installed. In this picture the mounting surface on the cylinder head hasn't been machined down enough so the valve tip isn't flush with the tool.

THE VALVETRAIN

A close examination of the wear pattern on these valves shows that the rocker arms are a tad too long for this combination of parts. This isn't a bad wear pattern but if it was shifted slightly toward the intake manifold it would be better. Unfortunately, there is no easy solution for situations like this.

This side view shows what happens when a rocker arm that is a little too long is used. Notice how far the roller tip is on the exhaust side of the valve.

Here is a side view showing a rocker arm that is a little too short for this valve location. The rocker arm is short enough that the roller is barely able to make contact with the edge of the valve.

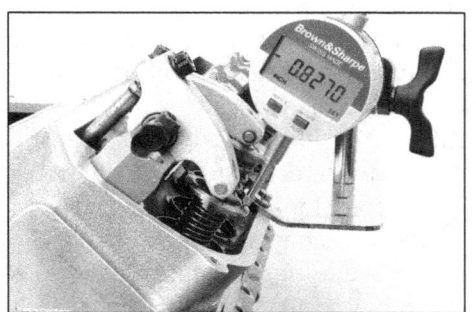

As you can see on the dial, this valvetrain is checked for proper function at over .800 lift. The Jesel rocker arms with their high-ratio capability and excellent geometry are about the only rocker arms that will work reliably at this high valve lift.

Here is an old trick that was used prior to the availability of the Jesel system. The stock rocker stands on this head have been machined away so that the rocker shaft could be mounted in a different location. The re-located rocker shaft provides correct geometry for extremely high-lift cams.

valves can cause issues for pushrod clearance and pushrod geometry at the rocker arms because the pushrod end of the rocker arm is in a slightly different location.

High-lift camshafts often require a more drastic solution to cure geometry issues. One technique is to completely machine away the support stands on the cylinder head and then locate the rocker arm shaft with machined blocks. The height of the blocks can be adjusted so the shaft is positioned for the correct mid-lift geometry. Using a stock-length valve, lower the shaft toward the head .100 inch for every .200 inch of extra lift. Since the rocker arm needs to be perpendicular to the valve at mid-lift as the valve opens more into the cylinder head, the rocker shaft must move down into the cylinder head in order to maintain the proper relationship. When moving the rocker shafts, the 15-degree angle between the valve stems and the rocker shaft bolts starts to cause an issue. As the shaft is lowered into the head, the distance between the center of the shaft and the center of the valve stem increases because of this valve angle. So as you lower the rocker arm shafts into the heads to correct a geometry problem, you will also need to use rocker arms that are slightly longer in order to keep the rocker tip centered on the valve tip.

Most aftermarket rocker arms are made in varying lengths and widths, and this can further complicate these geometry issues. Rocker arms are not built to any standard length, and many of the manufacturers won't tell you how long their rocker arms are. You might not be able to make a proper selection based on information in a parts catalog. This is not a significant problem for a moderate-performance build because most of these engines use a camshaft with .550 to .650 lift, and the typical aftermarket rocker arms work in that range. But the max-performance engine is sensitive to geometry issues, and you may need to be prepared to mix-and-match components if aiming for more than .750 lift. There is no guarantee that off-the-shelf rocker arms bolted into the stock stands will have anything approaching perfect rocker arm geometry. I have seen many valvetrain combinations in which the rocker arm travels very close to the edge of the valve tip and the rocker arms hit the retainer, or the rocker arms do not line up properly on the valve tips.

Rocker Arm Ratio

The production rocker arms for all big-block Mopars have a fairly conservative ratio of 1.5:1. With a 1.50 rocker arm ratio, a camshaft with a lobe lift of .400 inch equals a gross valve lift of .600 inch. This 1.50 rocker ratio works well up to about .750 lift at the valve, but it's difficult to obtain more than that because most camshaft profiles have less than .500 lobe lift. In order to lift the valves more than .750 inch, the rocker arms typically need to be replaced with higher-ratio units. Fortunately, the aftermarket has stepped in with multiple solutions, and there are now many rocker arms available for the big-block with 1.60, 1.70, or even 1.80 rocker arm ratios.

Rather than lengthening the valve side of the rocker arm, you typically move the adjuster closer to the shaft to increase the rocker arm ratio. However, if the adjuster moves too far toward the shaft, the pushrods rub the cylinder head or the rocker arm designer runs out of room for the adjuster ball to clear the rocker shaft.

Although most vendors sell the rocker arm assemblies as complete sets, there's no rule that says you have to run the same rocker arm ratio on the intake side as on the exhaust side. In fact, it has become fairly common practice for builders to use higher-ratio rocker arms on the intake than the exhaust side in an attempt to get more combustion charge into the motor. It's a similar approach to using split duration camshafts for valve timing. One common setup uses 1.60-ratio rocker arms on the intake and 1.50 on the exhaust side, but I've successfully used ratios as high as 1.85 on the intake combined with a 1.60 ratio on the exhaust. If the motor makes good power without the added stress of higher rocker arm ratios on the exhaust side, then do it that way. Often the only way to sort some of this out is on the dyno since the dyno can detect the small benefits.

People don't always realize that a higher rocker arm ratio will make the motor see a bigger camshaft. Besides the increase in valve lift, the motor will see an increase in duration even though the camshaft hasn't changed. Although this may not seem possible, let's consider duration at a fixed point such as .200-inch lift. The same camshaft profile, with a higher rocker arm ratio, will get the valve to .200 lift quicker than will a lower ratio.

Buying a half set of higher-ratio rocker arms can be an easy way to try out different combinations when using standard offset rockers. Shown is a full set of 1.50 rocker arms and a half set of 1.60 rocker arms. The 1.60 arms can be used on either the intake or exhaust locations, depending on what the motor will like best.

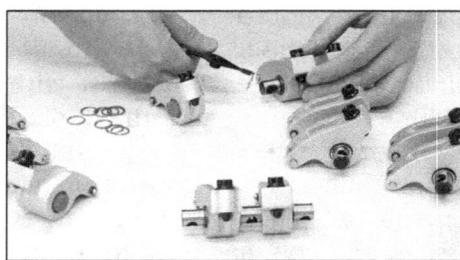

Small retainer clips hold the Jesel rocker arms in place. Having the correct tools allows you to quickly tear down the rocker arm assembly to change the ratio. (Photo courtesy of Joshua Finkbeiner)

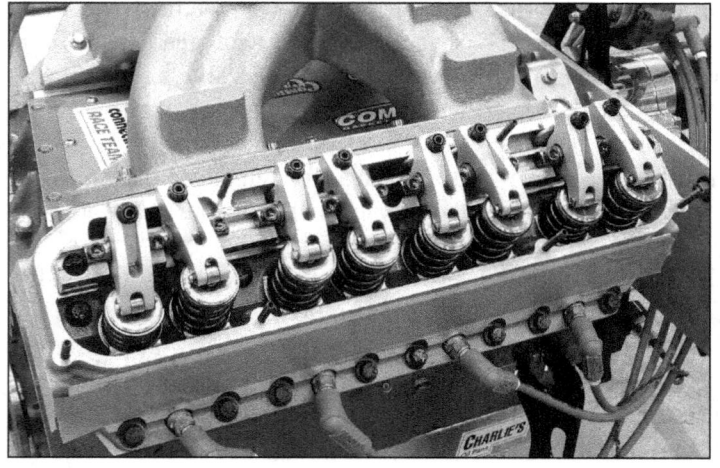

The Jesel rocker arm system becomes a requirement if you need high-ratio rocker arms or special offsets. The Jesel rocker arms are available in ratios from 1.55 to 1.85 and in a wide variety of offsets.

Not only will the valves move to the .200 lift point quicker when using high-ratio rocker arms, but the higher ratio will keep the valve at, or above, that lift point for a slightly longer period of time. So while the camshaft lobe hasn't changed, the area under the curve is greater when using higher-ratio rocker arms.

Along these same lines, the valve-to-piston clearance can significantly change with higher-ratio rocker arms because the valve accelerates much faster off of the seat. An engine with adequate valve-to-piston clearance and a 1.50 rocker arm might not have enough clearance with a 1.70 rocker arm because the intake valve will accelerate faster with the higher rocker ratio. It is possible for the intake valve to have plenty of clearance at TDC, but then the intake valve will accelerate and hit the piston during the intake stroke. So after changing to higher-ratio rocker arms, you need to recheck the valve-to-piston clearance at a range of positions.

The lash setting is one last item to adjust after making a change in the rocker arm ratio. The cam designer determines the valve lash, so the necessary clearance for proper operation of the valvetrain is predetermined. It is calculated based on an assumed rocker ratio. If the lash setting is .015 with a 1.50 rocker arm then it needs to be adjusted to .017 for a 1.70 rocker arm. This is a simple proportion calculation that maintains the same space for the clearance ramps on the camshaft lobe.

Scrub Distance

There is a neat little tool available from Mancini Racing that allows you to quickly measure the amount of sideways travel, or scrub, that the rocker arm has across the valve tip. Using basic math and a bisect arc tool, you can quickly calculate the minimum scrub distance that a rocker arm should travel across the valve tip for any given lift. If you then compare the theoretical minimum distance with the actual distance, you will quickly determine its deviation from optimal rocker arm geometry. With a rocker arm that is 1.50 inches long from the center of the shaft to the center of the roller tip, the sideways travel during .750 of valve lift is a maximum of .050 inch. If you mount up the scrub tool and it measures more than .050 inch, you have determined that the rocker arm shaft isn't located in the correct position. The scrub distance increases if the rocker arm shaft is mounted either higher or lower than the mid-lift point. In order to discover whether the rocker arm shaft needs to be mounted higher or lower, you need to closely observe the tracking pattern of the rocker arm on the valve tip.

The pushrod side of the rocker geometry doesn't get as much attention as the valve side, but the relationship of the pushrod to the adjuster is still very important. A pushrod that is too long or too short causes many problems. These problems can include rocker arm breakage and insufficient oiling of the pushrod cup. The manufacturer provides a setup specification for the adjuster in their instruction sheet. They usually recommend that only one or two threads of the adjuster screw should show

A simple sweep fixture such as this will help you sniff out potential valvetrain geometry issues. When the geometry is correct, the roller tip travel across the valve will be minimized.

under the rocker arm. If too many threads are showing, the adjuster ball moves away from the rocker arm, and the pushrod is forced into excessive sideways travel. Think of the adjuster as a lever arm: you can see that if it hangs too far out of the rocker arm, then there will be a sideways force that conflicts with the proper movement of the rocker arm. Also the ball on the end of the adjuster swings through a larger arc when it is adjusted away from the rocker body, and in turn this can cause clearance problems between the pushrod and the cylinder head.

Rocker Arm Material

The vast majority of aftermarket rocker arms are fabricated from aluminum alloy since it is easy to machine. A well-designed aluminum rocker arm must have enough stiffness to work effectively within its spring load rating. Aluminum is about 1/3 the weight of steel but it also only has about 1/3 the stiffness of steel. Given that, a properly designed aluminum rocker arm will be about the same weight as a steel rocker arm but will need to have additional size in order to have the same stiffness. This tradeoff works out fine as long as the extra physical size doesn't cause any interference with other parts in the valvetrain. The most common interference issue in the valvetrain is the underside of the rocker arm hitting the valvespring retainer, so that is the first place to look for problems.

Metal fatigue and failure are the primary concern with aluminum rocker arms. When aluminum rockers are used in an engine with cyclical loading, the number of cycles and the amount of stress on the rocker arm determines the time to failure. The force/area equation calculates the stress, so a bulky rocker arm has less internal stress than a narrow-profile rocker arm when used with the same spring load. It is difficult to determine the life expectancy of an aluminum rocker arm in a certain situation. In general, the higher the spring force the shorter the life. A rocker arm that works fine for 10 years on a street motor with 200-lb springs might fail within one season of racing with 750-lb springs. One of the most difficult duties for a rocker arm to survive is street driving with a solid roller cam. Street driving produces a lot of duty cycles for the rocker arm, and the solid roller produces fairly high spring loads. The combination of those two factors requires a high-quality valvetrain. If you use aluminum rocker arms in this type of application, it's wise to carry a couple of spares in your glove box!

There are currently a few non-aluminum rocker arms available for the big-block Mopar. Isky and Crane still make classic nodular iron rocker arms, and these are an excellent choice for use up to about .600 lift. These nodular iron rocker arms look a lot like the original Max-Wedge rocker arms and work really well with big flat-tappet cams, such as the MP .557 and MP .590. The nodular rocker arms tend to be fairly inexpensive to purchase, and they last a long time when used with a solid, flat-tappet cam. They are suitable for a mild street-roller camshaft, but most likely would be overmatched by the valvesprings required for a big

While most aftermarket rocker arms are made from aluminum, here are three that are not. The Comp Cams rocker arm in the upper left is an investment-cast steel rocker arm that has been bushed. The nodular iron rocker arm in the upper right corner is the classic Max-Wedge design and is a good choice for use with flat tappet cams. The rocker arm at the bottom of the picture is an inexpensive copy of the Comp Cams rocker arm and would not be the best choice for a performance engine.

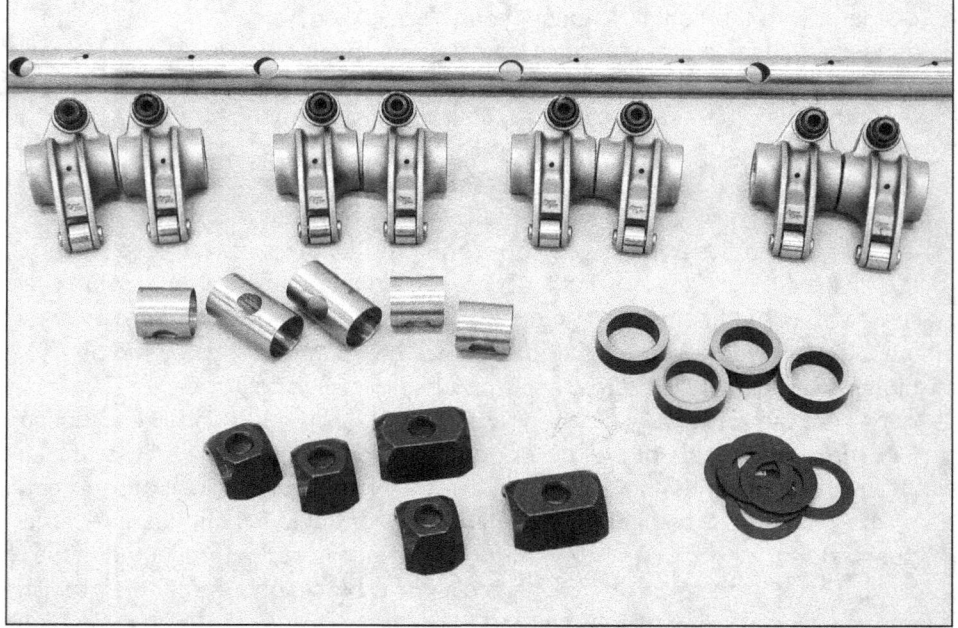

Here is an exploded view of a set of Comp Cams rocker arms that have been modified by RAS to work with high-load valve springs. The rocker arms have been bushed, the rocker shafts are smaller diameter with thick walls and multiple oil grooves, and the hold-down hardware has been upgraded with parts made from thick steel.

THE VALVETRAIN

solid-roller cam. The biggest issue with the nodular rocker arms is they don't fit onto a stock cylinder head very well. It is a strange problem; these parts have been around for 30 years, but they still aren't made quite right. You would need to do some grinding on the support stands in the cylinder head so these rocker arms fit, or grind on the body of the rocker arm so it will be narrow enough to fit the existing stands on the head. You can also send used nodular rocker arms to RAS (Rocker Arm Specialist) so bronze bushings can be installed and give them a new lease on life. This can be a great way to recycle a set of old rocker arms from a previous motor or a swap meet.

Competition Cams introduced a very nice set of steel rocker arms for the big-block Mopar a few years ago. These Comp rocker arms come complete in a kit with shafts and hold-downs, and they have been a successful product. The Comp rocker arms are designed to handle about 450 lbs of open spring force out of the box, but they can be modified to survive higher spring loads. Honing out the body increases the shaft clearance a small amount to handle higher spring loads, and it's the easiest mod for the Comp rocker arms. Extra clearance will help the rocker

The pushrod side of these rocker arms shows large oiling holes that are designed to squirt oil onto the valve cover. With this design, the spray of oil hits the valve cover and bounces back to lubricate the pushrod cup and adjuster ball.

At the top, an Edelbrock RPM head with an aluminum rocker arm system from Racer Brown is shown. The cast-iron head at the bottom has a set of nodular iron Isky rocker arms mounted in custom-built shaft supports. A professional has properly set up both of these heads, so they are good examples to follow. The picture shows the proper use of shims, rocker shaft studs, heavy-duty hold-down hardware, etc.

The RAS rocker arms are bronze bushed, and they come with very stout hold-down hardware.

These investment-cast rocker arms from Rocker Arm Specialist are perfect for a street driven engine that is running a roller cam. Since they are made from a high-grade steel material they can withstand higher operating stress than aluminum rocker arms without fatigue failure.

These lower-cost steel rocker arms have tangs on each side of the roller tip that hang down below the roller tip. This can cause a valvetrain failure if the tangs are allowed to contact the retainer or lock as seen in this picture.

arm handle higher loads because it provides more space for lubrication. RAS can also upgrade the Comp rocker arms by installing bronze bushings.

Rocker Arm Types

The original Max-Wedge rocker arms were a nodular iron material that rode on a hardened steel shaft. These Max-Wedge arms used the standard big-block oiling system; oil is pumped up from the number-4 cam journal into the rocker shafts and comes out of holes in the shafts at each rocker arm. These unbushed rocker arms work well because the combination of the softer cast iron riding on hard steel with an oil layer in between them is a good combination. This reduces the valvespring load that this system can handle before galling, but it does seem to work well for solid flat-tappet cams and even small street-roller cams. The original Max-Wedge rocker arms are no longer available from Chrysler, but Crane offers some that are a close copy. Competition Cams also has a steel rocker arm that is unbushed and rides on a hard steel shaft. The Comp rocker arms are a much newer design and they include a roller tip as well as a cup-type adjuster for a Chevy-style pushrod with ball ends. These Comp rocker arms seem to work well for solid flat-tappet cams and street rollers.

RAS sells an investment-cast rocker arm set for the big-block Mopar, which is designed for higher spring loads than the Comp or Crane rocker arms. These RAS rocker arms have a bronze bushing installed because the stainless steel material doesn't slide smoothly over a steel shaft as an iron rocker arm does. The bronze bushing adds a layer of protection for the rocker arm, but the rocker arm body has to be slightly larger to accommodate the wall thickness of the bushing.

Here is a set of T&D rocker arms mounted on a Mopar aluminum 452 head. These T&D rocker arms are one of the best single shaft rocker arms you can buy for the big-block Mopar. This picture shows the heavy-duty hold-down hardware, the studs used to mount the shafts, and the excellent fit of these rocker arms.

ARP offers a rocker shaft hold-down kit for the big-block that contains six short studs and four long studs as well as the nuts and washers. Studs are recommended with aluminum heads, especially when using a high-lift cam.

The B1 cylinder head uses a unique valvetrain setup with double-bolted hold-downs and high-offset intake rocker arms. (Photo courtesy of Koffel's Place)

Rocker arm shaft studs that have been turned down for extra oil flow are a good idea when using thick walled rocker shafts. A regular stud can impede the oil flow inside the shaft if the shaft walls are super thick. Shaft studs rather than bolts should always be used when running high-lift cams in aluminum heads.

THE VALVETRAIN

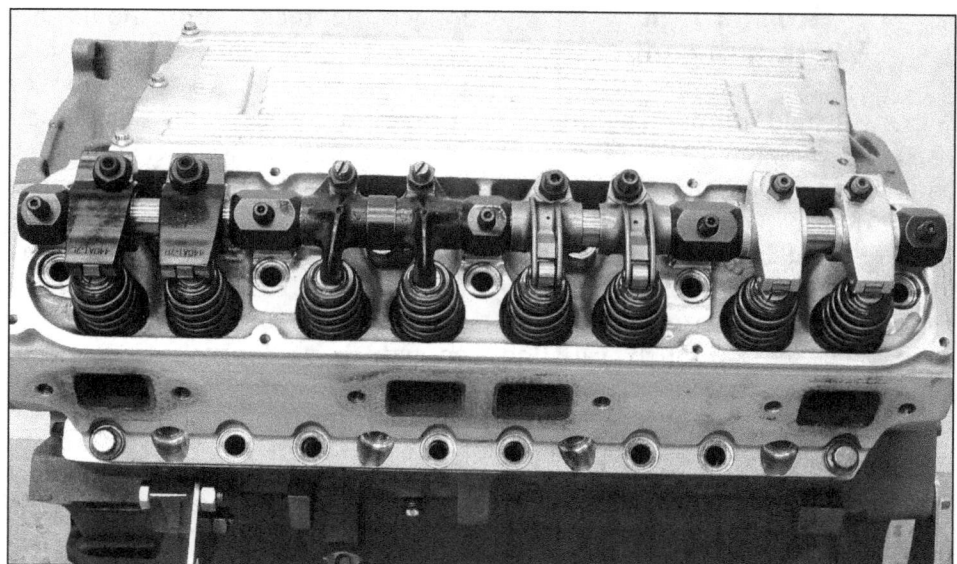

It is useful to keep a selection of rocker arms on hand in order to verify the fitment on different combinations. Here we see an arrangement of different rocker arms all mounted on the same shaft. This is for checking purposes only; the engine will not be run with different rocker arms on the same shaft.

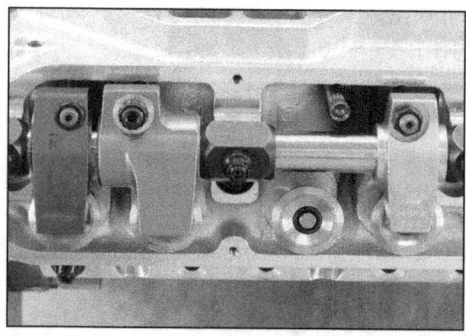

In this picture we're checking several brands of rocker arms to see what fits the best on the new Victor heads.

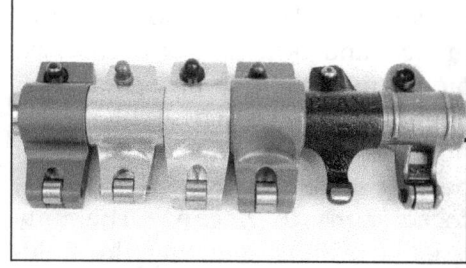

There is no standard rocker arm length in the industry for a big-block Mopar. As you can see, the lengths of the rocker arms vary quite a bit from brand to brand. The length difference has a dramatic effect on the rocker arm geometry, so be very careful when selecting a rocker arm for your combination of parts.

There are a large number of aluminum rocker arms on the market for the big-block Mopar. Some of these use an un-bushed design in which the aluminum rides directly on the rocker arm shaft. This design seems like it would be a problem at high valvespring loads because aluminum has the tendency to gall, but it actually works well. Some vendors such as Hughes advertise a cryogenic treatment designed to further improve the durability of their aluminum rocker arm.

Many of the aftermarket vendors use needle-bearing bushings for the aluminum rocker arms. These are a caged-type needle bearing that is pressed into the rocker arm. If you use these, the shaft needs to be specially heat-treated. The load on a needle bearing is focused onto a line contact where the needle contacts the shaft. There might only be two or three of the needles that are actually in contact with the shaft, so the entire load of the valvespring is carried on a small area. Look closely and you'll see that the more-expensive rocker arms use smaller needles, so they can have more contact with the shaft. The less-expensive rocker arms use larger needles and fewer of them to save money. The less expensive parts will work fine in lower-performance applications; you just need to match the parts with the intended use.

Several of the higher-end rocker arm systems use small-diameter shafts to leave room for the bearings. For example, the T&D system requires spacers in the stands in order to properly locate the smaller diameter shafts. They also use rocker shaft studs that have turned down waists so that the oil can flow down the shaft. These waists are required since the shaft diameter is smaller. The Jesel rocker arm system takes the smaller shaft trend further by using small solid shafts. These smaller shafts provide extra room for the needle bearing and make the needle bearings solid, so plenty of strength is maintained. The stock oiling system is shut off when using the Jesel rocker arms and the lubrication to the valvetrain is supplied either by the pushrods or by spray bars in the valve covers.

Rocker Shafts and Supports

The production-style rocker arm hold-downs are made from stamped sheetmetal and they work okay as long as the spring loads and engine speed are low. I was rather young and working on my first big-block Mopar years ago when I tried to save some money by using some stock sheetmetal-type hold-downs with my new

Isky nodular iron rocker arms. Everything seemed to be working just fine until I took off the valve covers to set the lash one afternoon and I noticed that the sheetmetal retainers were chewing up my new rocker arms. That was one experience that set me on the path of thinking about parts as a system rather than just bolting stuff together.

There are now many choices on the market that are more rigid and provide better support than the stock-type bent sheetmetal hold-downs. RAS, Hughes, Mopar Performance, and others offer hold-down blocks machined from either billet aluminum or steel. These thick, rigid hold-downs also provide a large flat bearing surface on each side for the rocker arms to ride on. The only issue is making sure that the hold-downs have the correct width so the rocker arms will be properly aligned on the valve stems.

The stock system uses five bolts to hold the rocker shaft down against the head. When installing the shaft, there will always be at least a couple of valvesprings that need to be compressed because the camshaft doesn't have a position where all lobes are on the base circle at the same time. This isn't too much of a problem with stock-type valvespring pressures, but it can become an issue with high-lift cams and heavy valvesprings. The worse case is when pulling the rocker shafts down against heavy valvesprings on aluminum heads because the threads are not very strong and can strip. The best solution is to use studs rather than bolts. The studs screw into the cylinder head and the stud material, rather than the threads, takes the force in the aluminum head. You can use an ARP stud kit to mount the rocker shafts onto most standard port and Max-Wedge cylinder heads.

Rocker Arm Width and Length

One would think that after 50 years of development, this area would be all sorted out, but that isn't the case. The current rocker arms on the market vary significantly from each other in both width and length. Line up a bunch of them on a common shaft and you'll see so much variation between manufacturers that it is a wonder some rocker combinations work at all. This variety is great for providing options, but can also cause confusion. The width issue is fairly easy to solve. Machine the rockerarms to make them fit, or use shims and spacers to move the rocker arms apart to resolve the side-to-side alignment on the valve tip. The length issue is much more difficult; you may need to purchase new rocker arms if the ones you currently own don't fit properly.

The length of the rocker arm from shaft to tip determines if the roller tip correctly aligns on the valve tip. If the rocker arm is too long or short, then the rocker tip will ride too close to the edge of the valve tip rather than applying the force to the center of the valve. Further complicating matters: there isn't really a single correct length for rocker arms. In general, the more valve lift that the engine will experience the longer the rocker arm should be. A longer rocker arm stays in contact with the valve as the valve moves through a longer path. Remember, the valve angle on a typical big-block is 15 degrees, so the valve is moving away from the rocker arm shaft. On a high-lift application, such as greater than .700 lift, the valve tip moves away from the rocker shaft enough that a longer rocker arm is needed to maintain contact.

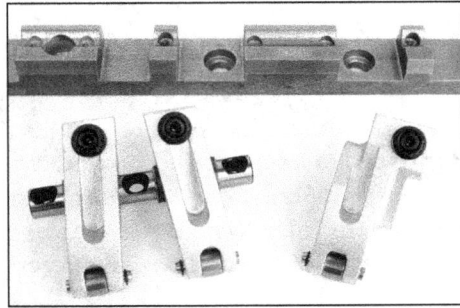

The Jesel rocker arm system uses a pair of rocker arms for each cylinder that are mounted on a small shaft. There are four pairs of rocker arms per cylinder head that are mounted on a steel stand. This system allows a pair of rocker arms to be removed without disturbing the others.

A close-up view of the T&D rocker arms illustrates the excellent alignment of the rockers on the valve tips. The large hold-down blocks and the thick spacers on each side of the rocker arms maintain precise alignment.

Make sure there is enough clearance between the rocker arm and the retainer when setting up the valvetrain for high-lift operation. Here, a valve spring retainer is set up for 2 inches of installed height. The retainer is close to the rocker arm but there is enough clearance for safe operation.

THE VALVETRAIN

One nice feature of the Jesel rocker arm system is the ease of valve spring replacement. The rocker arm pair is simply unbolted from the stand and the valve spring compressor tool is bolted onto the stand. A pair of valve springs can be quickly replaced without disturbing any of the other rocker arms on the cylinder head.

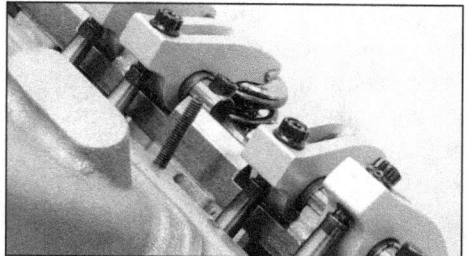

Jesel rocker arms must be oiled through the pushrod or via spray bar oilers because the stand blocks off oil from coming up inside the head. These pushrod ends burned up when the restriction in the oil line that feeds the spray bars was made too small. Sometimes it is a very small difference between a combination that works right and one that fails.

These Jesel rocker arms have been installed correctly and the wear pattern is perfectly centered on the valve tip. This installation was optimized for a .820-lift camshaft; an engine with more or less lift might require a slightly different stand height in order to get the wear pattern properly centered on the valve tip.

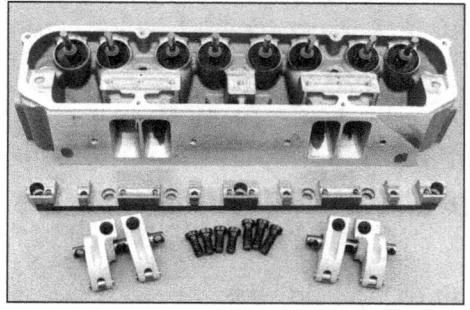

The rocker shaft supports on this Indy head have been machined away in order to provide a flat mounting area for the Jesel rocker stand. The Indy heads are designed with extra material in the rocker stand area for this operation. It is highly recommended to purchase new heads already machined for Jesel rocker arms rather than modifying existing heads.

The installation of Jesel rocker arms onto a cylinder head that were originally set up for shaft rocker arms requires substantial machine work. Here the rocker stands on an Indy EZ head are being machined away so that the Jesel rocker stand can be bolted in place.

After the stock rocker stands are machined away, the Jesel stand can be installed for a quick test fit. New mounting holes have to be drilled and tapped into the cylinder head in order to hold down the Jesel stand.

High offset rocker arms are available if the pushrod needs to be moved over to provide clearance for larger intake runners. In this picture a high-offset intake rocker arm has been installed on the first cylinder to see where the pushrod will line up.

To really complicate matters, the manufacturers do not publish information about the length or the width of their rocker arms. The only way for you to determine the best parts for certain applications is to actually buy the rocker arms and perform a test fit. The more experienced builders have notes and pictures detailing which rocker arms work well in certain applications. It is this type of experience that you're paying for when you have an engine professionally built.

One way to resolve the width issue is to purchase a complete rocker arm assembly kit from a vendor. The complete kit should include hold-downs, shims, spacers, etc. If the vendor does a competent job at engineering its kit, it will bolt onto a standard cylinder head and will be ready to go.

The production rocker arm shafts were made from a fairly thin material, and they will distort into an egg shape if the hold-down bolts are overtightened. This is a fairly common problem when people run adjustable rocker arms on the stock shafts. If the hold-downs have been overtightened, then the rocker arms cannot be removed from the shaft because the shaft becomes distorted into an oval shape. Thankfully the aftermarket has come to the rescue by offering a variety of thick wall shafts that can handle higher hold-down torques.

Besides checking the strength of the thick wall shaft, make sure the hardness of the shaft matches the type of rocker arm bearing. Needle bearing rocker arms require a shaft that has been heat-treated and ground smooth because the needle bearings have a high point load. Rocker arms with bronze bushings do not require a shaft that is as hard, but it should be okay to use hardened, ground rocker arm shafts with bushed rocker arms. Again, the best bet is to buy a complete system from a vendor who understands the system requirements. Fly-by-night eBay vendors are not the best place to buy rocker arms for a performance engine buildup!

Side Clearance and Alignment

For proper operation, the rocker arms need to have some side clearance. The side clearance isn't a critical spec like the main bearing clearance, but there should be enough clearance for oil flow past the rocker arms and to keep the rocker arms from binding as they get hot. About .030 of total side clearance should be acceptable for a pair of rocker arms.

A package of shims is included if you purchase a complete kit of rocker arms, shafts, and hold-downs from a quality vendor. These are hardened steel material, and they can be used between the rocker arms to take up extra clearance. The shims also provide a smooth, durable wear surface for the rocker arms to ride on. The small amount of offset in the rocker arm between the pushrod tip and the shims causes a twisting force on the rocker arm, which forces it sideways into the hold-down. A thin shim located between the rocker arm and the hold-down eliminates a wear pattern forming on the side of the hold-down.

Check the side alignment of the rocker arms to ensure that the rocker arm tips are properly lined up on the valves. The side-to-side alignment can be a real issue when using the cheaper brands of rocker arms, especially if the rocker arms do not come with hold-downs. This is a problem for the rookie engine builder who buys some cheap parts on eBay and then tries to get them to work on a big-block. Often, the hold-downs come from one vendor and the rocker arms from another vendor, and they either have too much side clearance or the whole assembly binds up and fails. There is not a standard design for either hold-down width or rocker arm width, so every

Double-check clearance on the pushrod side of the rocker arm also. Here we see that the cups on the pushrods are rubbing against the rocker arms at full lift. To fix this problem, new pushrods with smaller cups had to be ordered from the vendor.

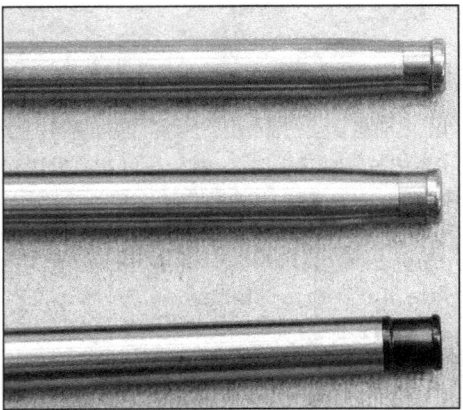

The shape of the pushrod cup becomes important at high valve lift, especially when using extra-large diameter pushrods. These pushrods are all 7/16 diameter, and there were interference problems with the rocker arm until the pushrod cups were turned down and contoured. This is typical of the problems that you'll encounter when building a max-performance Mopar.

There's plenty of clearance between the pushrod and the rocker arm when using a properly tapered 7/16-diameter pushrod and a small-diameter pushrod cup. This mock-up shows the valve operating at about .800 lift. More lift than this might require yet another set of parts for proper clearance.

vendor makes their parts to their own dimensions. So unless you have the capability to modify the parts or unless you know exactly what you are buying, stick with proven components from a single vendor.

Multiple Shaft Systems

Multiple-shaft systems are the ultimate rocker arm setups currently on the market. It seems a shame to machine away the solid rocker shaft stands that are cast into a Mopar cylinder head, but build an engine with a multi-shaft system once and you'll realize the many benefits. Since the heads are machined for the specific application, the shaft location can be optimized for your planned valve lift. In addition to having the geometry correct, the multi-shaft systems are designed to work with larger-diameter valvesprings, and are built from premium materials to handle high-speed operation. One of the really nice features of a multi-shaft system is that you can install the rocker arms for each cylinder while both cam lobes are on the base circle; you no longer have to pull down the shaft bolts against the pressure of the valvesprings. When using high-lift valvesprings having upwards of 1,000 lbs of force, not having to pull the shafts into place against the valvespring load is very important.

As you can imagine, the multiple-shaft rocker arm systems are much more expensive than the single-shaft systems, but needed when using high valve lifts at high engine speeds. Any engine with more than .800 inch of valve lift or 7,500 rpm operation typically benefits from a multiple-shaft rocker arm system. If you are considering changing over to multiple-shaft rocker arms, you need to plan how the rocker arms and

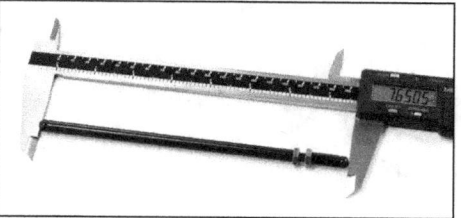

An adjustable pushrod is a good way to find the correct length needed for a custom installation. You'll also need a long set of dial calipers in order to accurately measure the pushrod when it has been removed from the engine.

pushrod adjusters will be lubricated. The multiple-shaft systems usually block off the internal oil feed from the block, so the valvetrain will need to be lubricated either from the pushrods or via spray bars located in the valve covers. Pushrod oiling requires special lifters and pushrods, which in turn can require modifications to the block. If you're considering a multiple-shaft system, you need to be sure the oiling system is capable of supporting it, and the block modifications are compatible with the desired setup. A little bit of research into this area can save a lot of problems later in the build.

Pushrods

The pushrods for the big-block Mopar have always been odd because they use a cup-style adjuster on the rocker arm end. Most of the more popular engines used a ball-style pushrod, which is easier to manufacture. Recently, however, some of the higher-end rocker arm vendors have started to offer the cup-style pushrod end as an upgrade so maybe the Chrysler engineers had this one correct 50 years ago.

The biggest change in pushrod technology over the last decade has been the move to larger diameter pushrods. Extensive testing on

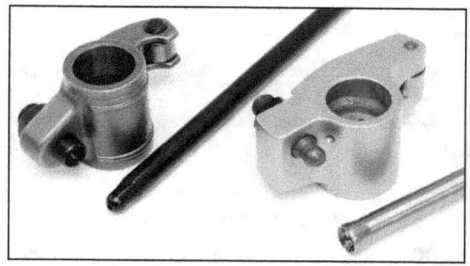

Big-block rocker arm adjusters are available for either ball end pushrods or the original cup-style pushrod.

Spintron equipment has shown that the pushrod deflection is quite extensive at high speeds, so builders have begun to increase the pushrod diameter as much as possible. The average street/strip engine these days uses a 3/8-inch-diameter pushrod with .080-inch wall thickness while the higher-performance engines with .800-lift-type roller-cam valvetrains will be using 7/16-inch- or even 1/2- inch-diameter pushrods. As you can imagine, finding the room inside the cylinder head for these large pushrods can be a challenge. If there isn't room for large-diameter pushrods, the other options available are to use high-strength materials or to increase the wall thickness of the pushrod.

When using pushrod oiling, the pushrods obviously need to be ordered with holes in each end, so the oil can flow up to the valvetrain through the pushrod. Smith Bros as well as other pushrod vendors will have pushrod ends that can oil. Smith Bros can also install oil restrictions in the pushrods as an option. Depending on how the lifter is designed and how much oil the valvetrain requires, the amount of oil that is flowing up the pushrod may need to be restricted. These pushrod restrictions are quite small and can be plugged up with any debris that is floating around in the oil, so frequent inspection is required.

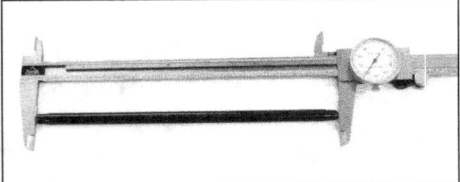

When ordering pushrods you can specify an overall length as measured by a pair of dial calipers. Just make sure that the pushrod vendor knows how you are measuring your pushrods because they might use a different method for determining length. It gets even trickier when measuring pushrods that have a cup on one end.

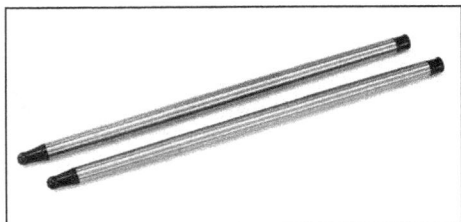

These pushrods are from Jesel and they are about as trick as you'll find in a big-block Mopar. These pushrods are a three-piece modular design using thick-wall 7/16-inch tubing. A set of these pushrods costs close to $500, so it is very important to order the correct length and style the first time.

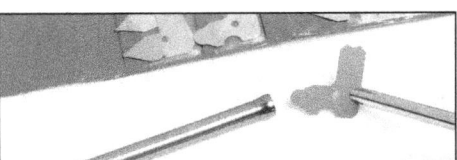

Mopar rocker arms and lifters often use 5/32-inch-radius ends but not always. Some lifters use a 3/16-inch-radius cup and some rocker arm adjusters use even smaller or larger ball ends. The bottom line is that everything needs to be measured before you order your custom pushrods or else the parts might not fit together properly.

When assembling a new combination there should be a final checkout of the valvetrain with a dial indicator to see if the rocker arm ratio is correct. This is also an excellent time to verify that there are proper clearances for all moving parts and that the rocker arm geometry is correct.

A pair of Comp Cams rocker arms are being checked for fit and function on an Indy cylinder head. Notice that these rocker arms use a pushrod with a ball end. It is very important to have the correct length of pushrod with these rocker arms because the adjuster screw can only lubricate the pushrod tip properly when it is in the right position relative to the rocker arm.

It is important to lubricate the pushrod tips liberally before final assembly. It can take a few moments for oil to reach the pushrod tips when starting up the engine for the first time and high spring loads can quickly cause damage if the parts are not lubricated.

You need to measure the radius of the cup in the lifter as well as the radius of the cup or ball adjuster at the rocker arm before ordering the pushrods. Usually the Mopar lifters and rocker arms use a 5/32-inch-radius ball and cup, but this is negotiable. Vendors are free to put whatever size radius on either the lifters or the rocker arms, so it is your responsibility to measure everything before ordering the pushrods.

Pushrod length has to be measured during a trial assembly process using the actual parts that will be used for the final assembly. The lifter's length will vary per vendor as well as per style. Also some cylinder heads are much taller than others; if you are building a new combination of parts, there is very little chance that you'll be able to reuse some existing pushrods.

It is also critical to get the pushrod adjusters in the correct location before measuring the length of the pushrod. This topic was discussed earlier in the rocker arm section of this chapter, but it bears repeating here. The adjuster screw typically should only have one or two threads showing below the rocker arm. If the adjuster is hanging out too far below the rocker arm, then the pushrod is traveling through a larger than necessary arc, and the adjuster is being put under greater stress. Also, if the adjuster isn't in the correct location, some rocker arms will not oil correctly because some rocker arms use a turned-down waist on the adjuster screw to provide oil to the pushrod cup.

CHAPTER 9

CAMSHAFTS AND LIFTERS

The desired power output as well as the operational RPM range of the engine primarily determines camshaft profile. The power output of the engine directly correlates to the amount of duration and lift of the camshaft. Selecting a camshaft profile for all-out racing is often a matter of selecting the right duration for a specific track or engine speed, without regard for low-speed manners. Selecting a cam for a street/strip performance engine is an entirely different matter because consistent and strong performance is required from idle to full throttle.

Duration

The duration of the camshaft is probably the most important factor when selecting the proper lobe for the engine. There seems to be a primal urge to select the biggest camshaft offered by the manufacturer. But a big cam doesn't make big power unless the rest of the system—heads, compression ratio, converter, or gears—is capable of supporting it. When the components don't match the cam, owners are disappointed by a poorly performing combination. Hot rodders who made this mistake often got tired of engines that wouldn't idle, didn't have any low-end response, and kept fouling spark plugs.

A 500-ci stroker motor primarily built for street duty will work great with a smaller camshaft, such as the Mopar Performance .528 solid. This is a very mild cam in a 500-ci motor that will idle smoothly at 750 rpm with plenty of manifold vacuum, but it will also produce 600 hp on the

A custom fixture makes it easy to dial in the camshaft. This fixture is mounted to the block with the head bolts, and it holds a dial indicator in alignment with either the intake or exhaust lifter.

These two camshafts have similar lift and seat duration numbers but obviously the roller cam on the left has a lot more duration at high lift than the flat-tappet cam on the right. The net result is that the roller cam will get the valve open earlier and keep it open longer.

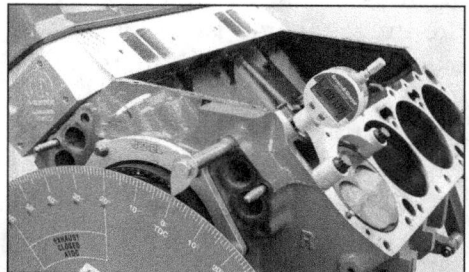
When installing a new cam into a performance engine it is a good idea to measure the duration at .050 and .200 as well as the cam lift at TDC. Some builders record the duration at .300 and .400 for future reference to other lobes and they might also check the cam lift at points other than just TDC.

HOW TO BUILD MAX-PERFORMANCE MOPAR BIG-BLOCKS

dyno. This is assuming a 10:1 compression ratio, a good intake, typical headers, and 850- or 950-type carb. On the other hand, that same 500-ci motor with 13:1 compression, Indy heads, a Dominator carb, and big headers would make about 750 hp when using a much larger cam, such as the Comp Cams MM305. The MM305 is a very large, solid flat-tappet cam when compared to the MP .528, but they both work well in a 500-ci stroker motor. The MP .528 performs well in a street/strip car and delivers solid idle quality, but can still run 11s at the drag strip. On the other hand, a Mopar race car equipped with the MM305, open headers, and a good chassis runs deep into the 9s, but it certainly won't have very good manners when driving around town.

Single Pattern vs. Dual Pattern

Obtaining the proper split between intake duration and exhaust duration fuels a lot of bench racing sessions. It's very difficult to come up with firm answers on this subject, so be prepared to hear "it depends" when discussing this ratio. The ratio of intake flow to exhaust flow is the fundamental issue, and most builders agree it should be in the range of 75 percent. That is, the exhaust should flow about 75 percent of what the intake flows in order to have a properly balanced system. If the exhaust doesn't flow this amount, then the engine is a good candidate for using more camshaft duration on the exhaust side than on the intake side. The theory is that the extra duration will help to evacuate the combustion chamber because the exhaust port needs the help.

The 75-percent flow ratio of exhaust to intake port is a good rule for a normally aspirated motor, but this ratio changes significantly for supercharged motors or one that uses lots of nitrous. Remember, the exhaust gases are extremely hot and under very high pressure, so they'll flow out of the engine much easier than the intake will flow in. The engine needs to suck the intake charge into the cylinder using nothing more than atmospheric pressure, while the exhaust gases have high pressure plus the piston pushing them out.

The camshaft design needs to reflect the ratio of intake to exhaust valve size and flow. If the exhaust flows about 75 percent of the intake, the duration on the exhaust lobe should be roughly the same as the duration of the intake lobe. If the exhaust flow is lower than 75 percent of the intake, you should consider adding some extra duration to the exhaust side. There are a few situations where the exhaust ports are so good that a smaller duration lobe is used on the exhaust side but this is usually not the case with big-block Mopar cylinder heads.

Besides the aspect of duration, you'll find that many of the cam vendors offer different lobe shapes for the exhaust side. There are several theories at work here. Since the exhaust gases are hot and under pressure, they act differently than the intake charge does. Even if the cylinder head has the recommended 75-percent ratio of exhaust to intake flow, the cam grinder might want to see a different rate of lift on the exhaust than on the intake. Remember, at higher engine speeds, you need to take more than flow rate into account. For instance, the intake valve is larger and heavier than the exhaust valve, so it can be more difficult to control with the same valvespring. At high engine speeds, you may need a different lobe profile to accommodate the extra

The Jesel rocker arms are available for Mopar big-block heads in ratios that vary from 1.55 to 1.85. Shown is a 1.85 ratio rocker arm on the intake with a 1.70 rocker arm on the exhaust. Engine builders often mix the rocker arm ratios like this in order to get more intake lift without having to compromise the base circle on the camshaft.

mass of the intake valve. As always, you need to think in terms of the whole system, rather than just one aspect of the system. The only end to the possible combinations is the depth of your pocketbook!

It is also very common on higher output motors to vary the rocker ratios between intake and exhaust. This is a fairly easy tuning mod that can be made quickly on the dyno or on the car, and sometimes the engine will respond very favorably. The exhaust side typically requires a lot less rocker arm ratio than the intake side, so a split of 1.70 on the intake and 1.50 on the exhaust is common. If the engine makes as much power with the lower ratio on the exhaust port, it will be easier on the valvesprings and rocker arms to use the lower-ratio arms and run with less exhaust lift. If you're planning on doing this type of testing, it's wise to do a trial fitment before final assembly with different ratio rocker arms to make sure that there is adequate clearance with the different parts.

Single-pattern cams work well for a milder-performance motor under 600 hp. One of the more interesting dyno test sessions that I worked on involved a low-deck 470 motor with a single-pattern cam. This moderate-performance motor with Edelbrock RPM heads, a dual-plane intake and solid flat-tappet cam made about 550 hp on the engine dyno and 475 rwhp on a chassis dyno. Many different cams were tested in this motor, but the very best power curve was generated when using the classic Mopar Performance .528 solid flat-tappet cam. I tried a variety of split duration cams that were either larger or smaller in duration than the MP .528, but the test sessions never found a cam that worked any better than the old-school purple shaft. This doesn't mean that the MP .528 is the best possible camshaft design, but it must be pretty darn good; after a significant investment in time and money I didn't find anything better.

Lifters

Selecting what type of camshaft and lifters to run used to be a fairly simple task. If you wanted a versatile street motor with strong idle and torque, you used a hydraulic cam. If you wanted a racing engine, you should use a solid-lifter setup. This simple selection criterion got a little more complicated after the development of the solid-roller camshaft, and then the development of the hydraulic-roller cam added yet another choice to the mix. Today, all four of these lifter types are viable choices for a performance big-block Mopar, but each choice does come with at least one severe drawback.

Hydraulic Flat Tappet

The hydraulic flat-tappet setup is still one of the least expensive and most reliable ways to build a moderate-performance street engine of 600 hp or less. The hydraulic flat-tappet camshaft can be used with stock-type non-adjustable rocker arms, but those stock-type rocker arms are limited to fairly low spring pressure. Using aftermarket adjustable rocker arms provides the hydraulic flat tappet with more performance potential. However, it doesn't solve all of the potential issues because the hydraulic portion of the lifter can still fail to operate properly at higher engine speeds, from pump failure or lifter collapse. There are some helpful marketplace options at the moment, such as the Pro Magnum hydraulic lifter from Comp Cams or the fast bleed-down lifters from Rhoads. Hydraulic flat-tappet cams are usually limited to less than 7,000-rpm usage, but that isn't necessarily a problem with a big-block stroker motor because the power peak will often be well below 7,000 rpm anyway. A hydraulic flat-tappet setup can be prone to failure without a proper break in procedure, and flat-tappet cams are sensitive to the type of oil used.

Hydraulic Roller Lifter

Hydraulic roller camshafts were never a production option on the big-block Mopar because this technology was released several years after Chrysler discontinued the big-block. Fortunately, the aftermarket has stepped in, and there are now several retrofit-type hydraulic roller lifters available for the big-block. The design offers excellent performance potential along with quiet operation, but it also suffers from the same pump-up problem as the hydraulic flat-tappet cam. In fact, the hydraulic roller lifter might be more prone to pump-up than the flat-tappet cam lifter because the roller lifters are bigger and heavier. Even with the extra weight of the roller lifter, it is possible to operate the hydraulic roller lifter past 6,000 rpm and maybe as high as 7,000 rpm if the components are carefully matched. Given that a 500-ci big-block with standard port heads will have peak power output somewhere around 5,500 rpm, the hydraulic roller lifter camshaft is a viable option. For a 500-ci motor with the large Max-Wedge ports, the hydraulic roller might not be quite as good a solution because the larger-port motors will see peak power about 6,500 rpm, which is pushing the limit of the design. You would typically select either a solid flat-tappet cam or a solid roller cam for a Max-Wedge port motor.

Solid Flat Tappet

The solid-lifter camshaft has been a high-performance street favorite since the original hot rod motors. The solid flat-tappet camshaft requires an adjustable valvetrain, which is more expensive than the non-adjustable type used on a hydraulic flat tappet, but most high-performance engines use an adjustable valvetrain anyway. I have had some experience with a 505-ci big-block that made more than 740 hp using a large solid flat-tappet cam, so the potential is certainly there.

The solid flat-tappet design worked very well for a long time, but when production vehicle technology changed to increase fuel economy and reduce emissions, motor oil was reformulated to reduce catalytic converter contamination. The new emission-reducing motor oils have reduced levels of zinc, and appear to be responsible for a rash of lifter

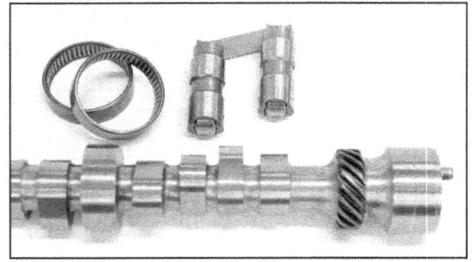

This is a custom hydraulic roller camshaft designed by Crane Cams to work in a big-block motor with roller cam bearings. Notice there is no provision to run a mechanical fuel pump. Full custom camshafts like this are quite expensive because the cam vendor must start with an oversize billet blank.

Comp Cams has recently introduced a line of retro-fit hydraulic roller cams and these matching lifters. A hydraulic roller camshaft is a great compromise for a performance street motor.

failures in older engines. A few "hot rod" and racing oils have higher levels of zinc. If you are going to run a solid flat-tappet cam, make sure the oil you chose contains the correct additives, including zinc. Since production vehicles haven't used solid flat-tappet cams for many years, the standard motor oils stocked at your local gas station will not likely be optimum for a performance motor.

The OEM's switch to roller cams produced another negative side effect: a large portion of flat-tappet-lifter manufacturing capacity went away due to a lack of demand. As you can imagine, new production vehicles used a huge percentage of the lifters made in the world, and the lifters used in high-performance engines were just a small part of the business. After the manufacturing lines switched to making roller followers, it no longer was economical to produce flat-tappet lifters, and several of the flat-tappet-lifter companies went bankrupt. Some smaller companies stepped into the marketplace, but a few of them didn't seem to have the capability of making a high-quality flat-tappet lifter. Consequently, hot rodders started to see more flat-tappet-camshaft failures. This situation may stabilize over time, but many builders have now decided to switch their customer engines over to roller followers rather than run the risk of very expensive camshaft failures.

Composite Lifter

A few years ago, Schubeck Racing introduced solid flat-tappet lifters that had a "button" of hard composite material attached to the bottom of the lifter. This extremely hard composite material was capable of higher spring loads, and it also allowed the lifters to be reused on multiple camshafts. With this innovation, racers who were using flat-tappet camshafts were now able to use one set of lifters with many different cams. This was a great tuning aid for racers and builders because it significantly reduced the cost of cam testing, even though the Schubeck lifters are quite expensive.

I have had excellent results using Schubeck lifters on large flat-tappet cams, such as the Comp MM305. For a big cam like the MM305 profile, I used the Comp 26094 valvesprings set up with 190 lbs on the seat and about 450 lbs over the nose. The Schubeck lifters worked great in all the motors I used them in and did not require any break-in process. Several builders have reported poor results with Schubeck lifters, primarily problems with the ceramic puck on the bottom of the lifter shattering and causing engine damage. Problems like these could be a result of a manufacturing defect or they could be due to valve float.

Special Coatings

NASCAR has required solid flat-tappet cams as a "cost saving" measure for many years. Usually this cost-saving measure is actually more expensive because the engine builders have been forced to use special materials, such as DLC, will live for 500 miles at 8,000 or more RPM. We rarely need to consider NASCAR technology for a big-block Mopar because it would be more cost effective to change to a roller cam, but there might be a little bit of technology trickle-down that could benefit some readers. There are several vendors who are now offering NASCAR-type tool steel lifters with DLC coatings and EDM oil feed holes. These lifters represent fairly new technology, but builders need to

Schubeck flat-tappet lifters have a hard composite facing that allows them to be used with high spring loads and aggressive cam lobes. The hard surface treatment also allows these lifters to be re-used on different camshafts. These particular lifters are drilled for pushrod oiling.

determine if it's necessary to run a big flat-tappet cam in their Mopar. Typically these coated tool steel lifters are designed to work on a steel-billet cam core rather than a cast cam core so you need to verify material compatibility with your camshaft engineer before trying these tricks.

Comp Cams has recently begun to offer a nitrided surface treatment for their solid flat-tappet cams and lifters. This surface is harder and has better wear properties than untreated materials, so this could be a solution for the builder who wants to run a big flat-tappet camshaft but can't afford to use trick NASCAR lifters and tool steel camshafts.

Mushroom Tappet

Mushroom lifters are an old technology that isn't used much these days. Typically, the mushroom tappet has a large face that allows for a more aggressive cam lobe, so you can get roller cam performance on a flat-tappet budget. The typical mushroom lifter was 1.00 inch in diameter, which is a substantial increase over the stock diameter of .904 inch. Mopar Performance used to sell mushroom-tappet lifters and a couple of mushroom-tappet cams. This lifter design does function well, but the lifters have to be installed from the bottom of the lifter bore and this is usually difficult. Some builders use clothespins to hold the lifters in the bore while installing the camshaft. Others drill a hole through the lifter and then use a piece of wire to hold up all the lifters while installing the cam. The bottom of the lifter bores in the cylinder block need to be machined for clearance when using a mushroom-tappet cam, and the adjacent lobes on the camshaft need to clear the mushroom base on the lifter.

Solid Roller Lifter

The solid roller lifter was popular for racing in the 1970s; shortly thereafter it migrated to the street. Many street and street/strip cars use a solid roller camshaft these days, but there are still some ongoing problems with them in Mopar engines. One of the biggest issues is durability of the roller bearing during extended street duty, especially if the engine sees a lot of idling. Evidently roller bearing doesn't get enough oil during lower engine speeds, and, over time, this often leads to lifter failure. Another potential issue is with roller cam followers; the main oil gallery where the lifters are located is also the gallery that feeds the main bearings. If one of the roller lifters pops out during operation from a bent pushrod or other failure, the engine will see a sudden drop in oil pressure that will most likely result in total engine failure.

The fuel-pump drive and oil-pump drive can also affect durability in a roller-cam-equipped big-block Mopar. Roller cams are built from billet steel material rather than the cast material used for the flat-tappet cams. This billet material is much harder than the stock cast material, and isn't compatible with the production-type oil-gear drive or the factory fuel-pump pushrod. Aftermarket vendors now offer bronze-tipped fuel-pump pushrods as well as oil-pump drives with bronze gears so the problem can be remedied, but the bronze material doesn't have the life expectancy of the production-type parts. Therefore if you are going to run a solid roller cam on a street-driven application, you should follow a maintenance schedule and remove the bronze-tipped parts every few thousand miles to inspect them for wear. The life expectancy will vary per your application, but you should be able to determine the life of the parts in your engine. Veteran builders, manufacturers, and suppliers should provide the information, so you know when to replace certain parts before they break.

Solid roller lifters currently available for the big-block Mopar usually use a .750-inch-diameter roller wheel, but other sizes are also available. Mopar Performance used to sell roller lifters that had .850-inch-diameter wheels, and there are a couple of other diameters that are also commonly available. The diameter

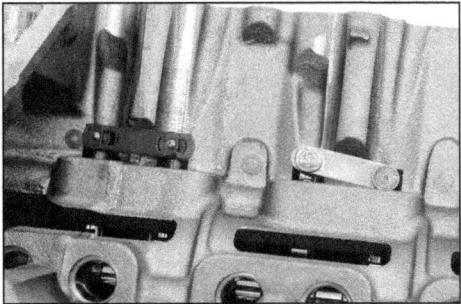

The World Products block has tall lifter bores, which will not work with short roller lifters. Many of the newer lifters are tall enough to fit these lifter bores but not all of them are. This is one more thing for you to double-check before ordering parts.

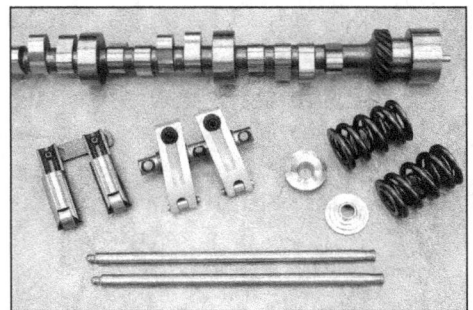

Here are the ingredients of a performance valvetrain. This is a high-lift solid roller cam from Comp Cams along with high-quality roller lifters, Jesel rocker arms, Ti retainers, triple valvesprings and 7/16-inch-diameter pushrod. You start to use parts like these when the power level gets into the 800-hp range or when engine speeds start to approach 8,000 rpm.

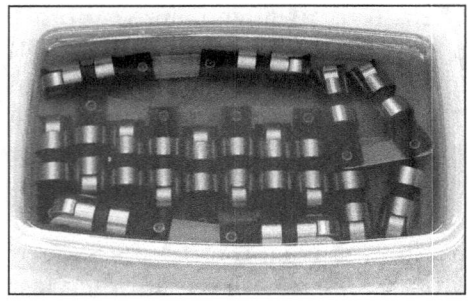

One easy trick is to store your roller lifters in clean engine oil. A small Tupperware-type of storage container with a sealing lid keeps the lifters clean and ready to use.

Solid roller cams usually use the three-bolt cam gear and are ground on steel billet cores. Some roller cam vendors delete the fuel pump eccentric so double-check with the vendor if you are planning on using a mechanical fuel pump.

of the roller wheel is important because camshaft lobes are designed to operate with only a certain size roller wheel. A mismatch between the lobe profile design and the roller wheel size can cause valvetrain instability at higher engine speeds and could potentially fail. A larger-diameter roller wheel operates at a slower speed and, depending on the design and material, it can be stronger, so there are some valid reasons for using a larger roller wheel. Just make sure the camshaft vendor knows what size roller wheel you'll be using when you order camshafts so you don't end up with mismatched parts.

When purchasing roller lifters for an aftermarket block, make sure that the lifter is tall enough to clear the extra material around the lifter bores. The Mega block and the World block have extra-large lifter bores and the shorter roller lifters will not clear the block. Fortunately, several of the lifter vendors have developed taller roller lifters that will work. It is also possible to order roller lifters with offset seats for the pushrods. An offset pushrod cup is needed on the intake lifter only when using the high-offset rocker arms, such as the ones used on the Indy 440-1 cylinder head. The lower-deck B motor might have a greater need for an offset pushrod seat than an RB block because the pushrods are shorter and the angle of the pushrod is greater. This is one of the many things to check during a trial assembly, and it is one reason that engine builders tend to keep a lot of extra parts on hand. It's a painful learning experience to purchase some brand-new lifters and pushrods and then find out that they don't quite work with your new heads and your new rocker arms.

Roller Lifters and Valvetrain Oiling

We'll probably open up a bit of a can of worms with this subject, but it is something that needs to be addressed. As described earlier, the main oil gallery intersects all bores for the passenger-side lifters. Given that, the passenger-side lifters all see main gallery oil pressure, and the flow of oil in this gallery cannot be regulated or else the main bearings will be starved. If the lifters supply oil to the pushrods for valvetrain oiling, this poses a problem because the lifters must each properly regulate oil fed directly from the main gallery.

If the lifters do not properly regulate the oil flow from the main gallery, too much oil will flow through the lifters and damage the engine.

The lifter can expose the oil gallery at high lobe lift, and this condition can cause severe problems for solid roller lifters in a big-block Mopar. A leak in the oil gallery that feeds the main bearings is obviously a very bad event, and this can quickly lead to engine failure. Most solid roller lifters that are made for the big-block Mopar will have a "shielded" wheel design or will be a "full body" lifter. In any case, be very careful when buying roller lifters for a big-block if you are using a production-type block because you must not allow the oil gallery to become exposed during operation.

In an effort to better understand the relationship between lobe lift and lifter dimensions, I designed a small test fixture that mimics the relevant dimensions of a production block. This fixture has a cut-away window in it so I could quickly determine if the lifter in question will expose the oil gallery or not. Another valuable thing that can be checked with this fixture is to see where the oil feed holes on the lifter are during the full cam cycle.

If you are using a lifter that is designed to oil either the roller wheel or the pushrods, there must be an oil-feed hole in the lifter body that picks up oil and directs it into the lifter. Some roller lifters are designed for use in Chevy motors, which are less sensitive to the placement of this oil feed hole because the lifter gallery oil flow and pressure can be regulated in a Chevy motor. On a Mopar, you are pulling from the main oil gallery at full pressure, so if the oil feed hole in the lifter is tapped directly into the main oil gallery without any restriction, the

CAMSHAFTS AND LIFTERS

These lifter bushings have been drilled so that they will work with a hydraulic roller camshaft. The hole needs to be drilled in the correct location so that the oil from the main gallery can provide pressurized oil to the lifter during the full range of operation.

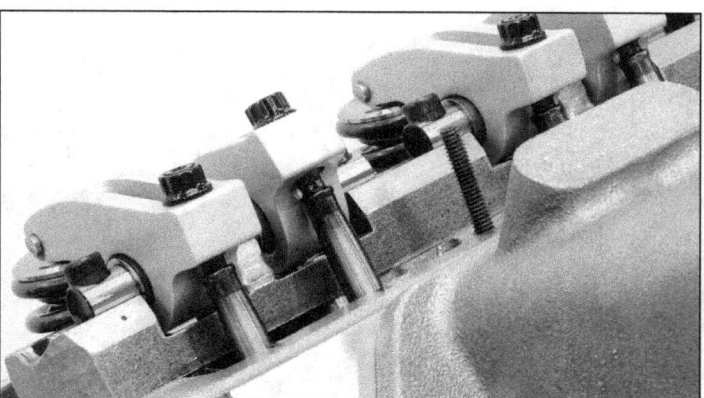

Valvetrains with high spring loads might work better if the pushrod cup is provided with pressurized oil rather than splash oiling. These pushrods were used with splash oiling and they burned up after a few pulls on the dyno. Pushrod oiling requires special lifters or modifications to the lifter bushings.

lifter will be overwhelmed by the volume of oil flow.

Some lifter designers have been placing the oil feed hole parallel to the axis of the roller lifter axle to solve this problem. By placing the feed hole parallel to the axle, it can't intersect the main gallery and will only pick up oil from the clearance area around the lifter.

A quick study of the lifter in its bore shows that there should be about .0015 to .0025 inch of total clearance around the lifter in the bore. That means that the clearance on each side of the lifter is one-half that, or .0007 to .0013 inch. Since the lifter bore is about 1 inch tall, the oil feed hole is supplied by the equivalent of a .001-square-inch restriction or about the same area as you would get from a .035-diameter hole. This side clearance restriction is very effective at limiting the amount of oil sent into the lifter, and it should eliminate the issue of pumping excessive oil to the top end of the motor. Another way to accomplish the same trick is to use pushrods that have internal restrictions for oil flow.

A very small oil feed hole in the lifter or pushrod can become a restriction because small particles that are circulating within the engine could plug up the feed hole. Use the clearance around the lifter as a way to meter the oil flow; it is very effective and costs next to nothing. You can also use lifter bushings to meter the flow of oil to the lifters, but there is a substantial expense involved with the installation of the bushings into a production block.

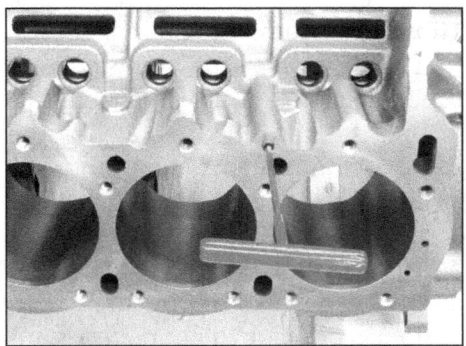

The new World Products blocks feed oil to the rocker arms directly from the main oil galleries. There is a restrictor that is screwed into the oil feed hole that reduces the amount of oil flowing to the valvetrain. This system is easier to modify than the production system, which uses a timed port in the camshaft to feed oil to the top end.

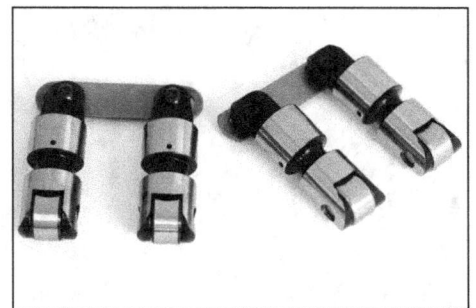

These two sets of solid roller lifters are both designed to provide pushrod oiling as well as pressurized oil to the roller wheel. The set on the right will work in a stock block since the oil feed holes are drilled parallel to the gallery. The set of lifters on the left has the feed holes aimed directly into the main gallery, which can cause excessive internal oil flow.

Rev Kits

The rev kit has been around for a long time, but it seems to be currently out of favor with professional drag racers. Sometimes the bracket racer and street/strip crowd falls into a monkey-see, monkey-do trap. If

CHAPTER 9

Isky Cams makes a rev kit for big-block Mopar. This rev kit only works with specially designed Isky solid roller lifters.

the Pro Stock guys aren't running a part, then they don't want to either. In the case of the rev kit, this might be a mistake because there are some very good reasons to use a rev kit in any engine with solid roller lifters that will see street duty.

The rev kit design is fairly simple. Basically, it consists of a set of springs that push directly on the lifters. The cylinder head positioned against the lifter body holds these springs in place. The spring pressure on these springs is usually light: about 50 lbs of force when open and upwards of 100 lbs at full lift.

There are three primary benefits of the rev kit design. First, the roller lifter is kept in contact with the camshaft lobe at all times. This constant force on the roller wheel keeps it spinning on the lobe and prevents a sudden shock of taking up the lash. Second, a lifter is less likely to be ejected from the valvetrain because the spring holds the lifter in the bore. The loss of a lifter will lead to a total loss of oil pressure and engine failure. Third, the valvespring load can be split between the two springs with a rev kit. Moving some of the valvespring load to the pushrod side of the rocker arm reduces the stress on the pushrod and the rocker arm.

The rev kit has fallen out of favor for high-speed race engines because it contains extra parts, which provide extra complication and weight. While those might be good reasons not to use it in a professional race engine, there does still seem to be significant benefits to using it for lower-speed motors, especially any engine equipped with a solid roller cam that will see street duty.

Lifter bore bushings are required in some blocks to correct the lifter geometry. The bushings can also be used to control the oil flow in an engine, and they might be required to use some special roller lifters. Installing lifter bushings takes special fixtures and many shops are not capable of doing this procedure.

Lifter Bore Bushings

I referenced the lifter bore bushings in the block chapter (Chapter 2), but I should again address the interaction between the oiling system, roller lifter, and valvetrain operation. Installing lifter bushings can correct various valvetrain alignment issues. The bushings can be also drilled with a small hole into the main gallery so the lifter only gets a metered amount of oil rather than full flow and pressure. This then allows you to use less-expensive Chevy-style lifters that might have additional features, such as pushrod offsets, that aren't available in the Mopar body style. When drilling a hole in the lifter bushings, take care to see that the hole in the bushing does not line up directly with the oil feed hole in the lifter. If these two holes line up, the lifter will be fed oil directly from the main gallery rather than from the clearance area around the lifter.

At press time, the Crower PN 66255 lifter is the only roller lifter on the market that allows pushrod oiling in an un-bushed big-block Mopar. Those lifters have shielded bearings, so they'll work with the stock oil gallery location, and the oil feed hole in the lifter is drilled parallel to the gallery. Comp Cams does not currently offer a pushrod-oiling lifter design that will work with an un-bushed block. Isky can custom-build lifters for pushrod oiling in an un-bushed block but they aren't a standard shelf item.

Camshaft Bearings

The production big-block design uses five different cam bearings. The rear bearing is the smallest—the front is the largest. Each bearing is slightly smaller than the one in front of it in a kind of stair step pattern.

The OD of the fourth cam bearing determines the height of the cam lobes, because the lobes must fit through bearing shells number-1 through number-4. The cam lobes never need to fit through the fifth or last bearing because the cam is always removed from the front. For some unknown reason, the cam bearings in a production block are rarely aligned properly. On a rebuilt engine, it's common to have trouble sliding a camshaft into a set of newly installed cam bearings. Given the stair-step-type bearing system, it is difficult to align-hone the bearing bores, so most builders scrap the offending bearing down by hand until the camshaft spins freely.

Large-Diameter Cam Bearings

As valvetrain loads have increased, larger cam cores and larger lobes on the camshafts have been needed. The strength issue is fairly obvious if you think of the camshaft as a part that is applying a force through the lifter to the valvetrain. The force on the cam from each lifter is the force from the valvespring multiplied by the rocker arm ratio. This could be as much as 1,000 lbs from a stiff triple valvespring and a 1.70 rocker arm ratio, which means close to one ton of force for each cam lobe. There are four lobes between each bearing, so a tremendous load can be applied to the cam, which is like a beam suspended between supports.

Increasing the diameter is the best way to increase the strength of a shaft, but the diameter can't be increased too much without causing other problems. The aftermarket has started to grind camshafts on cores with larger bearing diameters, but using these larger cores requires that the cylinder block be machined for larger bearing bores. A 52-mm roller bearing avail-

Standard sleeve bearings are available from Mopar or various other sources. The stock cam bearings come in a set with five different sizes.

able from Ford will fit in the Mopar production block with some machine work, or a 55-mm sleeve bearing can also be used in the production block. The stock block wasn't designed for really large cam bearings, so there is a limit to how much the machine shop can bore out the cam tunnel.

The aftermarket blocks are designed to handle at least a 55-mm roller bearing and maybe even larger. The KP 440 block accepts a 60-mm camshaft bearing in either a stock location or a raised location. These larger diameter bearings can be either a sleeve bearing like the production bearing or you can install roller bearings.

A camshaft with large-diameter bearing journals and base circles can become quite heavy. A 60-mm cam journal is a little over 2.360 inches in diameter—a very large chunk of steel that is spinning in the engine. One way to reduce the weight is to have the center of the cam drilled out. The gun-drilling process reduces the weight without reducing the torsional strength, but it will also add significantly to the cost of the cam.

Several builders have reported positive gains by balancing the camshafts. Balanced cams prevent any harmonics generated by the spinning lobes from affecting the rest of the valvetrain. Having the cam balanced might not be practical for most big-block Mopars because the maximum engine speed is rarely over 7,000 rpm, but it is something to think about if an engine builder is using a large 60-mm core at higher engine speeds.

Roller Cam Bearings

The Babbitt-type sleeve bearing used in the production blocks works well until the valvespring loads become too heavy to support. There might not be an exact point at which the bearings start to fail, but it's probably about 1,000 lbs of open force on the valvesprings. At spring loads higher than that, you should consider changing over to a roller-type cam bearing. The roller cam bearing would typically be installed only when larger-than-stock-type bearings are being used because it is practically impossible to find a set of five roller bearings that would fit a stock-type cam bearing size. You would probably decide to install a camshaft with the larger 55-mm journals and then decide whether or not to just use large-diameter Babbitt bearings or to machine the block for the roller bearings.

While you must assume that a roller bearing will have less friction than a plain-type bearing, this shouldn't be the case as long as the hydrodynamic layer of oil isn't breaking down. A camshaft spinning on a layer of oil has roughly the same friction as spinning on needle bearings. The big difference is at engine startup. When the motor first cranks over, there will not be enough oil pressure to float the camshaft. This isn't a problem at lower spring loads, but can be with high valvespring loads.

CHAPTER 9

A conventional flat tappet cam and camshaft bearing set is shown at the top of the picture, while a custom roller cam designed to work with roller cam bearings is shown below.

Another option for the cam bearings would be to use a coated bearing rather than going to the expense of the roller cam bearing. Roller cam bearings take some special care to install, and they make the block a little more difficult to clean during rebuilds, while a coated bearing is a fairly routine install. Also, the roller cam bearing does not allow the production-type oiling system to send oil to the top end of the motor because the bearing shell blocks the oil passage. This can be fixed by either providing an external oiling line to the cylinder heads or else by machining a groove behind the number-4 cam bearing. Remember: if you use the groove method, you'll have full-time oiling to the top end, which will deliver too much oil unless you restrict the flow.

One way that camshaft needle bearings might save a little horsepower is by reducing the amount of oil flowing inside of the engine. This is a fairly advanced area to consider, but the needle bearings operate from splash oiling rather than pressure fed, so there are now five fewer pressure-fed bushings being fed by the oil pump. So perhaps a person could reduce the volume of the oil pump and save a little bit of power. Also, reduced oil splash might reduce the windage. With a performance Mopar, you are probably not searching for these small horsepower gains unless you're in a very competitive racing class.

Firing Order

The stock firing order for a big-block Mopar is 1-8-4-3-6-5-7-2. This is the same firing order for many GM and Ford motors, so it is fairly conventional. Some builders feel that the 6-5-7 firing sequence hammers the number-4 main bearing, so they change the order to 1-8-7-3-6-5-4-2. This is called the 4/7 swap, and it is popular enough that Comp Cams currently has a large selection of cams for this firing order in the catalog for Chevy motors. At this time, they do not have cams for big-block Mopars with alternative firing orders though. While some people consider this 4/7 swap to be a trick idea, it is merely the same firing order that was used on the old Ford Flathead motors.

Another firing order that is considered to be trick to use is the 1-8-7-2-6-5-4-3 arrangement. This is also called the 4/7-3/2 swap because those four places swap from a stock Mopar firing order. This 1-8-7-2 firing order is also called the LS1 firing order because the new Chevy motors use this firing order. Again, what is new is also old since this same firing order was used on the Ford 351W motors as well as the later Ford 5-liter engines.

Changing the firing order is a fairly common trick in the world of Chevy motors but at the moment it isn't cost-effective for a max-performance big-block Mopar unless you can find a cam manufacturer

A production block can be machined to accept 52-mm roller bearings such as the ones available from Ford. Aftermarket blocks such as the World block can be machined for an even larger 60-mm roller bearing.

who has the necessary core. Changing the firing order means that the lobes on the cam be ground in a different order. Since the lobes on a typical Mopar cam blank are arranged in the standard order, there isn't enough material to put the lobes into new positions. In order to create a different firing order the camshaft manufacturer needs to start with a round billet of steel and grind the new lobe pattern. This is very expensive because it is time-consuming. I had some round lobe cams created for an engine project and they cost more than $500 each. Maybe someday one of the cam companies will tool up a Mopar blank with either the Flathead or the LS1 firing order and then people can experiment with this latest trick idea.

CHAPTER 10

Camshaft Drives and Valvesprings

You need to select the timing chain, cam drive (belt or gear driven), valve springs, and related parts that match the cam and the power output of the engine. This chapter will provide the pertinent information so you can choose the best and most compatible equipment for your valvetrain.

Timing Chains

There are many types of timing chains available for the big-block Mopar, ranging from a low-end stock replacement all the way up to top-end units with billet gears and adjustment capability. The timing chain system is fairly inexpensive and simple to install, but it does have some limitations. When replacing the timing chain, most builders quickly toss away the factory-style timing chain with the nylon gears and use a roller chain timing gear. The primary limitation of the stock-type chain drives is the lack of ability to easily adjust the cam timing. In years past, builders would need to drill out the timing gear for an offset bushing and then rotate the bushing to get the correct advance or retard desired. That required a lot of work to dial in correctly, so a person can now thankfully purchase chain drives that come with built-in cam timing adjustment capability. There are also top-end chain drives that have Torrington-type bearings behind the cam gear to reduce the sliding friction between the block and the gear.

In summary, the timing chain system is probably the best one to use for the majority of performance Mopars. A premium timing chain system and an aftermarket timing chain cover can be relatively expensive. If you are building an engine that is going to see significant tuning or cam changes, it could be time to invest in a belt drive. The basic belt drive system can be re-used from motor to motor by just replacing the belt, so the investment can be spread out over time. The belt system isn't suitable for street driving, but a gear drive system can be used on the street. The gear drive is more like a Pro Street system. Some like it because of the aggressive sound on the street, and they don't care about the small power loss.

Roller Cam Thrust

Any time a roller cam is used there needs to be a positive stop setup to keep the camshaft from moving forward out of the block. The cam manufacturers recommend limiting the end play to .005 to .015 inch. With a traditional cam drive and timing-chain cover, you need to

The Cloyes Hex-A-Just timing chain provides a fairly quick way to dial in a few degrees of advance or retard at the camshaft.

High-quality timing chains are available for the single-bolt cam even though most performance camshafts are ground on three-bolt cores.

CHAPTER 10

A shim stack rather than a cam button controls camshaft end play when using the Jesel belt-drive system. The shims can be easily changed if the end play needs to be larger or smaller.

Since the end of the camshaft is exposed with the Jesel belt drive, it is very easy to use a dial indicator to check the end play.

install a cam button of some sort that will ride on the inside of the timing-chain cover. Some aftermarket covers have a removable center section that makes setting and adjusting the end play a little easier. There currently doesn't appear to be any off-the-shelf end-thrust systems that bolt in and work perfectly with timing chains, so fabrication is often required in this area.

The gear- and belt-drive systems require different methods for setting the end play. In our observance, the belt-drive system is very easy to set up and adjust. The Jesel belt-drive system that we've used on dyno motors uses shims to set the camshaft end play. It is very easy to measure the end play of the camshaft and then change the shims as necessary to achieve the correct amount of clearance. The Jesel-belt drive system is expensive to purchase, but the ease of use sure pays dividends in an application where there is constant maintenance or constant modifications being performed.

Timing-Chain Covers

In the past there were few options for covers, but the aftermarket has finally started to provide a few solutions for the big-block Mopar. There are a couple of cast-aluminum timing chain covers that are now available as well as couple of ones made from billet aluminum. The billet covers have removable centers at the camshaft that allow you to quickly get to the cam drive for inspection or adjustment. The cast covers do not have this feature, but they are still nice for rigidity and better gasket seal.

Some of the aftermarket covers do not fit under a stock water pump or fit with a stock-type harmonic damper. Several of the other aftermarket covers will fit both stock dampers and stock water pumps, so be sure you know what you're buying. The Indy chain cover doesn't have a timing pointer, so you'll need to fabricate your own. Any of the aftermarket covers should accept a stock seal but some of them allow the seal to be replaced from the front, while others use the older style of replacing the seal from the rear.

A small cam button can be installed in the center of the cam gear when using a roller cam. The cam button usually needs to be machined to provide the correct amount of end play.

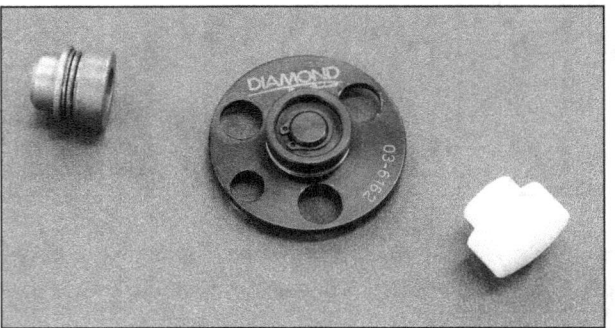

There are various cam buttons available for the big-block engine, including these three styles. Rarely will any cam button provide the proper end play right out of the box, so be prepared to modify either the button or the timing-chain cover.

CAMSHAFT DRIVES AND VALVESPRINGS

This billet front cover has an inspection cover that allows a quick way to determine the end play of the camshaft.

With the center plate of the billet front cover removed, the camshaft advance can be easily adjusted. A hex key driver is used to adjust the camshaft advance after the three cam gear bolts are loosened.

Belt Drive

A belt-drive system for the camshaft has become a standard item on most Professional-class racing engines, and they are starting to show up with more frequency on the Sportsman-class engines. A belt drive is not required for a performance engine, but it does have some merits that should be considered, especially for a dedicated drag race setup.

The drive on a belt-driven camshaft is exposed and easy to adjust. You can change the cam timing in just a few minutes without having to remove any covers or scrape any gaskets. A cam swap is also much easier using the belt drive than with a normal chain drive because there is no timing-chain cover to remove. The block plate on the belt drive system stays sealed to the block and to the oil pan during the cam swap, so there is much less chance of dirt getting into the engine. One more advantage to the belt drive is your ability to easily set and adjust the camshaft end play. With a chain drive, a cam button needs to be installed and set to the proper end play. This can be difficult with a typical timing chain cover because it has to be removed for each adjustment. With the belt-drive system, you use a stack of shims to set and adjust end play.

A belt drive is rarely used on a street-driven vehicle because the exposed belt can be vulnerable to dirt and debris tossed up from the road. There is also a shorter life span for the belt than for a chain drive. Jesel recommends changing the belt once a year with their system, while the normal life for a chain can be many years.

The cam pulley on the Jesel belt-drive system is marked for up to 10 degrees of advance or retard. The cam position can be easily adjusted by loosening the nuts on the four retaining screws and rotating the cam pulley as needed.

The Jesel belt-drive system is designed for quick camshaft changes. With the Jesel system, there is no front cover to remove and the oil pan gasket doesn't need to be disturbed during a cam swap.

CHAPTER 10

The Milodon gear-drive system is designed for high-load conditions, such as a supercharged engine or an off-shore marine engine. These gear drives are also a good choice when a fuel pump or an oil pump needs to be driven off the nose of the camshaft. (Photo courtesy of Milodon)

Gear Drive

Milodon and Keith Black offer a couple of different models of gear drives for the big-block Mopar. Gear drives are often used in supercharged applications or for extended, heavy marine use. Some builders feel that the gear drive transmits harmful harmonics from the crankshaft to the camshaft, while other builders feel that they need the precision and stability of the gear drive.

The gear drive is expensive to purchase and install, with a total price comparable to the belt-drive systems. There are some options with the gear-drive systems, such as the ability to run camshaft-driven fuel pumps, that aren't available with other drive systems. Gear drives tend to produce the "blower whine" noise that some people really like, although their neighbors probably aren't as thrilled! The gear-drive setup is usually easier to work on than the timing chain when performing cam changes because you can slide the cam out without removing the full front cover assembly.

Gear drives have their place, which is why you typically see them

The Milodon gear drive on the front of this RB block gives the motor a tough, racy look. Gear drives are popular for certain engine combinations. (Photo courtesy of Koffel's Place)

The beehive springs from Comp Cams are becoming a popular choice for flat-tappet and hydraulic-roller applications.

A high-quality dual-valve spring with a heat-treated spring cup and a titanium retainer is a good combination for most performance engines. Parts like this work with roller cams well into the 700-hp range.

on supercharged motors, especially the blown/alky-type motors used for drag racing. You won't find gear drives on most bracket cars or the high-speed NA motors used in Pro Stock or Comp Eliminator.

Valvesprings

The valvespring choice is usually influenced heavily by the camshaft design as well as by the physical limitations of the cylinder head and valvetrain components. Normally, if the camshaft has less than .700 inch of lift, you would use a good-quality

The Battleship triple valvespring is a classic design that goes back many years. These springs are designed for roller cams with less than .750 lift.

Several vendors are now offering lightweight tool steel retainers that weigh about the same as titanium but don't cost as much. Another benefit to the tool steel retainers is that they usually provide some extra clearance for the rocker arm.

CAMSHAFT DRIVES AND VALVESPRINGS

dual valvespring in a performance big-block motor. Most big-block Mopar cylinder heads have room for a valvespring that is 1.900 inches tall and 1.550 inches in diameter, and this size of spring can handle almost any flat-tappet camshaft profile. A high-lift roller cam often requires a taller valvespring than can be fitted using stock parts, so special retainers and locks must be used to increase the installed height. Most aftermarket cylinder heads are machined for larger-than-stock-diameter springs, but they still might need to be machined further to accommodate the springs required by the specific engine combination that is being built.

Installed Height

The distance between the spring seat and the valvespring retainer is called the installed height. Most Mopar big-block heads will allow at least 1.900 inches of installed height using standard parts, and this dimension can be increased up to 2.000 inches on most heads without any machine work. The easiest ways to increase the installed height is to use special valve locks and/or valvespring retainers. Vendors, such as Manley, Isky, and Comp Cams sell locks and retainers that will increase the installed height by .050 or even .100 inch.

The installed height needs to be at least .060 greater than the total of the net valve lift, plus the coil bind height of the valvespring, so adequate clearance is provided during operation. For instance, if the valvespring coil binds at 1.140 inches and the valve lift is .700 inch, then the installed height needs to be at least 1.140 + 0.060 + .700 = 1.900 inches. If the installed height is too great, spacers placed under the spring can reduce the height.

Spring Diameter

The outside diameter of the valvespring is an important dimension. If the valvespring is too large in diameter, rocker arm interference becomes a problem. There are many valvesprings that measure 1.550 inches in diameter, and these springs fit most big-block rocker arms. The larger 1.625-OD valvesprings used for high-lift applications will not fit all of the available rocker arms, so this area needs to be double-checked before running the engine.

In general, the larger the diameter, the better for the valvespring because it allows the spring to operate at lower internal stress. But there is a tradeoff between diameter and weight, so sometimes it isn't really obvious which option to choose. For highly stressed valvetrains it is best to contact the spring engineers directly to discuss whether a large-diameter spring should be used or maybe the engine will work better with a taller spring that isn't quite as large.

Beehive Valvesprings

Comp Cams recently introduced a line of beehive valvesprings that have some unique characteristics, which can be helpful in certain situations. The beehive spring gets its name from the unique tapered shape that looks like a honeybee hive. The tapered shape makes the beehive spring less prone to surge and may allow higher operating speeds before valve float. The beehive spring is especially useful when running hydraulic flat-tappet and hydraulic roller camshafts; so if you are having issues with valve float, you might want to look into the beehive spring as a possible solution.

Seat Load and Spring Rate

The seat load is the amount of spring force that is exerted on the valvespring retainer when the spring is in the installed height. This value is usually about 200 lbs when running a mild roller cam but can be much higher for really aggressive cams and is typically lower for flat-tappet cams. Compressing the spring from its free length down to the installed height generates the seat load. The seat load changes as you vary the installed height, so be careful when using springs at installed heights that are different than what the spring was

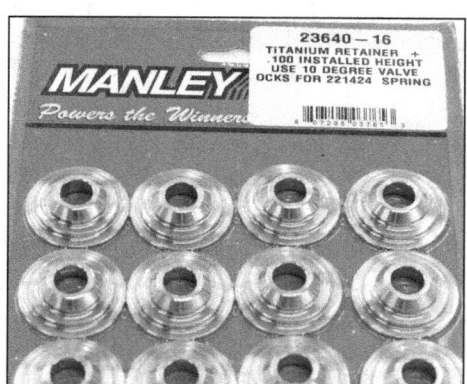

Various vendors, such as Manley, offer valvespring retainers that increase the installed height of the valve spring. These titanium retainers increase the installed height by .100 inch but other heights are also available.

High-quality triple valvesprings are often used when the valve lift gets over .800 inches. With high-ratio rocker arms, such as these Jesel units, the valve lift can easily exceed the capacity of most valve springs.

The tapered upper portion of the beehive springs provides a lot of extra clearance around the rocker arms. Beehive springs are currently available for flat-tappet and hydraulic-roller cams.

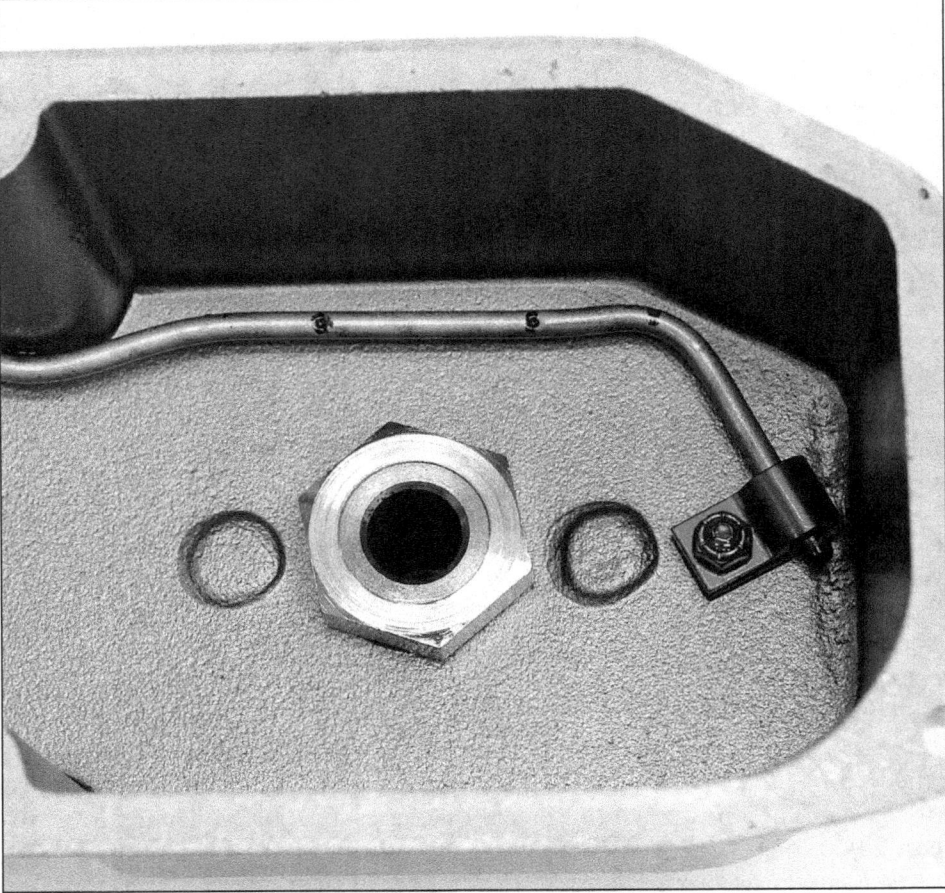

These Indy valve covers come equipped with a spray bar that directs oil onto the pushrod adjusters. This same idea could be used to direct oil spray onto the valvesprings.

The beehive springs are significantly lighter than conventional springs even with a steel retainer. Some titanium retainers are available for beehive springs for the ultimate in weight reduction.

designed for; this creates a lot problems and could lead to failure.

The spring rate tells you how stiff the spring is, or in more technical language, how much resistance the spring will have to being compressed. The spring rate is measured in pounds per inch, and high-performance springs usually have rates in the range of 400 to 500 lbs per inch. If you know the seat load, spring rate, and valve lift, you can quickly calculate what the spring force will be over the nose of the cam. The spring force is found by multiplying the lift by the spring rate. This amount is then added to the seat load to find the total force over the nose. For example, a spring with a rate of 500 lbs per inch will have 350 lbs of force when compressed by .700 inch. If this spring has a seat load of 200 lbs, then the total force at full lift will be 350 + 200 or 550 lbs.

Valvespring Oiling

Valvesprings get very hot during operation, and the higher the forces involved, the hotter the springs will get. The highly stressed valvesprings benefit greatly if oil is sprayed directly onto the springs during operation. The oil will lubricate the valvesprings but more importantly, the oil will carry away any excess heat. Engines built for high-speed operation sometimes have the valvesprings located in pockets, and these can be filled with oil in order to keep them cool. Of course, this type of construction requires paying special attention to valve stem seal since it is not desirable to have oil getting into the combustion chamber.

CHAPTER 11

INTAKE MANIFOLDS

Such a large selection of intake manifolds is available for the big-block Mopar that it can be overwhelming to discuss them all. To minimize the confusion, I'll split the choices into two categories: standard-port-size intakes, and Max-Wedge-port-size intakes. Within those two categories, I'll discuss dual plane vs. single plane, 4150 flange or 4500 flange, single carb vs. multiple carb, and so on. Port sizes that are even larger than the Max-Wedge size are a specialized niche, which I will briefly cover toward the end of the chapter.

Standard Port Intakes, B and RB

Single Plane with 4150 Flange

A variety of single plane intakes for the B and RB motors with standard-size ports is available. Edelbrock has several choices ranging from older X-style intakes, such as the Torker and Torker II, to the newer Victor designs. Weiand offers their Team G intake for both B and RB motors while the Holley Street Dominator is only available these days for the RB. Mopar Performance has the popular M1 intake available for both B and RB applications. The Victor 383 and Victor 440 intakes typically produce the highest peak power, but they are rather tall intakes that will not likely fit under a flat hood. The Holley Street Dominator is low-profile design that makes excellent power and allows the use of most production hoods.

Single Plane with 4500 Flange

There aren't a lot of intakes designed for Dominator carbs, but Mopar Performance does have very nice M1 intakes for both the B and RB motors with the 4500 flanges. These Mopar Performance intakes are part numbered P4529724 for the B and P4529725 for the RB. Either of these intakes will work great combined with standard port heads on a 500-ci short-block. Edelbrock has a 4500 flanged Super Victor that fits standard-sized ports, but it is only available for the RB motor. Weiand has a Team G intake with standard runners and the 4500 flange, but again, this intake is an RB-only item.

The big-block Mopar enjoys a fairly wide selection of intake options.

HOW TO BUILD MAX-PERFORMANCE MOPAR BIG-BLOCKS

CHAPTER 11

The Holley Street Dominator intake is a classic design that really works great. It is only available for the RB block with standard ports and a 4150 flange. This is a low-profile intake with EGR and a choke stove.

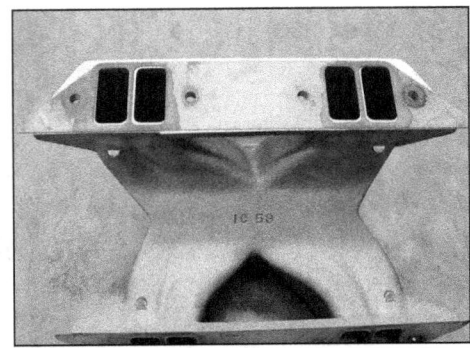
Most intake manifolds exhibit some core shift right out of the box. It usually doesn't take more than a few minutes with a die grinder to perform a gasket match.

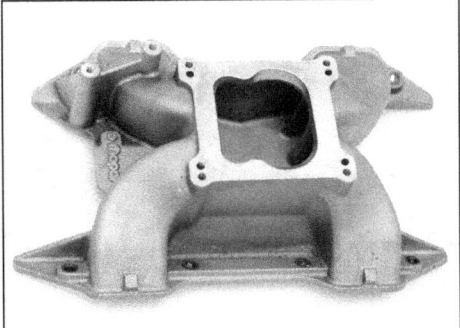
Mopar Performance offers their M1 single plane intake with a 4150 flange and standard-port-size runners for both the B and RB engines.

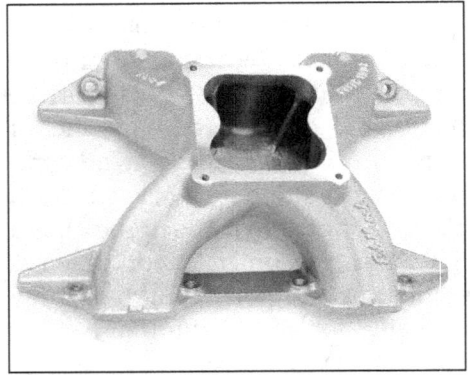
Edelbrock recently introduced their Super Victor intake manifold for the RB block. The Super Victor has a 4500 flange and it is available in either a standard port version or a Max-Wedge-port-size version.

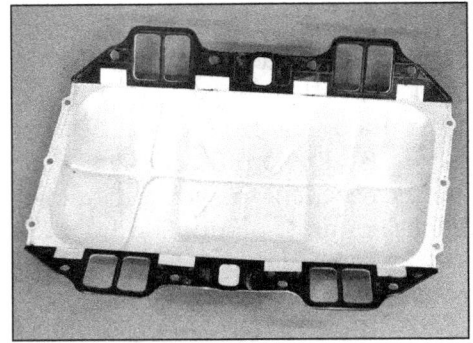
The classic bathtub intake gasket only works with standard port intake manifolds. These gaskets work pretty well if the head surface is milled down .060 so paper gaskets can be fitted to each side of the tin bathtub gasket.

A 1,000-hp Holley carb mounted on a Holley Street Dominator intake manifold is a good combination for a 500-inch performance big-block. Pictured is list number 80513, which has down-leg boosters for excellent high-speed operation.

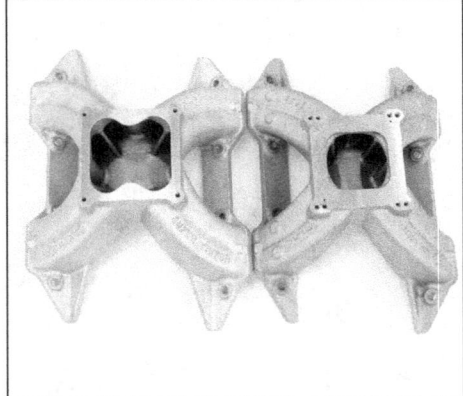
The Edelbrock Super Victor on the left has a substantially larger plenum area than the Victor intake. This should be beneficial on a larger engine.

The B1 intake manifold is designed to fit the B1 heads on a low-deck block. This intake is only available with a 4500 flange.

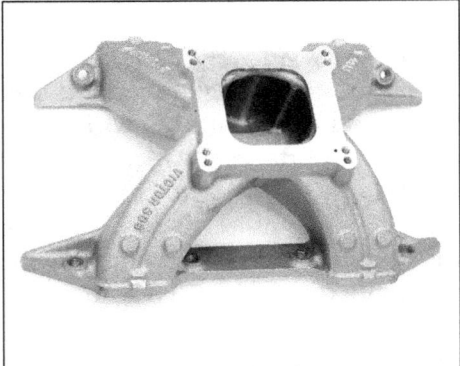
Edelbrock has both a Victor 383 as well as a Victor 440 intake. The Victor intakes are tall single 4-bbl designs with standard port sizes and a 4150 flange.

HOW TO BUILD MAX-PERFORMANCE MOPAR BIG-BLOCKS

Dual Plane Intakes

On most street motors, a dual plane intake works better than a single plane with a large plenum because the dual plane will deliver higher air velocity inside the intake. Dual plane intakes can produce uneven flow between the top and bottom runners because of the long passages. Dual plane intakes also tend to have runner lengths that vary between the cylinders, which leads to mixture variation between cylinders. This isn't a critical problem for most high-performance engines; but as the engine size and speed go up, the air speed becomes more critical, and at some point the dual plane intake isn't a good choice anymore. For a big-block Mopar, the crossover point is probably about 650 hp. If you're planning to make power above that range, then it makes sense to use a single plane intake manifold.

If you are going to use a dual plane intake, Edelbrock has the Performer RPM intake manifolds for both the B and RB motors. The Performer RPM intakes are excellent choices for

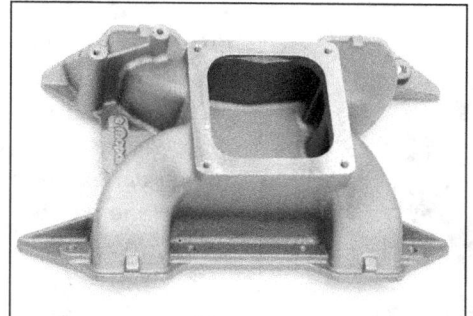

Mopar Performance also has the M1 single plane intake with a 4500 flange for both the B and RB engines. These M1 intakes are designed to work with the standard port size.

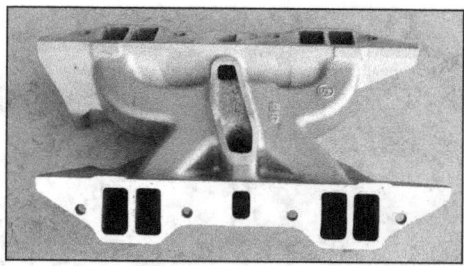

If you use a dual plane intake on a combination with a flat valley tray, you'll need to machine away most of the exhaust crossover. This shouldn't cause an issue because most aftermarket heads do not have a provision for exhaust crossover anyway.

dual-purpose (street/strip) cars running standard port heads. On a 500-ci motor, the torque output is outstanding down in the 2,500- to 4,000-rpm range, but output will drop off rapidly past 5,000 rpm. I ran a 470-ci stroker motor with a Performer RPM intake on a street car for a number of years, and it was a stoplight monster. The power peak was around 5,500 rpm, and I needed to shift by 6,200 rpm or else the car slowed down a bunch, but it was a ton of fun to drive on the street.

Indy Cylinder Heads also offers a dual plane intake for the RB motor with standard port heads. This intake has generous runners, so it can be ported out to work with the Max-Wedge port size. The Indy dual plane intake is only available with a 4150 flange but, if you were determined, it could be welded and re-machined in order to mount up a 4500 carb.

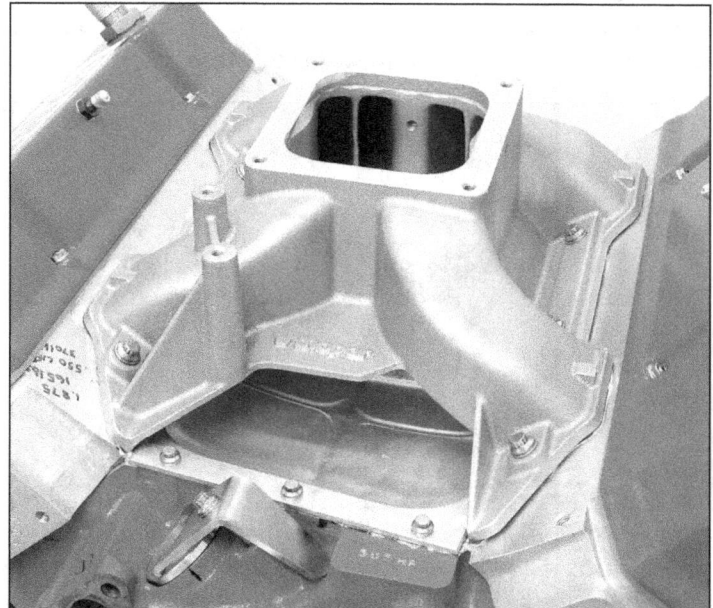

The stock-type bathtub intake gasket works well with standard port heads.

The throttle bracket and throttle return spring brackets need to be modified when using a taller than stock intake manifold. Several vendors such as Mancini Racing sell special throttle brackets that are designed to work with tall aftermarket intake manifolds.

CHAPTER 11

The Indy dual plane intake is an excellent choice for big street motors. The runners in the Indy dual plane can be ported to work with Max-Wedge cylinder heads. The special throttle return bracket is available from Mancini Racing.

Multiple Carb Intakes

Mopar Performance offers the classic six-pack intake for both the B and RB motor while Edelbrock only offers the six-pack for RB engines in its catalog. The six-pack intake has excellent torque for a street car, but the dual plane design does limit the power on the top end, especially when used on a large stroker motor. The difficulty of adjusting these carbs has always been a major drawback to the six-pack design. The factory installed metering plates in the end carbs—these aren't as easy to work with as jets—but the aftermarket has developed solutions for this. Several companies, such as ProMax and QuickFuel offer metering plates with removable jets that fit into the stock fuel bowls. Replacement base plates for the six-pack carbs allow the idle mixture to be adjusted while the engine is running. These types of fixes make the six-pack setup easier to dial in on a hot street car.

In the category of low-rise, dual carb, dual plane intakes, Edelbrock has a CH-28 dual quad intake for the RB motor. This is an excellent setup for a heavy street car or even a

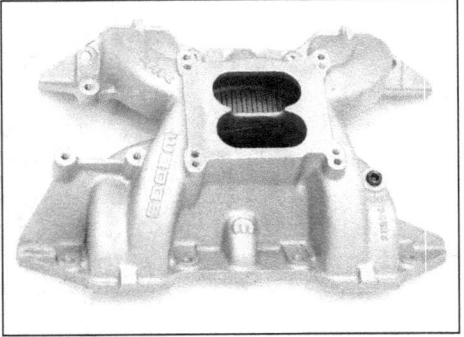

Mopar Performance has this tall dual plane intake available for the RB motor with standard port heads and a 4150 flange. This is basically an Edelbrock Performer RPM intake with the Mopar Wedge script on it.

Edelbrock offers the tall dual plane Performer RPM intake for both the B and RB engines. The Performer RPM is an excellent street/strip setup when used with standard port heads and a large 4150 flange carb.

Mopar Performance used to sell tunnel ram intake manifolds for both B and RB engines but they have been discontinued now for some time. Dual Holley carbs on a tunnel ram is a classic look for a big-block Mopar.

Using dual Edelbrock carbs on a tunnel ram rather than Holley carbs saves about 10 pounds. The Edelbrock carbs don't have quite the same classic look as dual Holley carbs but they work very well on a tunnel ram and are easy to tune.

INTAKE MANIFOLDS

street/strip setup if you want to be a little different. A pair of Edelbrock 600-cfm carbs is probably the ticket on this intake. There are a few bracket racers who run the CH-28 intake in heavier vehicles with excellent results. The low-profile design limits the top-end power capability, but it certainly makes enough power to put a B body deep into the 11s or high 10s.

The cross ram was of course the original Max-Wedge induction system, but recently A&A Transmissions released a standard port version of the cross ram for RB motors. The combination of long runners in the smaller standard port size probably isn't the best for maximum performance, but this might be an interesting option if you want the looks of a cross ram and aren't concerned about wringing the last bit of horsepower out of the combination.

For more than 30 years, the tunnel ram intake has been the proven combination for ultimate power production. The tunnel ram features short runners, high airflow capacity, and good alignment of carb to runner to create substantial horsepower. However, for some reason, the availability of tunnel rams for the Mopar big-block has continued to decline over the years. It could be that single 4-barrel intakes are making excellent power with less hassle, or it could be that the serious builders have all moved on to sheetmetal tunnel rams. In any case, it appears that the Weiand PN 1987 tunnel ram is the only standard port tunnel ram still available for Mopar big-blocks, and it is only available for the RB motor. Mopar Performance used to have tunnel rams for both the B and RB motors but they have been discontinued for several years.

Max-Wedge Port Intakes, B and RB

The Max-Wedge port size wasn't very popular until recently, when aftermarket vendors began to produce cylinder heads with the larger port size. Until then, the only heads available with the bigger ports were the original factory heads, and they were expensive and hard to find. The other issue with the Max-Wedge port size was that for a very long time there wasn't any intake manifold, other than the cross ram, that would bolt onto them. All of this started to change a few years back when Indy Cylinder Heads began to produce both cylinder heads and intake manifolds that used the Max-Wedge port size. Indy produced intakes that would fit both the B and RB blocks, and that led to a wider use of the larger port size. In addition, Mopar Performance started to reproduce the original heads and the cross ram intake manifold as well as making some single 4-barrel intakes with the larger port size. With the recent introduction of the Victor heads from Edelbrock, there is now quite a bit of activity in the Max-Wedge space, which should lead to even more intake choices in the future.

Indy Cylinder Heads sells single 4-bbl intakes for both B and RB motors with Max-Wedge ports and a 4150 flange.

The Mopar Performance 337 intake manifold is a perfect fit when using Max-Wedge replacement heads on an RB block. The floor of the intake fills in the valley area, so a bathtub-style gasket is not required.

Single 4-Barrel Intakes with Max-Wedge Ports

The small selection of intake manifolds for the larger Max-Wedge ports is one reason many builders opt out of using the low-deck B motor for a performance build. At press time, Indy Cylinder Heads is the only vendor that makes a Max-Wedge intake manifold for the B motor. The Indy intake is available with either a 4150 flange or the larger 4500 flange. Fortunately, this low-deck Indy intake is an excellent intake manifold that will handle the requirements of an 800-hp low-deck motor, so don't let the lack of available intakes stop you from building a low-deck motor.

The RB enjoys a much wider selection of single 4-barrel Max-Wedge intake manifolds than the B motor. Indy Cylinder Heads offers a 440-2 intake with a 4150 flange as well as a 440-3 with the larger 4500 flange. Indy also offers an extra-large plenum 440-3X intake that is designed for large-cubic-inch motors. Edelbrock has recently introduced a Super Victor intake that fits the Max-Wedge ports on an RB block. The Super Victor intake has the larger 4500 flange, so a Dominator carb

CHAPTER 11

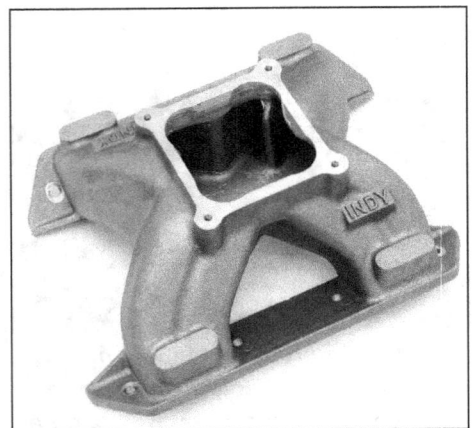

The Indy intakes are also available with the larger 4500 flange. All of these Indy intakes are designed to fit the Max-Wedge-sized ports.

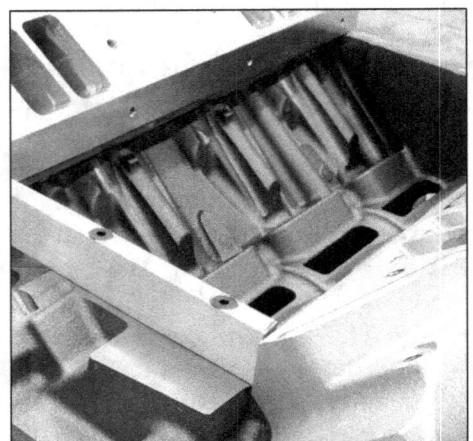

These end rail spacers are not available from any vendor, but they were fairly easy to fabricate out of some bar stock.

The big Indy single plane intakes make good power on the dyno, especially when equipped with a Dominator carb.

The Mopar Performance Max-Wedge intake manifold can be used on the Victor heads but you need to fill up a large gap on each end with end-rail spacers

bolts right on. Mopar Performance also lists a single 4-barrel intake with MW ports under the part number P4876337. The 337 intake only comes with the smaller 4150 carb flange, and it is unique because it has a cast valley pan. The built-in valley pan on the 337 intake makes it the only single 4-barrel intake that will bolt on to stock Max-Wedge heads on a RB block. The 337 intake will also fit Victor heads on an RB block if you fabricate some custom spacers to raise the valley rails. One advantage to the 337 intake is that it is about 1.25 inches shorter than either the 440-2 or the Super Victor intake. So the 337 intake might fit under the hood of some vehicles where the taller Super Victor and Indy intakes would require a hood scoop.

Mopar Performance also has a selection of intake manifolds that are designed for the Max-Wedge versions of the Stage VI head. Remember, the Stage VI heads have raised intake ports, so it takes a very wide manifold to fit Stage VI heads on a RB block. These extra-wide intakes are unique and will not fit

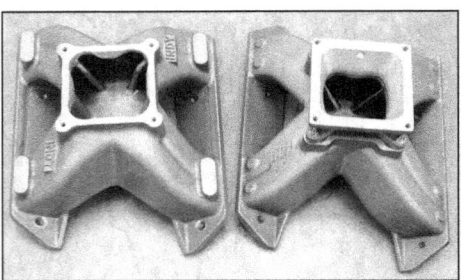

There is some debate about which intake manifold is best to run with a Dominator carb. While it seems obvious that an intake with a 4500 flange would be best, some builders feel that a 4150 intake plus an adapter is capable of making more power. We did not see much of a difference between the two options during the dyno testing performed for this book.

An original B1 intake manifold can be installed onto Max-Wedge heads if special tapered adapters are used. This used to be worth the effort back in the days when the B1 intake was the only race intake available but now there are other choices available.

INTAKE MANIFOLDS

The combination of an Indy 440-3X intake on a set of raised port Edelbrock Victor heads creates a very tall induction system.

The Mopar P4876337 intake will also fit raised port heads such as these from Indy but you end up with a double valley tray. The double valley tray wouldn't necessarily cause any problems, but it is extra weight and complication.

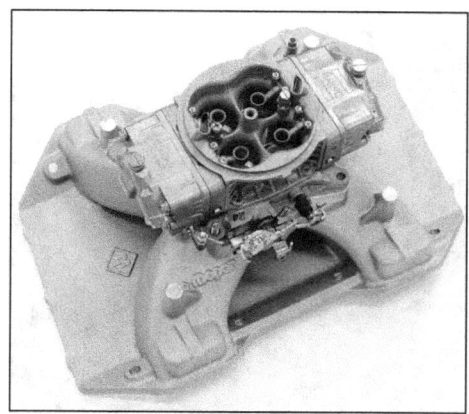

The Mopar Performance P4876337 intake manifold is a single 4-bbl intake designed for use with Max-Wedge heads. The built-in valley tray eliminates the need for a bathtub gasket.

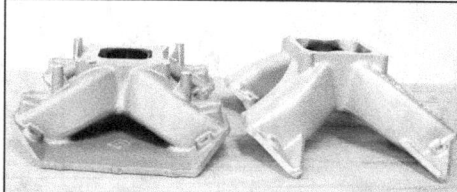

The Mopar P4876337 intake on the left is substantially shorter than the Super Victor intake on the right. This low profile Max-Wedge intake might possibly fit under a stock hood on some vehicles.

any other engine combinations. The Mopar Performance intakes for the Stage VI heads are available in either a 4500 or 4150 flange.

One problem with using a Max-Wedge-sized intake, such as an Indy 440-2 or an Edelbrock Super Victor on a set of production Max-Wedge heads is that there isn't a bathtub-style intake gasket available at the moment. The Max-Wedge single plane intakes work fine on either Indy or Edelbrock Victor heads because those heads have raised intake runners. However, the production Max-Wedge heads require the use of a bathtub intake gasket, which currently does not exist. You could try to fabricate a Max-Wedge gasket from a standard port gasket by cutting out the ports, or weld a valley plate onto the bottom of the intake manifold. It isn't apparent why, after all these years, nobody has designed a bathtub-style intake gasket that fits the Max-Wedge port size, but so far nobody has produced one. So if you want to run original Max-Wedge heads on an RB block you need to either use the Mopar Performance P4876337 intake, or else you'll need to fabricate a special valley pan.

Cross Ram

The cross ram is probably the most appealing of the factory induction systems offered for the big wedge motor. There is no denying the fun of popping the hood and seeing that huge intake manifold with the carbs spaced across from each other and the linkage setup that operates them. The Max-Wedge was the only one to use the cross ram and it was only available for a few years during the early 1960s. The cross-ram-equipped cars were rare back in the day and original cars are so rare today that they rarely see the light of day. The cross ram intake manifold itself was just a collector item until a few years ago when a couple of vendors started to reproduce it. At this time it is again possible to purchase the intake and the necessary linkage kit to assemble a cross ram induction system. The original Carter carbs are no longer available new, but Edelbrock currently offers carbs that closely resemble the originals in appearance and operation. The cross ram is an expensive induction system because the total package requires the cross ram intake plus the two carbs, linkage kit,

CHAPTER 11

The cross ram is a classic Mopar intake manifold. Mopar Performance has recently re-introduced this intake, so they are again available. The original Carter carbs are not available, but the Edelbrock carbs can be adapted to this intake without too much work.

The Edelbrock carbs require a slightly different linkage than the original Carter carbs. Also the Edelbrock linkage hangs down farther than the Carter linkage, so either use a spacer or trim off the linkage for clearance.

The reproduction cross ram has bosses that interfere with tall valve covers. These bosses can be trimmed at a 45-degree angle without compromising any functionality.

The cross ram setup is very impressive looking, but it doesn't really make a lot of power on the dyno. Long intake runners evidently cause enough internal restriction to hurt the power output more than you would suspect.

Replacing the factory cross ram with this box-style cross ram from Indy Cylinder Heads improved the power output of this 505-inch motor by more than 80 hp.

fuel line kit, and dual air cleaners. There is also the issue of hooking up a kickdown rod to work with the cross ram linkage as well as finding the room under the hood for all of this stuff.

One thing to remember is that the cross ram was designed for the 413- and 426-ci engines, and it doesn't seem to perform strongly on larger stroker motors. It is possible that the runners inside the cross ram manifold are too small and long to work well with a larger displacement engine, or maybe the sharp 90-degree turn the air makes under the carb base is the cause of the problems. In any case, dyno testing has shown that a reproduction cross ram intake on a 500-inch big-block will produce about 100 hp less than a big single plane intake with a 1050 Dominator carb. This isn't necessarily true for the exotic, sheet-metal cross rams that are used in Super Stock racing, and it might not be true for cross rams that have been extensively modified. But we do know that an unmodified cross ram right out of the box will make much

Changing the jets on a dual-carb intake is fairly easy when using Edelbrock carbs because the jets are accessible from the top.

INTAKE MANIFOLDS

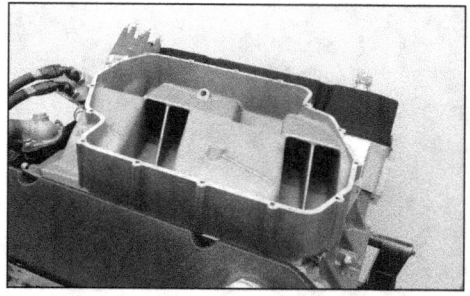

The cross ram intake manifold from Indy Cylinder Heads has internal ports that are both larger and shorter than the original Max-Wedge cross ram.

An internal view of the Indy cross ram shows how the runners cross over from side to side inside the manifold.

less power than a big single 4-barrel intake right out of the box when tested on a 500-ci stroker motor.

Indy Cylinder Head offers a cross ram intake that works very well on the larger displacement motors, but it doesn't look like a cross ram. The Indy 440-25 intake looks like a tunnel ram, but inside the plenum box the runners cross over from side to side. So it is technically a cross ram intake, but it looks more like a tunnel ram or box ram. I've run the Indy cross ram against the Mopar Performance cross ram on back-to-back dyno tests with a 500-ci motor. The same engine on the same day with same carbs, cam, etc., made 80 more horsepower with the Indy ram than the Mopar cross ram. A number of cars have picked up several tenths at the track when switching from the Mopar cross ram to the Indy ram intake, so that confirms that there is a significant power difference between these two cross ram intakes.

Tunnel Ram

Since it was first developed, the tunnel ram has been the ultimate way to make power on a drag-race motor. A properly set up tunnel ram outperforms the very best single 4-barrel intakes on a performance engine. The tunnel ram isn't very popular on street cars because of the extra cost of the second carb and complications with the linkage kits, fuel lines, and air cleaners. Indy Cylinder Heads is the only vendor at the moment that is selling cast tunnel rams with the larger Max-Wedge runners. They offer their tunnel rams for both the B and the RB motor with the large runner size as well as a variety of different tops available for 4150 carbs and 4500 carbs.

For extreme output motors, there are a variety of vendors that fabricate tunnel rams from sheetmetal. This flexible approach to manufacturing allows the fabricator to change the length of the runners or the taper angle and the plenum volume to suit the customer's requests. These specialty intakes are expensive, but they do provide the ultimate power available from a normally aspirated engine.

B1 Intake Options

Koffel's Place sells an excellent intake manifold that is designed for the B1 cylinder heads on a low-deck block. The B1 intake has very large runners, which match the runner size in the B1 heads and the carb flange is designed for a 4500-series carburetor.

The B1 intake has very large ports with long smoothly curved runners. This intake is one of the very best race intakes available for use on a performance big-block. This intake is designed to fit B1 heads on a low-deck block but spacers can be used to mount the intake on an RB block.

The intake bolts on the B1 heads thread in at a slight angle to the head surface. Be careful that you get these bolts properly engaged in the head before tightening them down; you could strip the threads if you try to force them in straight.

CHAPTER 11

If you are interested in building your own EFI system then this Victor EFI intake manifold might be a good place to start. Edelbrock sells this RB block intake with the injector bungs already finished and ready for assembly.

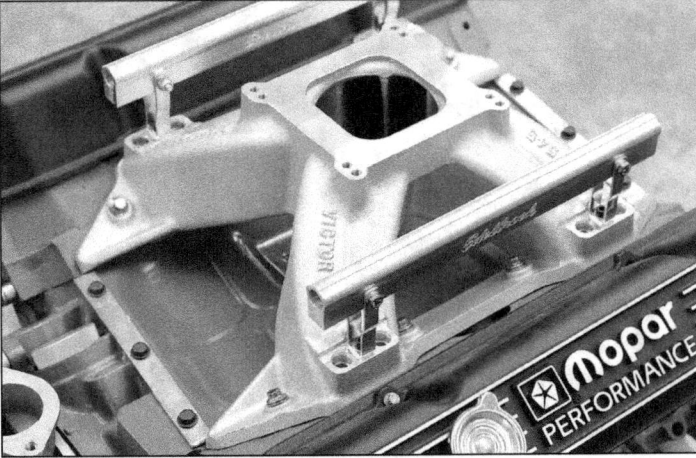

Edelbrock also sells fuel rails that bolt directly onto the Victor EFI intake manifold. The only items left to be installed are injectors and a throttle body and this system is ready to run.

This same intake can be used on an RB block by sandwiching spacers between the intake and the cylinder heads to fill in the extra width. There currently is not a version of the B1 intake that bolts directly on to the RB block. There are adapters available that make it possible to mate the B1 intake to Max-Wedge heads on an RB block, but this combination probably isn't worth the effort because so many other high-performance manifolds are available that don't require adapters.

EFI

Electronic Fuel Injection is certainly the slickest way to go for a performance motor that is going to be run on the street because it has the capability of using a feedback loop to optimize the air/fuel mixture. For pure drag racing duty, the carb setup seems to work okay, but EFI sure is nice for cold engine operation as well as mileage and reduced oil contamination. EFI hasn't really caught on yet in the big-block Mopar world because there are only a few bolt-on kits. Edelbrock does offer a kit for the RB motor using a modified Victor intake manifold. At this time, there aren't any EFI intakes available for the Max-Wedge ports, but certainly any of the Indy intakes can be modified for EFI. In fact, most intakes sold during the last decade have pads on the runners that can be drilled and tapped for either nitrous injectors or fuel injectors. Due to the popularity of EFI with other engine makes, there is a wide variety of injectors, controllers, and throttle bodies currently available. The vast majority of these items use generic bolt patterns and interfaces, so they can easily be adapted to the big-block Mopar. One of the last remaining items to be produced for the big-block Mopar was the necessary distributor and now that is available.

EFI will allow you the flexibility of having a very large throttle body for high power at WOT while maintaining very good low-speed operation.

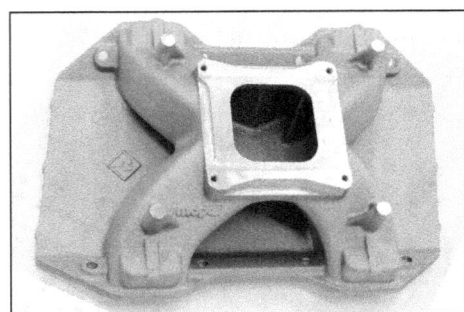

Some Mopar Performance intake manifolds, such as the P4876337 shown here, have bosses located above the intake runners that can be machined for injectors. The Edelbrock fuel rails have the same center-to-center spacing as the bosses on the intake so the conversion is quite simple to carry out.

The Indy intake manifold on this RB engine has been modified for fuel injection. This Indy intake had bosses cast into the intake so welding was not required. (Photo courtesy of FAST Man EFI)

INTAKE MANIFOLDS

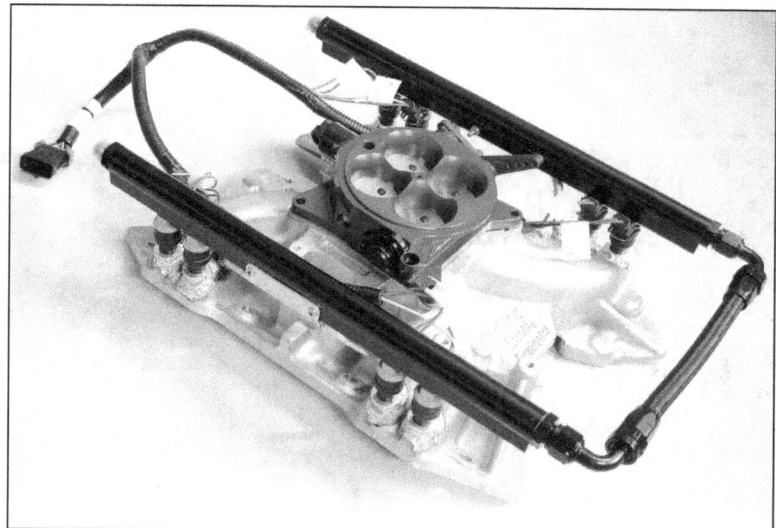

This Holley Street Dominator intake has been modified for use in an EFI application. This intake needed to have injector bosses welded onto the runners since the stock intake didn't have enough material for the injector bungs. (Photo courtesy of FAST Man EFI)

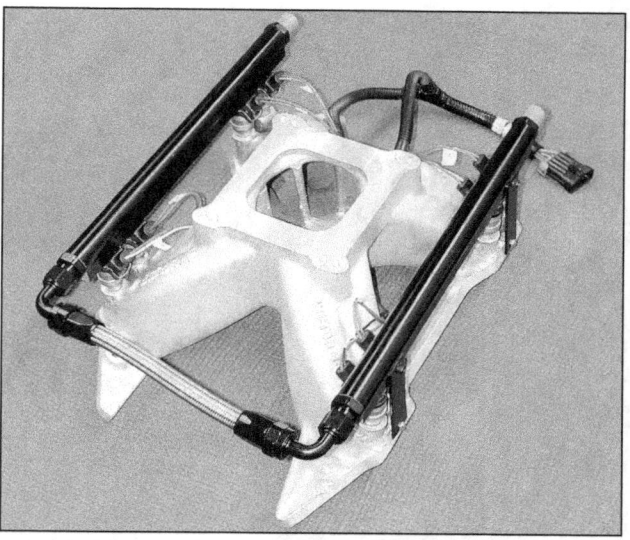

Edelbrock sells an EFI version of the Victor 440 intake but they do not currently have an EFI option for the 383 intake so this one had to be fabricated. (Photo courtesy of FAST Man EFI)

This RB engine uses custom-fabricated injector stacks for each cylinder that mimic the look of a quad Weber setup. (Photo courtesy of FAST Man EFI)

EFI also provides the flexibility of closed loop operation, which allows the system to automatically react to changing conditions such as altitude and temperature. Tuning can be quickly handled from inside the car with a laptop rather than under the hood with a screwdriver.

The primary issue with EFI is the initial cost of the components as well as the learning curve required to operate the system. By deciding early on in the project, the cost investment can be minimized because many parts cost about the same. The EFI intake is about the same price as a carb intake, the throttle body is about the same price as a carb, and EFI fuel pumps are roughly the same cost as fuel pumps for carburetor systems.

There are some people who are very experienced in using EFI systems on big-block Mopars, so help can be found if a person wants to pursue such a project. Also, *Building and Tuning High-Performance Electronic Fuel Injection*, by Greg Banish would be useful as a guide to the general topic.

CHAPTER 12

CARBURETORS

For our target 500-ci performance buildup, there are really only a couple of good choices for carburetion: either one of the larger 4150 flanged carbs, or a 4500 flange carb. The 4150 flange carb is available in cfm ratings up to about 1,000 cfm, which is plenty for a 700+hp motor. However, a performance big-block will almost always make more power with a 4500-series carb because of the superior flow characteristics.

Classic 4150 Double Pumper

The 4150 flange measures 5.156 by 5.625 inches and is definitely the most popular bolt pattern available for aftermarket intake manifolds. This bolt pattern also works with the currently available Edelbrock carburetors as well as most Demon carbs. Besides the offerings from Holley, Demon and Edelbrock, there are many specialty carb manufacturers such as Braswell and BLP who also produce 4150 flanged carburetors.

Selecting a proper carburetor for a street/strip vehicle is somewhat similar to selecting the proper camshaft profile; a little too small is better than a little too large. The airflow velocity will be higher in the smaller carb, which will allow

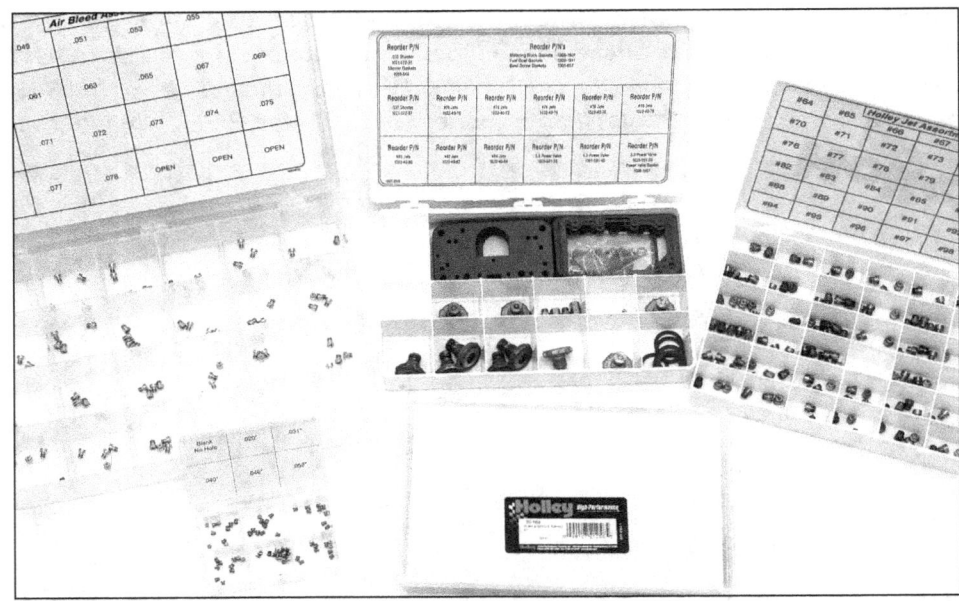

A fairly significant inventory of parts is required before an engine builder is ready to become a carb tuner. This is especially true when working with the newer carbs that have replaceable air bleeds and emulsion jets.

A high-quality fuel regulator is required when using an electric fuel pump. Carburetors work best when the fuel pressure is properly set and maintained.

A Holley 950 Ultra HP makes an excellent choice for a smaller performance big-block. This 950 carb is mounted on a Mopar dual plane intake and it has been fitted with a custom-built dual-inlet fuel line.

CARBURETORS

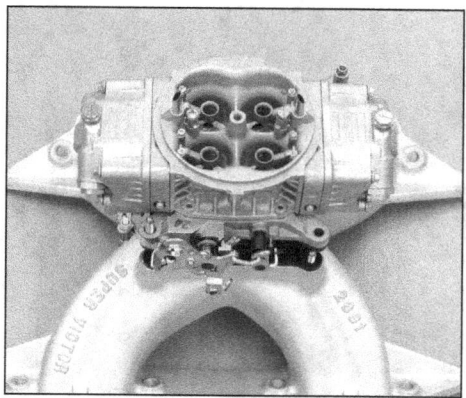

The Holley 1000 HP carb is an excellent choice for a larger performance big-block motor. The 1000 HP has large 1.56-diameter venturis that are best suited to motors that are larger than 500 ci.

The Holley 1000 HP carb is a good choice on top of a 500-ci motor with a dual-plane intake. When using a dual-plane intake a slightly larger carburetor can be used since each cylinder only sees one half of the carb.

This Holley 950 Ultra HP carb has holes drilled into each of the throttle plates. These holes provide extra air in order to run a higher idle speed without opening up the throttle blades. This modification works very well with large motors that have a lot of camshaft duration.

The classic Holley carburetor's zinc die-cast body is quite heavy. This 1000 HP weighs about 12 lbs.

the metering system to work better, especially at part throttle. The smaller carb may give up a little bit of power to the larger carb at WOT, but the typical street/strip vehicle spends very little time at WOT so this is a good tradeoff. For a street-type engine, a 750-cfm carb will work well at the 600-hp level while the 850-cfm carb is a good choice for a 700-hp motor.

For a street/strip car you should seriously consider selecting a carburetor with a choke, as well as the vacuum ports necessary for operating the PCV, distributor advance, and the power brakes. Holley has the Street HP-series of carbs, which would work fine for many street big-blocks, while Edelbrock has the large 800-cfm AVS carb that also works well in this application.

The 4500 Dominator

The big 4500-series Dominator carbs have a rich racing heritage and have been linked with big-block Mopars for many years. The pure racing design of the Dominator carb makes it a great choice for any large-displacement drag racing engine and there is often a substantial power increase a large-displacement racing engine when you replace a 4150 flange carb with the bigger 4500-series carburetor.

The 4500 flange uses a square bolt pattern that measures 5.375 x 5.375 inches. The wider bolt pattern allows for the larger throttle bores to be arranged in a square pattern, and this allows the carb spacers and intake manifold plenums to be more symmetrically shaped. Holley currently offers the Dominator carb in ratings of 1050, 1150, and 1250 cfm. The 1050-cfm rated carbs will certainly handle an 800-hp big-block Mopar, but you might want to go one step larger if you are planning on 900 hp. The larger carb makes more power on the dyno, but it might not get the car down the track any faster. So some actual testing is required at these power levels to determine the optimum combination.

Holley Dominators are available in either a two-circuit configurations or as a three-circuit carb, which has an additional intermediate circuit. The large venturis on the Dominator require a fair amount of airflow before they start to really work, so the intermediate circuit adds more fuel during the transition from the idle circuit to the main circuit. If

CHAPTER 12

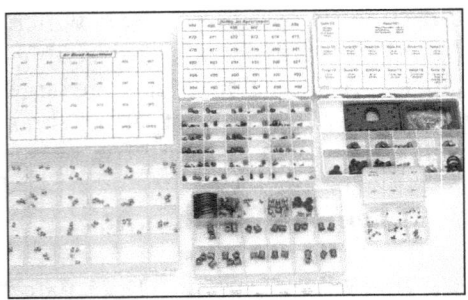

There are a lot of parts available for tuning the Holley carburetors. The 4500-series carbs share many parts with the smaller 4150-series but some parts are unique so if you're tuning both styles of carbs you will need some additional tuning supplies.

On the left is a 1000-cfm Holley HP carb while on the right is a 1050 Holley Dominator. These carbs have similar flow ratings, but the venturis in the Dominator are larger with smoother inlets. Because of this, the Dominator carb often produces an additional 20 to 30 hp more than a 4150 carb of the same size.

The large 4500 Dominator carbs look right at home on a performance big-block. This 1050 Ultra HP is mounted on a high-compression 505-inch motor that made more than 800 hp on the dyno.

the airflow is a too slow to get the main circuit going, there may be a lean spot or a bog. The problem is that the intermediate circuit can be too eager to please, and these carburetors have a tendency to run very rich during part-throttle operation. A rich condition at part throttle can help a car launch off of the trans brake, or help it during shift recovery at the drag strip, but it can also foul the spark plugs on a daily driver. The important thing to remember is that these higher-end carburetors are designed for specific applications, and that you need to select the one that is the best fit for your application.

Holley doesn't recommend the larger 4500-series carbs for street-driven vehicles, but with the tuning capability that exists today, it is possible to get them to work fairly well for street cars. I'll address this topic more in the tuning section but basically, with the introduction of the wide band oxygen sensor systems, the average hot rodder can now solve tuning problems that were very difficult in the past. The most important guideline is to start off with the appropriate carb in the first place. If you select the correct carburetor for your application, then the tuning will be fairly straightforward.

Tuner-Friendly Carburetors

There is a fairly recent and most welcome aftermarket trend toward carburetors that are easier to tune. The classic double pumper from the 1970s had main jets that could be replaced, but the rest of the circuits were fixed. If a person had a carb that didn't operate properly for their combination, then drilling out the restrictions in the metering blocks was often the only solution. If those modifications turned out to be wrong, then sometimes the builder needed to start over by purchasing new metering blocks or a new carburetor body.

In contrast to that situation, the latest HP and UltraHP carburetors from Holley have metering blocks, which are drilled and tapped for jets in most of the fuel and air passages.

This big Holley 1050 Ultra HP carb is only 1 lb heavier than the smaller 4150 carb. The Ultra HP carbs have aluminum metering plates that are significantly lighter than the die-cast zinc parts.

There currently are not any dual plane manifolds available for the big-block Mopar engine that are designed to work with a 4500 series carb, but an adapter can be used to mate the two parts together.

CARBURETORS

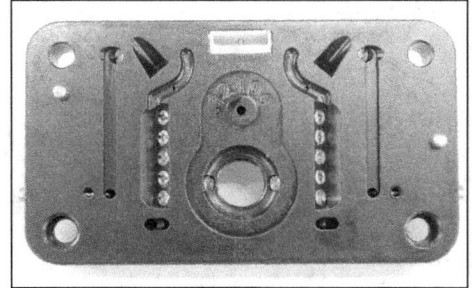

A welcome trend for carburetors is the new billet metering blocks that are fully threaded for metering jets in all of the circuits. This Holley Ultra HP metering block has replaceable jets in the emulsion circuit, the idle feed circuit, the main circuit, and the power valve restriction channel.

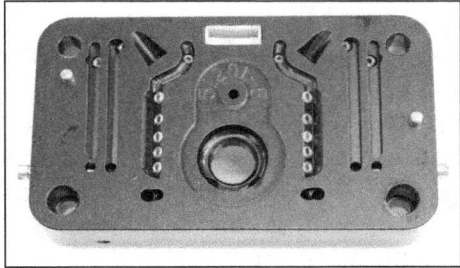

This metering block from BLP is for a three-circuit Dominator. The channels closest to the edges of the block feed the extra intermediate circuit. Every circuit in this metering block has jets installed and can be easily tuned.

This Edelbrock 800 cfm is mounted on a 470-ci low-deck stroker motor. This combination made 475 rear-wheel horsepower on the chassis dyno and was very drivable on the street. The two-step metering rod design allows the Edelbrock carbs to be dialed in for great street manners while still providing plenty of top-end power.

These additional jets allow for easy tuning as well as a quick return path to the original setup if necessary. Also, most of the newer carbs have idle circuits at all four corners, and many designs also allow adjustment of the secondary throttle blades for additional air at idle speeds. These newer HP carbs also have replaceable air bleeds for additional tuning capability while the UltraHP carbs have screw-in emulsion jets for even finer tuning capability. The newest carbs have so much adjustment capability that people will be confused by the complexity. It is possible to be overwhelmed by the tuning choices that

The Holley Ultra HP uses three sizes of jets to tune the various circuits: the large jets on the left are main jets, the jets in the middle are for the air bleeds, and the small jets on the right are for the emulsion, idle, and intermediate circuits.

come with a modern carburetor but, as long as you keep good notes that show which jets were changed and what the results were, you should be able to find your way back to the initial combination.

Edelbrock and Carter Carburetors

Anyone who has been around Mopar engines for a while knows about the legacy of the Carter carbs. While those carbs worked great for many years, the business side of things didn't work out so well, and Carter eventually abandoned the marketplace. Edelbrock was able to step in and acquire the rights to not only continue making the basic Carter design, but they also have expanded the selection to include a larger 800-cfm version. Edelbrock currently offers both an AVS-style 800-cfm as well as an AFB-style 800-cfm carb. These two carbs are very similar with the main difference being the operation of the secondary air valve. For a street/strip-type

Edelbrock offers several versions of their 800-cfm carburetor including the AVS version on the left and the AFB version on the right. The AVS version is a little easier to adjust and is a little more expensive than the AFB version.

CHAPTER 12

The secondary throttle blades should always be inspected to see if they are opening fully when the linkage is pulled fully against the stop.

The 800-cfm Edelbrock carburetor works really well on a 600-hp street engine. The use of two-step metering rods in these carbs makes them easy to dial in for street/strip use.

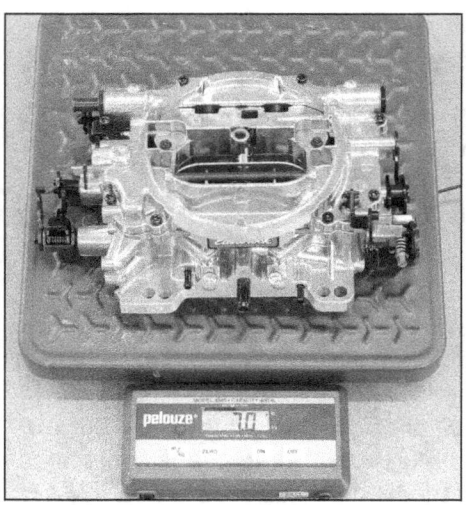

The Edelbrock 800 cfm carb is almost 5 lbs lighter than a Holley carb. On a dual carb setup the weight savings would be about 10 lbs which becomes significant.

application on a big-block Mopar, either of the 800-cfm Edelbrock carbs will perform well; I have used these carbs on several big-block projects with excellent results. They deliver strong performance when used in pairs on the cross ram intake manifolds from either Mopar Performance or Indy Cylinder Heads.

The Edelbrock-style carburetor uses vacuum controlled metering rods to adjust the fuel curve between cruising and WOT. These metering rods are quick and easy to replace and the jets can be replaced from the top without draining out the fuel, which is why many builders like this style of carb. The top access also allows much quicker tuning when used on a dual-carb application, such as the Indy cross ram, because the carb body does not need to be removed from the manifold in order to change the jets. Due to the differences in construction and design, the Edelbrock carburetor weighs about 5 lbs less than a traditional Holley carburetor. This weight difference becomes 10 lbs for a dual carb setup, which can be a significant amount of weight sitting up high in the engine compartment.

There is not room in this book to cover the internal details of either the Holley- or Edelbrock-type carburetors because that level of detail alone would fill a book. Fortunately, there

One nice feature of the Edelbrock carbs is that the top comes off for jet changes so fuel spillage is eliminated.

This Indy cross ram intake manifold has been modified to use a three 2-barrel setup from Barry Grant.

CARBURETORS

are several books on the subject. *Super Tuning and Modifying Holley Carburetors* by Dave Emanuel is a good place to start if you are going to use a Holley carb. *How to Tune and Win with Demon Carburetion* by Ray Bohacz is also available for the Demon users. For those who will be running the new Edelbrock carburetors, a great reference book would be *How to Rebuild and Modify Carter/Edelbrock Carburetors* by Dave Emanuel.

Carburetor Spacers

The subject of carb spacers could fit into Chapter 11 on intake manifolds or even Chapter 16 on dyno tuning, but I'll cover it here with the carburetors because the two are tied closely together. There are a surprising number of carb spacers available for both the 4150-bolt pattern and the 4500-bolt pattern. Spacers are available in open style, with four holes, with internal tapers, and with shear plates.

Carburetor spacers basically break into three different categories: simple spacers, merge spacers, and shear plates. I will take a quick look at each style just to give you information on what is available. The subject is surprisingly complex in terms of actual engine performance, so the only way to tell what will work on a specific engine is to actually try some different spacers and track the results. One type of spacer might make more power on the dyno, but another type might get the car down the track faster. The nice thing about carb spacers is that they are fairly inexpensive and easy to change; so you can keep a small selection to try out on each motor you build.

Simple Spacers

A simple spacer raises the carburetor up from the intake manifold without trying to modify the airflow in any form. These spacers come in many different thicknesses and either have one large hole that matches the opening in the intake manifold, or four individual holes that match the throttle bores in the carburetor. The simple spacer can improve power by raising the throttle plates away from the floor of the intake manifold. This extra space causes two effects: the size of the plenum area is increased, and the airflow has more time to make the turn into the intake runners. The bigger the motor, or the higher the engine speed, the more need there is for plenum space and turning room. The downside to the simple spacer is that throttle response typically suffers because it takes longer for the accelerator pump shot to actually reach the combustion chamber.

Merge Spacers

The merge-type spacer has become fairly popular in the last 10 years. Wilson Manifolds released some very elegant designs that were widely used by circle track and drag race engine builders. The merge spacer provided a smooth path from the four separate throttle bores into the common plenum area in the intake manifold. While the simple spacer has an abrupt transition from the throttle bore to the plenum, the merge spacer design smoothes out the transitions in order to improve the airflow. Builders

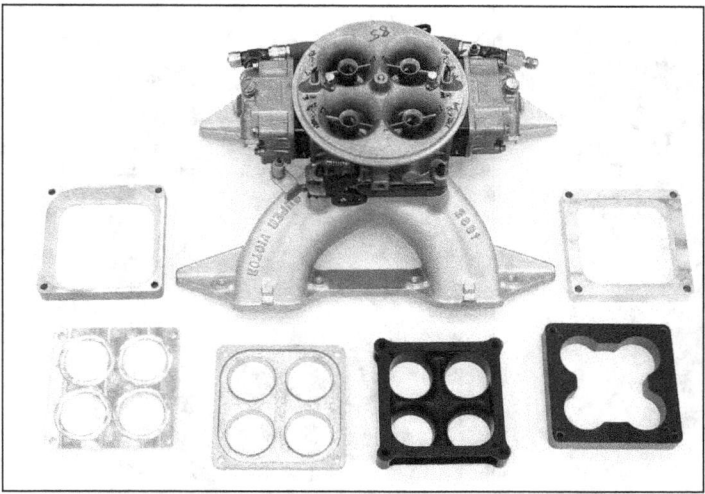

A wide variety of carburetor spacers are available for either the 4150 or the 4500 bolt pattern. Plain, cloverleaf, and tapered spacers are shown in this picture as well as a couple versions of shear plates.

A phenolic carb spacer is a good idea on a street/strip-type of motor since it will help to keep heat away from the carb base. Phenolic spacers are available in different heights and styles. This one is a tapered four-hole spacer.

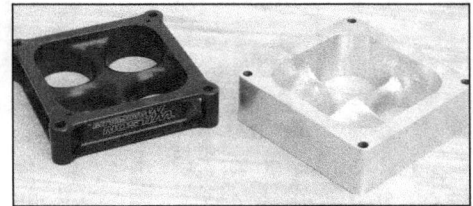

Tapered spacers are available from many different vendors in different materials, heights, and shapes.

HOW TO BUILD MAX-PERFORMANCE MOPAR BIG-BLOCKS

CHAPTER 12

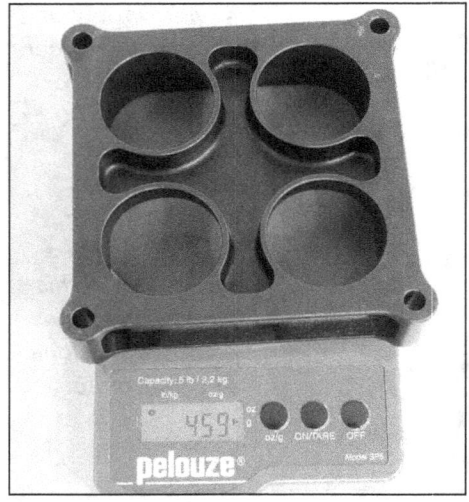

Wilson spacers are expensive, but the extra machine work on the exterior makes them the lightest design available. The 4500 tapered spacer weighs just 459 grams.

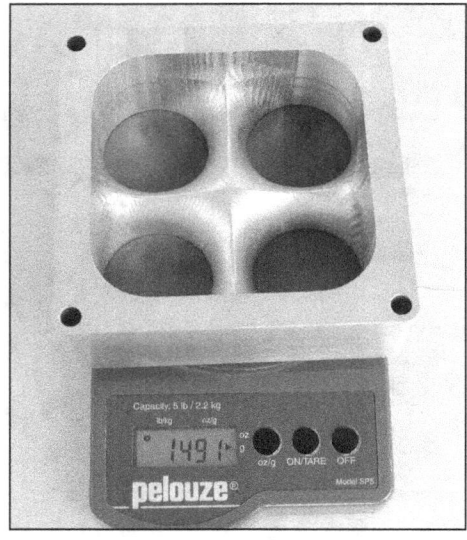

This 4500 tapered spacer weighs almost 1,500 grams, which is more than three times what the Wilson spacer weighed.

The tapered 4-hole to 1-hole type of spacer is often the most effective design to use for a performance-type engine. At high engine speeds, the shear plate design seems to work better.

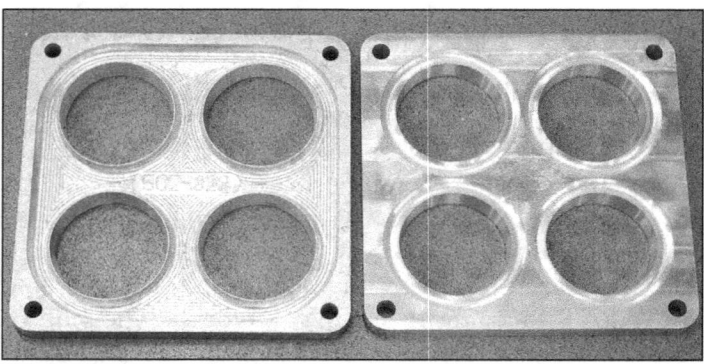

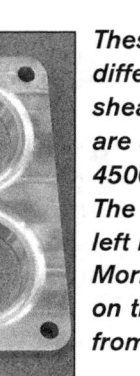

These are two different styles of shear plates that are used under 4500 flange carbs. The plate on the left is from Reher-Morrison; the plate on the right is from Holley.

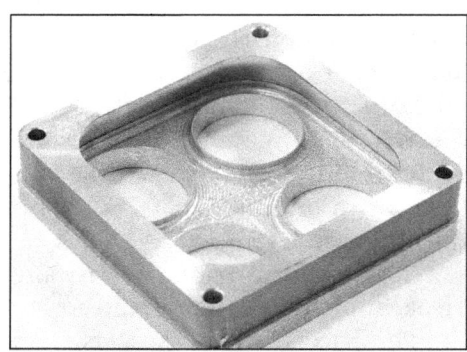

The complete shear plate assembly from Reher-Morrison includes a tapered spacer that fits under the shear plate. This assembly is designed to break up the fuel droplets in the airflow as well as block reversion from the intake manifold. These shear plate spacers are most effective on high-RPM motors.

commonly report power increases on the dyno of 5 to 15 hp when using a merge spacer over a simple spacer. Of course, there are always certain combinations where the merge spacer doesn't seem to work but that is the kind of results one sees when performing a lot of testing.

Shear Plate Spacers

The shear plate has been around for a few years, but it hasn't gained much acceptance among the average street/strip guy. Many of the higher-end professional class drag racers use shear plates on their intakes, but the bracket racers don't. In contrast to the merge spacer, the shear spacer is designed to have abrupt transitions at the entrance to the intake plenum. The shear plate looks like a simple four-hole spacer, but under close examination, you'll see that the throttle bores have a slight taper to them and then they have a sharp edge at the exit. This sharp edge is usually surrounded by a groove or a cavity that further isolates the throttle bore from the plenum.

When a shear plate is working correctly on a motor, it will sharpen up the intake signal to the carburetor enough that the jetting in the carburetor will need to be leaned down several jet sizes. The induction system efficiency is improved, so the motor will make the same amount of power with smaller jet sizes. I've run the shear plates on big-block Mopars before and have had to remove four jet sizes from the main circuit in order to get the air/fuel ratio back to where it was with a simple spacer.

CHAPTER 13

IGNITION SYSTEMS

There are a large number of ignition system choices in the marketplace. Hence, you need to determine the requirements of your system, and then select the aftermarket unit that has the necessary features. Ignition boxes can be equipped with exotic features such as traction control, individual cylinder timing adjustment, timing curves for each gear, and programming from a laptop computer. Most of the extra features will not increase the power output of the engine, but they can make it more reliable in the car.

Electronic Ignitions

Chrysler was an early adopter of the electronic ignition system, so the Mopar aftermarket got a boost years ago when the Direct Connection engineers released the hotter chrome box. For many years, a production electronic distributor with the chrome box delivered the strongest ignition, but hotter aftermarket systems have steadily replaced the production-based ignition systems over time. Direct Connection kept up with the aftermarket systems for a while with the Super Gold ignition box and then a rebranded MSD ignition system, but the aftermarket systems eventually took over this space.

This custom-built ignition plate is used for dyno testing. A plate like this could also be used on a race engine in a dragster body. This is a high-powered ignition system with a MSD 7AL-2+ box and a HVC coil with 2 amps of peak current.

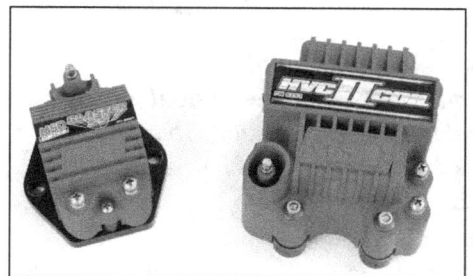
Modern coils have evolved away from the traditional cylinder shape with many these days looking more like a box or cube. Custom mounting brackets are usually required for these coils.

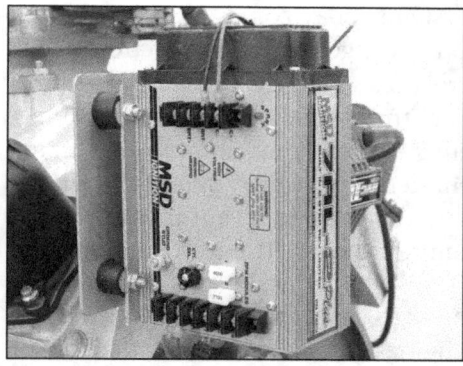
The MSD 7AL ignition box is one of the most popular choices for performance race engines. MSD has several other ignition boxes with slightly different features so consult a catalog or the sales line before making a final decision on which ignition box to run.

This MSD coil has been mounted to the factory location on the intake manifold using a custom-fabricated billet mount.

CHAPTER 13

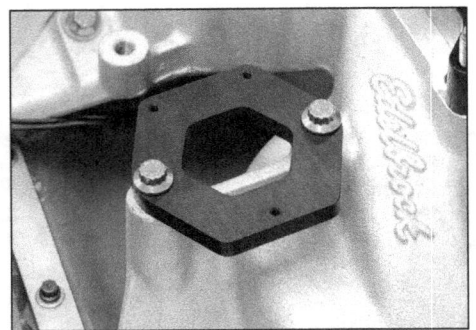

With the coil removed the shape of the custom bracket required for the MSD coil can be seen. Most machine shops could fabricate a bracket like this.

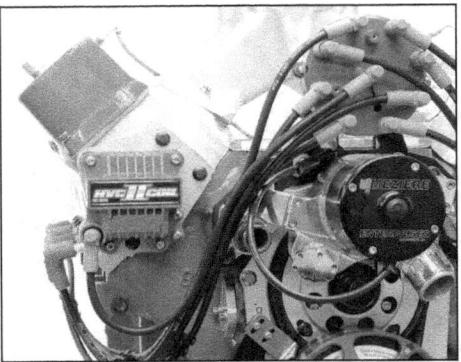

If you are not running an alternator in the stock location then the end of the cylinder head is a good place to mount a high-output coil.

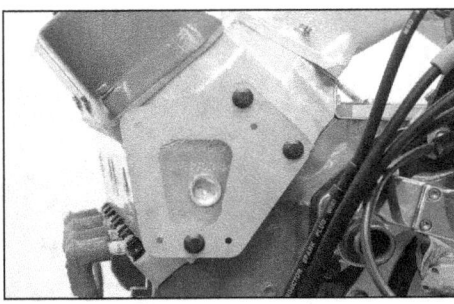

A custom bracket to mount a high-output coil can be quickly cut out on a laser or water jet. This bracket was cut from 12-gauge stainless steel to hold a big MSD racing coil.

One of the most popular ignition systems today comes from MSD. They offer a large number of electronic control boxes with a wide range of features that the production boxes never imagined. Now you can commonly find rev limiters, starting retards, nitrous retards, etc., in even the lower-end ignition boxes. The lowerend ignition boxes will typically provide a strong enough spark to power 800- or 900-hp engines on the dyno, but they won't necessarily have all of the features that a person might want in the car. So select the ignition box first, and then the other components such as the distributor and coil can be matched to the needs of the ignition system.

Distributor

You need to decide between a vacuum or mechanical advance distributor. The addition of vacuum advance allows for an extra level of tuning, but it often isn't required for a performance build. The ignition can be advanced significantly while cruising at light throttle with a vacuum advance. If you are planning to spend significant time driving your big-block Mopar on the freeway, you should strongly consider a vacuum advance distributor. The additional advance while under high-vacuum cruise conditions improves fuel economy and will help to keep the engine cooler and operating more efficiently. Vacuum advance should not have any negative effects on WOT power output because it doesn't operate at low manifold vacuum.

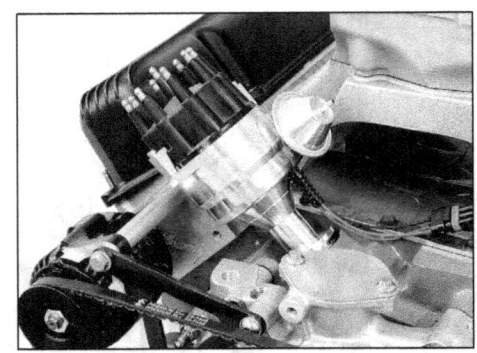

The MSD all in one distributor has a large main body but it will fit with stock heads and most stock replacement heads.

This original cast-iron tach-drive distributor has been updated with an electronic pickup unit. This distributor would work in a performance engine, but it is very heavy.

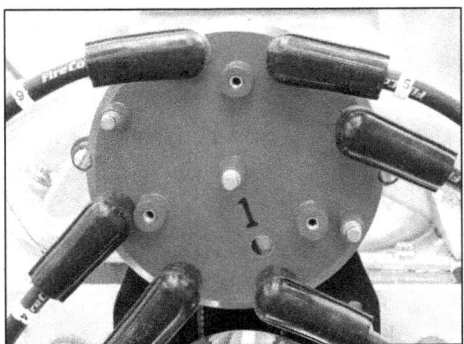

A hole drilled in the distributor cap provides an easy way to double-check that the rotor is correctly aligned. Shining a timing light into the hole while the engine is running will show the location of the rotor. If the rotor isn't pointed directly at the number-1 spark-plug terminal when the number-1 plug fires, then the rotor phasing needs to be adjusted.

The classic Mopar Peformance distributors have a lightweight aluminum body, electronic pickup and an adjustable vacuum advance can. MP distributors still use the old-style spark plug wire plug while MSD distributors use the more modern HEI tower.

IGNITION SYSTEMS

The newer distributors from Mopar Performance are based on a Mallory distributor mechanism. After the distributor is taken apart, the advance curve as well as the total advance can be easily adjusted in these distributors.

The older Mopar Performance distributors had a stock-type advance mechanism, which is difficult to adjust. The center shaft needs to be removed and the slots welded up in order to limit the total advance in this type of distributor.

The MSD distributors are easier to work on than some other units because the advance mechanism is accessible right under the rotor. A bushing located on the back side of the center plate controls total advance.

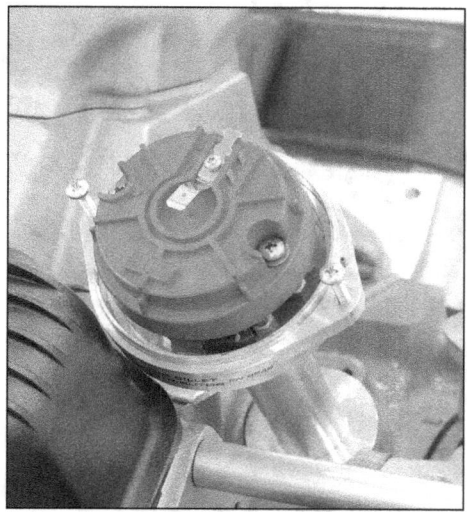

The MSD distributor uses a full-size rotor that is held down with two screws.

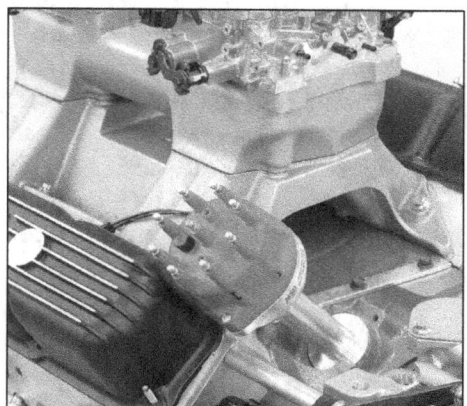

The MSD Pro-Billet distributor is tall with a turned down housing in order to clear aftermarket heads. These Pro-Billet distributors do not have a vacuum advance mechanism.

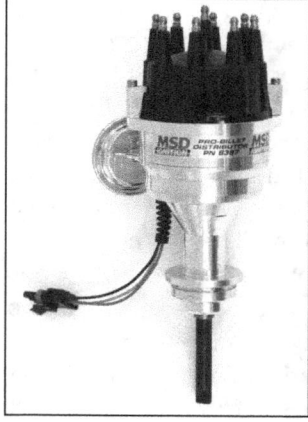

The MSD ready-to-run distributors have a built in ignition box, so no external wiring is required. The three-wire harness on the distributor connects to the coil and ground.

An exploded view of the new Mopar Performance distributors shows the parts that have to be removed in order to adjust the advance curve.

A kit of springs is available from Mopar Performance to tune the advance curve of their distributors. The red plastic keys are used to set the total advance.

However, the additional hardware involved can cause issues, so racers tend to remove it.

Any performance distributor on the market these days is an electronic rather than a breaker points system. There are different styles of electronic pickups in use in modern performance distributors, including the magnetic reluctor in the production units, the LED system used in the Mallory Unilight, and the magnetic design in the MSD units.

The most popular system for the big-block Mopar seems to be the MSD billet distributor. The MSD distributor

CHAPTER 13

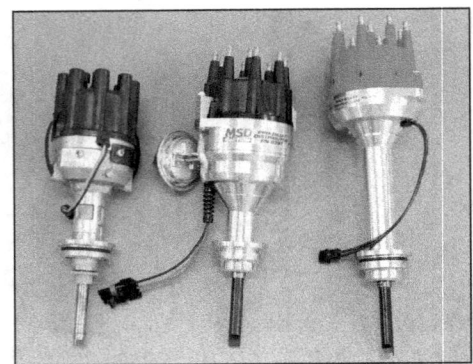

A lineup of the MP distributor, MSD ready to run distributor and the MSD Pro Billet shows the differences in length and diameter between these models. The shorter and wider distributors will not fit with some of the taller aftermarket heads.

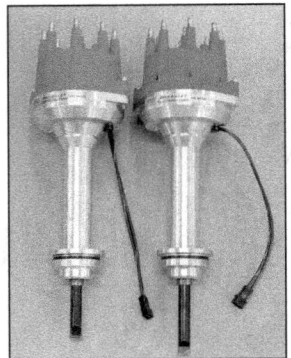

B and RB distributors do not directly interchange because of different shaft lengths. Here the longer distributor shaft for the RB application is shown on the right.

A belt-driven distributor can be mounted anywhere that the belt drive will reach. On this engine the distributor was offset to the driver's side in order to provide clearance for the water pump.

The Jesel belt driven distributor mounts in the same location where the thermostat housing usually sits. There are several ways to solve this interference issue but they all require custom fabrication.

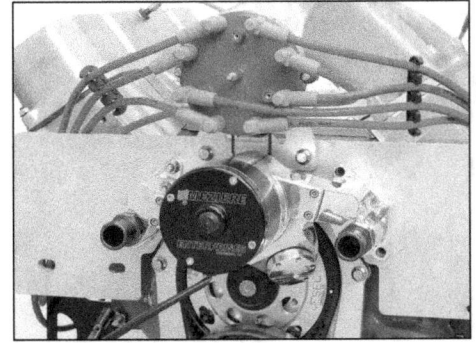

A Jesel belt-driven distributor works well when combined with a reverse-flow water pump because the outlet ports on the reverse-flow pump point forward rather than upward into the distributor.

is a plug-and-play unit with the popular MSD ignition boxes, and it is fairly easy to set up internally. The mechanical advance system is controlled with a bushing that sets total advance while the advance rate is controlled with two springs. There is no vacuum advance capability on the MSD distributor. The MSD uses a HEI-style cap so new plug wires are required.

Mopar Performance still produces an electronic distributor. This unit has a redesigned advance system that is much easier to work with than the old production-based distributors. It also has vacuum advance ability so it is a useful street/strip distributor.

There are still some distributors available with the old-style cable drive for a mechanical tachometer. The mechanical tachometer is simple and accurate, but most people have switched over to electronic tachs because the digital capability of data capture and playback helps builders tune for a specific power curve. There is also a much larger selection of electronic tachs to choose from than the cable driven models, but the mechanical tachs are kind of a cool retro item to see under the hood.

Belt Driven Distributor

The Mopar big-block distributor is located at the front of the engine, so it is out of the way of the firewall and fairly easy to access in most cases. There are some situations—when larger cylinder heads are used with larger valve covers— where the stock location gets tough to access. Also, when using a crank trigger ignition system, there is no longer any need for the electronics inside the distributor, so a rotor and a cap is all you need. In either case, a belt driven distributor often makes sense. It is run off of the front of the camshaft with a small pulley and belt system, and available from Jesel, MSD, and Mallory.

I have had very good results recently with the belt driven distributor, even on lower-horsepower engines. The belt driven distributors have a very simple internal design that makes them easy to work with. Because they are a no-compromise design with a large cap and robust components, they work well and are fairly rugged. The central front mount location provides easy access and the spark plug wire routing is shorter and more symmetrical. The only issue is that you then need to locate the water pump forward for clearance, or else use a different style of water pump without a center outlet. We have

IGNITION SYSTEMS

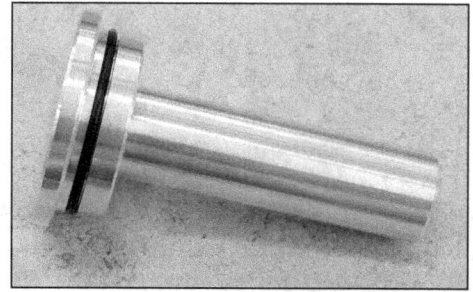

When using a belt-driven distributor, there needs to be some sort of block-off to plug up the existing distributor hole in the cylinder block. This block off has an O-ring seal as well as an extended nose that keeps the oil drive shaft from backing out of position.

A stock-type distributor clamp holds down the distributor block-off plug.

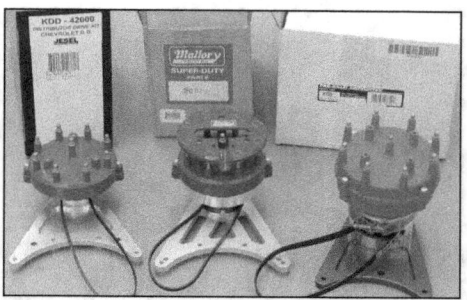

There are at least three different vendors selling belt drive distributors for the big-block Mopar. The Jesel distributor on the left is the smallest and lightest of the three choices.

been using the Meziere WP307 reverse flow water pump during dyno development, and it seems to work well. The reverse-flow Meziere water pump has the outlets located on the sides of the pump, rather than in the center of the housing, so there isn't an interference issue with the belt drive distributor.

Crank Trigger

Chrysler engineers developed one of the very first crank trigger ignitions for the Motown Missile Pro Stock program. They took the magnetic pickup out of the distributor and mounted it on a bracket next to the harmonic damper. They then put the triggers on a wheel that bolted to the front of the damper. By mounting the trigger and pickups on the front of the crankshaft, the ignition signal is tied directly to the crankshaft position rather than referencing the distributor shaft. The distributor shaft is linked to the crankshaft through the timing chain and the oil pump shaft, and as a result, there are multiple areas where slop and backlash can affect the distributor timing. When using the distributor as an ignition source, an engine can experience chain whip, camshaft twist, and oil pump gear engagement, but these issues are eliminated when using the crank trigger.

The crank trigger arrangement was once too exotic to use on a bracket-type motor, but the invention of digital ignition boxes with built-in start retard has made it a lot easier to install. The crank trigger arrangement does add some parts to the front of the motor, but these parts are fairly simple and robust. The distributor no longer requires any type of advance mechanism in it, so it can be reduced to just a rotor and a cap. Often, the original-style distributor is completely removed in favor of a belt driven distributor. The signal from the crank trigger could also be used to fire a distributorless system where individual coils are used for each spark plug.

A crank trigger ignition is often used on the more serious race engines. Ignition timing should be rock steady when using a crank trigger ignition because the variation of the cam drive and oil pump drives are eliminated from the equation.

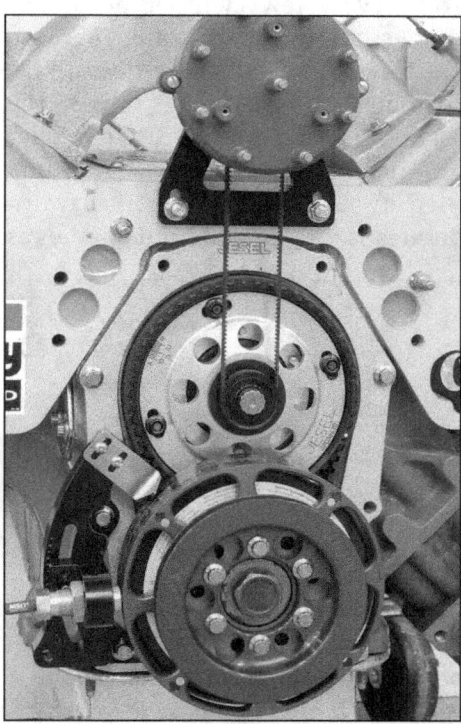

A belt-driven distributor is a perfect match for a crank trigger ignition because all the distributor needs to do is to pass the spark from the coil to the cylinders.

CHAPTER 13

When using a crank trigger, the distributor doesn't need to have any advance mechanism so it can just be a simple rotor spinning in the housing.

An adjustable TDC pointer is essential when working with aftermarket crankshafts and dampers. Higher-end timing chain covers, such as this billet cover from Mancini Racing, come with an adjustable pointer.

Spark Plugs

The production spark plugs for BB Mopars used a 14-mm thread with a short 3/8-inch reach and a large 13/16-inch wrenching hex. Today, very few cylinder heads use that style of spark plug because almost all of the vendors have switched to sparkplugs with the longer 3/4-inch reach and the smaller 5/8-inch wrenching hex. These are used in almost all aftermarket cylinder heads for GM and Ford engines as well as some Mopar production engines. Given that large popularity, there is a vast array of plug choices in this size as well as a wide selection of heat ranges and tip designs.

Indy Cylinder Head recommends the use of Champion race plugs for their cylinder heads. These Champion plugs have a cut back electrode that makes the spark plug very robust. It is very difficult to damage the electrode on these because they are so short and stiff. Indy recommends a Champion C59CX for 13:1 compression motors and the hotter C61CX for lower-compression motors.

Many builders use the popular NGK racing plugs. The NGK spark plugs are available in a wide selection of heat ranges as well as projected and non-projected tips. We've had good results using the NGK 5671A-9 non-projected tip plug with Indy heads and domed pistons. The projected tip version of this plug is a 5672A-9, which works well with a flat-top piston.

Edelbrock recommends using a Champion RC-12YC or equivalent spark plug when using their popular Performer RPM cylinder heads. These RC-12YC plugs are quite common because several OEM vehicles used it. So it is possible to find replacement plugs in most any auto parts store as long as you know what to ask for.

Indexing the Spark Plugs

Installing the spark plugs so that the ground strap is in a particular location is referred to as indexing. A domed piston can interfere with the ground strap on the spark plug, so check for interference before starting the engine. Projected tip spark plugs will be more likely to have interference issues so you need to select a standard tip spark plug when using domed pistons. In some cases the spark plugs must be installed so that the ground strap is located toward the top of the combustion chamber to avoid a contact with the piston dome. Several companies, such as Moroso, sell washers that can be used to index the plugs, but many builders prefer to just start with a large selection of plugs and then try them in each cylinder until they find a set that fits properly. It is easier to keep track of things if each spark plug is marked with its ground strap location and the cylinder number.

Aftermarket aluminum heads typically use 3/4-inch-reach plugs like the ones shown here. Close inspection will show that the plug on the right has a projected tip while the plug on the left has a more recessed tip. Projected tip spark plugs might make a little more power but they can also interfere with domed pistons.

The ground strap on this Champion racing plug is cut back away from the center tip. Indy Cylinder Heads recommends this style of racing plug for use with its heads. These plugs are very durable and come in heat ranges suitable for very-high-compression engines.

IGNITION SYSTEMS

Good spark plug wires are required when building a performance engine. Thankfully several vendors such as MSD have a great selection of spark plug wires that will fit the Mopar big-block.

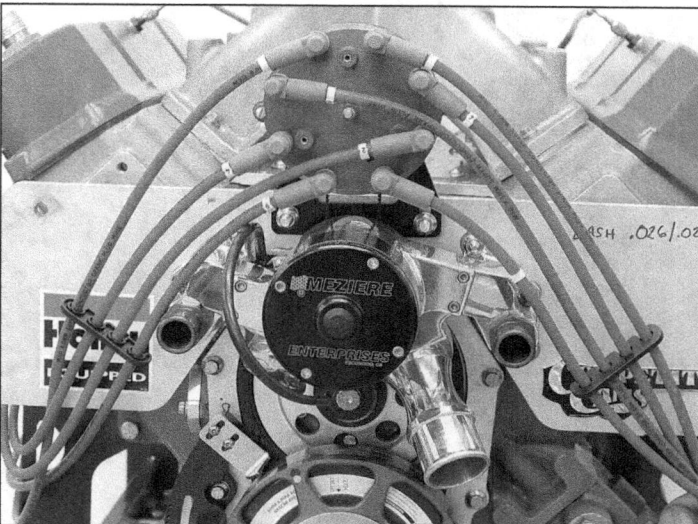

Routing the spark plug wires with a centrally located distributor is a little easier because the wires are almost a mirror image of each other. Remember, when using a belt driven distributor the distributor rotates CW rather than the usual CCW direction.

A few builders feel that if the spark plugs are indexed properly with the ground strap opening pointing in the correct direction, then the engine will make some additional power. Some builders theorize that the ground strap opening must point toward the intake valve, while others will say the exhaust valve. If you have access to a very accurate engine dyno and have a lot of spare time on your hands, this might be an interesting experiment to run.

Spark Plug Wires

There is certainly a much larger selection of spark plug wires on the market than ever before. Over the years, wire size has increased from the production size to 7 mm and now to 8 or even 8.5 mm. In general, more insulation is better because it helps to prevent cross talk and breakdown. The restoration-type engine builder typically uses OEM-type spark plugs. The performance engine builder wants wires that deliver the full ignition energy to the spark plugs without causing harmful interference to any other electronic devices.

Years ago solid-core ignition wires used to be the hot trick. Now, with all of the sensitive electronic controls in the engine compartment, it is best to use a high-quality wire that has suppression built in. This isn't so your radio will work; it is so your high-dollar ignition system or EFI system will work properly. The spark plug wires carry a very-high-voltage pulse that can disrupt or even damage other electronic devices if the proper wire insulation isn't used. Most new spark plug wires use a spiral core, or wound-type construction, that creates resistance to electronic interference. When combined with the newer silicon coverings and high temperature boots, these modern wires should provide excellent service for a performance engine.

One trend over the last several years has been toward the use of HEI-style connectors at the distributor rather than the original type of connector. The availability of wires is much greater with the HEI-style end on them, so that might be another good reason for people to finally switch their distributor caps.

When using the standard firing order for a big-block Mopar, the number-5 and number-7 cylinders will fire in sequence. This places an extra burden on the insulation because you do not want cylinder number-5 to false trigger number-7. Builders usually take care to separate these two wires in the loom so they do not run parallel to each other or in close contact.

There are some smaller companies in the spark plug wire business who are willing to produce custom-fitted wire sets. If you have an unusual engine compartment, or a strong desire to have a perfect-fitting set of spark plug wires, then you might want to contact a firm such as Custom Wires. I've used their wires before for belt driven distributor motors and have found them to be an excellent company to work with.

HOW TO BUILD MAX-PERFORMANCE MOPAR BIG-BLOCKS

CHAPTER 14

ACCESSORIES

If you're investing $10,000 to $20,000 in a max-performance engine build, you want to protect your investment by using the most compatible accessories and ancillary components, but these parts should also complement your wedge's performance package. Therefore, this chapter examines and advises you how to select the ideal water pump, alternator kit, motor plate or elephant ears, hoses, and fittings.

Water Pumps, Electric and Belt Driven

Electric water pumps have become very popular over the last several years because several vendors offer models reliable enough for a street/strip-type cruiser. Meziere is probably the best-known supplier of electric water pumps for Mopar big-blocks, and they sell several different models. An electric water pump is very popular for dyno testing or drag racing because it eliminates the need for a belt-drive pulley and it can be operated without the engine running for quicker cooling. Pumps are available that bolt into the factory water pump housing or there are models that replace the entire manifold and pump assembly.

This street/strip car has a small electric pump that runs the water pump while at the track. These small electric motors will not keep a performance engine cool on the street, but they'll work okay at the drag strip.

When working in a tight engine compartment it might be easier to use a remote water pump. In that case, cold water is pumped into the lower fittings and the upper Y fitting directs the hot water back to the radiator.

Reverse-flow water pump systems are available from both Indy Cylinder Heads and Meziere. The reverse-flow

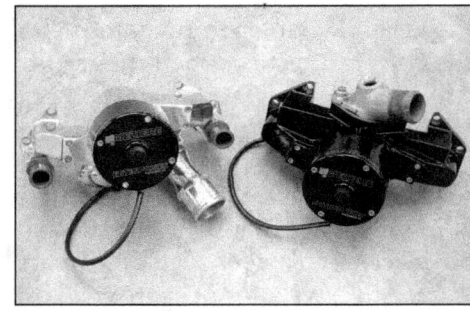

Several different electric water pumps are available from Meziere. On the left, a reverse flow pump is shown and a more conventional standard flow unit is on the right.

system works by sending water to the cylinder heads first and then down into the block. The hot water exits from the front of the cylinder block and returns to the top of the radiator through two hoses. You have the routing of the radiator hoses when using a reverse-flow system, so this modification is not a simple bolt-on. Reverse cooling is also a dramatic change away from the original

ACCESSORIES

A Dayco 70678 lower radiator hose has enough curve to clear a Milodon external oiling system. This is a handy little trick that uses an off-the-shelf part to solve a difficult fit.

Finding a good location for the alternator takes a little creativity when running a motor plate. This picture shows a custom-built mount that hangs a small Denso alternator beneath the motor plate. An external water pump was used on this motor so the alternator was the only belt driven accessory.

Using a bracket kit from Mancini Racing, a lightweight, one-wire racing alternator from Powermaster has been fitted to this 440 motor.

design intent so be cautious about making such a change. You can have trouble with air bubbles trapped inside the engine when using reverse cooling because the coolant flow might not be strong enough to force the air bubbles down and out of the engine. I have used a Meziere WP307 reverse-flow pump many times on the engine dyno without seeing any problems. But dyno cells are equipped with a large supply of freshly chilled water for cooling, so these results might not correlate with what you would see during street driving.

Alternator Kits

The factory alternator hung on the majority of big-block engines is heavy and bulky compared to modern alternators. And at 37 amps, the factory units don't put out enough juice to run an engine compartment full of electric fans and electronic ignition. There are a few different kits these days that provide the brackets and spacers to run a modern 60-amp alternator that is internally regulated. There are also kits available to retrofit the 120-amp alternator that was used on 1980s vans to the big-block engine.

Determining the correct pulley size to use for the accessory drive on a max performance engine can take a little thought. For an engine that is going to see substantial street duty, the ratios should be left close to stock to ensure adequate speed for the water pump and the alternator during low-speed operation. For a vehicle that is going to spend more time at the track than the street, changing the pulley ratio can slow down the driven accessories. Using larger pulleys on the driven side or a smaller pulley at the crankshaft can slow the accessories down. Large diameter alternator pulleys are available from vendors such as Moroso while smaller crankshaft pulleys are available from March, DMI and Moroso.

Engine Mounting Systems, Motor Plates and Elephant Ears

The big-block Mopar is very easy to hang from a motor plate because the six bolts that mount the water pump housing are on the front plane of the motor and they are spread apart far enough to provide a very stable mounting system. Builders tend to use either a 1/4- or a 3/8-inch-thick plate of aluminum that is sandwiched between the block and the water pump housing as the front motor plate. This plate is then connected to the frame of the vehicle on each side of the engine, either with solid mounts or through a system of bushings. For a tube frame race car, the motor plate will most likely be connected to both the upper and lower frame tubes, and in this case it acts as a cross member for the frame.

CHAPTER 14

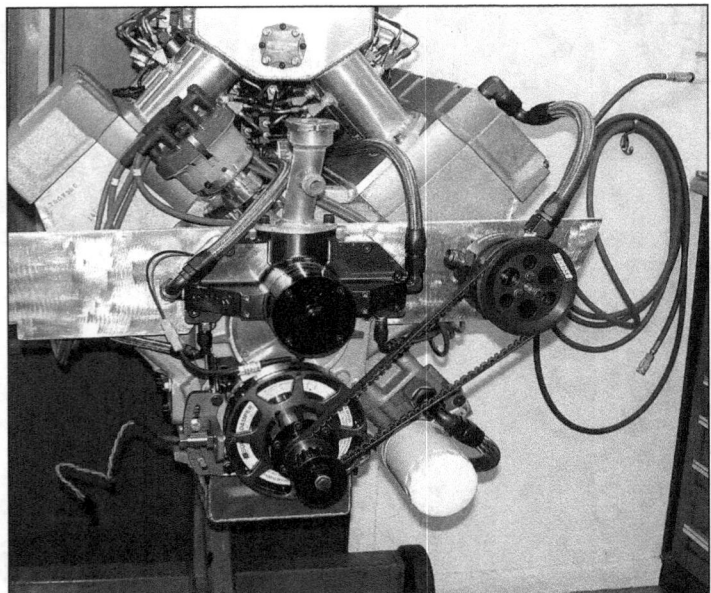

A vacuum pump can often be mounted directly to the motor plate as long as there is enough room for a long drive mandrel on the crankshaft. If the V-belt gets too long you can have problems at high-speed operation, so try to mount the accessories as close to the crankshaft as possible. (Photo courtesy of Koffel's Place)

This big-block has been set up with both a V-belt driven vacuum pump and a Gilmer belt driven fuel pump. Crankshaft mandrels are available that allow you to mix and match pulleys according to which accessories are going to be used. (Photo courtesy of Koffel's Place)

I highly recommend using a motor plate if the power level of the engine tops 750 hp. The forces associated with transmitting such high power levels to the chassis can really strain the stock-type motor mounts and the ears that are cast into the side of the cylinder block. A motor plate mounting system can also help to reduce weight by getting rid of the stock-type mounts as well as the mounts on the frame. The elimination of the motor mounts will also free up space for external oiling lines as well as additional room for the exhaust system.

One problem with the use of motor plates or elephant ears is that the water pump mounting location will be moved forward of the thickness of the plate. This will change the alignment of the pulleys and belts. This isn't a problem if an electric water pump is used but it will cause a problem for a belt driven pump. You can buy a spacer for the crankshaft pulley, to move it forward the same amount as the water pump when using a motor plate, but that still leaves an issue with the alternator and any other belt driven accessory. Also, if you're using a motor plate, the stock alternator mounting system will no longer work so you will need a custom solution. These are not new problems so vendors such as Mancini Racing will have several solutions in stock.

High-Performance Hoses and Fittings

An engine builder will often require custom hose assemblies when building a performance big-block. The oil lines for an external oil pump have to be made specific for each application, as will hoses for vacuum pumps and reverse cooling water pump systems. There are a variety of hoses available, among which the classic braided-steel type is one of the most popular. The classic braided-steel hose is a little more expensive than rubber hose but the real cost difference comes from the fittings. High-performance aluminum fittings are very expensive and they can be easily

There is a fairly large selection of pulleys currently available. The four on the left are crankshaft drive pulleys while the five on the right are alternator pulleys. The crankshaft drive pulleys are available in different depths to compensate for damper thickness and motor plate spacing.

ACCESSORIES

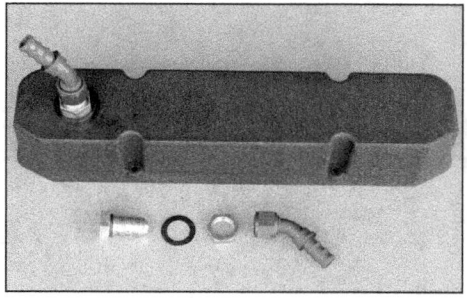

Valve cover breathers are often an issue on a performance engine. These valve covers have been drilled out to accept a set of number-12 AN bulkhead fittings that securely bolt to the valve cover. The hoses from these fittings go to a catch tank.

High-volume air cleaners are available for both 4150 and 4500 carbs. This Flow Control air cleaner from K&N measures 14 by 4.5 inches and can flow 1,200 cfm.

Complete fastener kits for big-block Mopars are available from ARP. The kit pictured uses stainless bolts with 12-point heads.

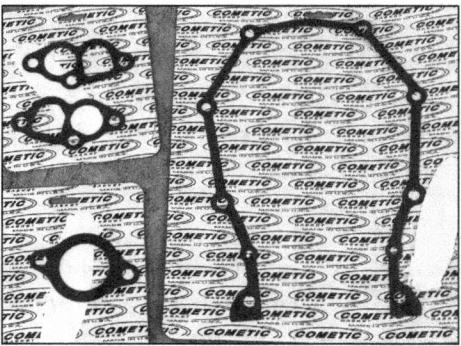

Cometic Gasket has introduced many special gaskets for big-block Mopars. These gaskets are made from a foam-covered steel material that provides excellent sealing properties.

Moroso recently introduced these steel-shim valve cover gaskets that are covered with a pliable silicone coating. These valve-cover gaskets work very well with cast valve covers that have a flat sealing surface.

damaged during assembly. For a street-driven vehicle it can be more cost-effective to use the industrial grade of steel fittings because these are much less expensive and are very durable. When competing in competitive racing classes where weight reduction is important, builders will use lightweight crimped fittings and lightweight hoses. The lightweight hose components are extremely expensive to purchase and special tools are required for assembly. I have had excellent results with fittings and hoses from Aeroquip over the years and have rarely needed to use a different supplier for any hose or fitting.

CHAPTER 15

EXHAUST SYSTEMS

The best exhaust system guide for street/strip vehicles is the one written by Jim Hand in his book, *How to Build Performance Pontiac V-8s*. I won't even try to duplicate the wealth of information that Jim captured in that book because I have not duplicated the amount of testing that Jim performed. The small amount of testing that I have done correlates with Jim's results and further validates his work.

The basic requirement for a streetable exhaust system behind a performance big-block is the ability to handle the large amount of exhaust gas generated at higher engine speeds, without allowing too much noise while cruising around town. While it might seem that high flow and low noise are conflicting requirements, actually there are mufflers and exhaust systems that can meet both requirements. What Jim Hand showed in his research is that the large case turbo-style mufflers such as the DynoMax Super Turbo can meet these conflicting requirements of low noise and high power. Jim's data shows that a good muffler can be much quieter than some of the inferior mufflers while flowing more air and allowing more engine power. Jim's research also showed that some of the really popular mufflers that are known for being loud do not make the most power.

The size of the exhaust system is also an important design consideration; most performance engines require a minimum of 3-inch-diameter exhaust pipes. The 3-inch rule is only for the portion between the headers and the mufflers. Exhaust gases cool off enough after the restricting muffler that the tail pipes can be slightly smaller without sacrificing performance. Customizing with smaller tail pipes is almost a requirement in some vehicles after larger tires are mounted at the rear axle. Moving the mufflers as far to the rear as possible also permits quicker exhaust cooling for some performance improvement. Another side benefit is that the weight distribution of the vehicle will improve anytime heavy items such as mufflers can be located closer to the rear axle.

One other item that should be considered when installing a custom exhaust is the use of a crossover. The classic H-style crossover has been used successfully for many years with high-performance exhaust systems but current data is showing that the X-style crossover might be superior. There are many proponents of the X-style crossover who claim reduced noise and increased power after changing over from a traditional H-style crossover. I haven't personally performed any X vs. H crossover tests but plenty of others have and reported gains on the order of 10 to 15 hp when replacing the H- with an X-style. Alternatively, some people report that they do not like the sound of the X-style crossover so you might want to listen to a few different exhaust systems before you decide which way to go.

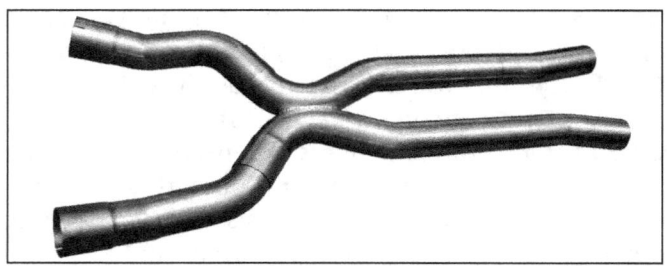

X-type exhaust systems are available in either 2½- or 3-inch tubing. Any engine larger than 500 cubic inches would benefit from the larger 3-inch size, although noise levels do increase a bit. (Photo courtesy of Tube Technologies)

EXHAUST SYSTEMS

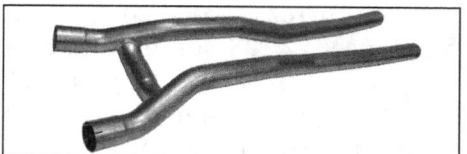

The classic H-type exhaust system is also available in different tube sizes to fit either headers or cast manifolds. (Photo courtesy of Tube Technologies)

Cast Manifolds

The factory cast-iron exhaust manifold is usually one of the first things to be tossed into the trash by the average hot-rodder, and often with good reason. The factory manifolds are restrictive and heavy. However, I have had reasonable success running a 470-inch big-block Mopar with cast-iron manifolds and there are others who are interested in the sleeper look as well.

The factory produced a few different versions of the HP exhaust manifolds during the 1960s and early 1970s. These manifolds have a distinct curved shape that looks completely different than the log-style manifolds that came on the lower-performance engines. If you're going to run cast-iron exhaust manifolds on a performance engine, then at least start with the best possible castings that you can find.

The cast-iron exhaust manifolds seem to work pretty well when they exit directly into a 3-inch head pipe. It might be possible to find a vendor who sells a 3-inch head pipe that fits the manifolds in your chassis but the odds are that you will need to fabricate this part. In the situation that I worked on, both the head pipe and the head pipe flange were custom-fabricated because there was not a 3-inch flange kit available that bolted directly to the cast exhaust manifolds.

The exhaust system that I used with the HP cast manifolds consisted of custom 3-inch head pipes hooked

Cast HP manifolds can easily make enough power to push a B body car to an 11-second time slip. One trick to making power with the cast manifolds is to hook them directly to 3-inch head pipes as shown in this picture.

to a full 3-inch exhaust system from TTI. This system included an H pipe, DynoMax mufflers, and full 3-inch tail pipes out to the rear bumper. This system was quiet enough for daily driving although it wasn't nearly as quiet as a production vehicle. There was a noticeable rumble at idle and people would notice the car if it was throttled hard in traffic, but the noise level was not obnoxious. This setup worked well enough to consistently see 475 hp at the rear wheels when testing on the chassis dyno, which put this vehicle right into Viper power territory.

One important lesson I learned during testing was that the camshaft profile is tremendously important when setting up a performance engine with cast exhaust manifolds. I performed a number of dyno tests trying to find the best camshaft profile to work with the restrictive exhaust manifolds. This work showed that mild is often better than wild when dealing with restricted exhaust systems. The best cam tested to date, with a 470-stroker engine, was the old Mopar Performance .528 solid flat-tappet cam. The MP .528 is a fairly mild cam with only 243 degrees of duration at .050 lift and it has a lot of recommended lash, which decreases the effective duration even more. This cam seems too mild to make serious power in a stroker big-block but it was enough cam to make more than 550 hp on the engine dyno with Edelbrock Performer RPM heads.

What we noticed during chassis dyno testing of the cast-iron exhaust manifolds was that any cam we tried with more duration than the MP .528 generally lost power below the torque peak, and rarely made significantly more power above the torque peak. What that told us was that the extra duration of the larger camshafts basically caused more problems from reversion than it solved at higher speeds. But when we tried cams with less duration than the MP .528, we found only slightly more low-speed power and significantly less upper-speed power. All this dyno testing showed us that you must make a definite compromise when selecting a camshaft for use with exhaust manifolds. Too small a camshaft and you'll never build the power that you want; but if you go too big, the restrictive exhaust system will force the exhaust back into the combustion chamber and you'll end up with even less power.

Headers

There is a decent selection of exhaust headers available for the big-block Mopar installed in the more popular chassis combinations such as the B and E body cars. The options get fewer for A-body cars and even fewer for C-body cars. Most aftermarket headers are designed for the street/strip-type of motor and will typically have a 1¾- or 1⅞-inch-diameter tube size with a 3-inch collector. There are a fair number of larger-tube-race-type headers available with the 2-inch-diameter tube size and a 3-inch collector, and a few vendors offer even larger sizes than this for very limited body styles.

Sometimes the larger-diameter headers will have one or maybe two tubes that exit out the fenderwell because there isn't enough room to fit it all under the car. The room is especially tight on the driver side where the header tubes are trying to fit between the steering column, the starter and the clutch linkage. Mopar B and E body cars are getting so valuable these days that many owners are not willing to cut holes in the fenderwells for the larger headers, so people often use slightly smaller headers that fit without any cutting. There are several header vendors in the industry, though, and they are always developing new products. The best thing to do is look over the Web sites and catalogs to see if you can find what you need.

Picking a Header Size

Common sense will tell you that, as the engine size gets larger or the RPM increases, there will be a need for a larger exhaust system in order to prevent exhaust restriction. But common sense isn't so good at telling what these exhaust tube sizes should be, how long the pipes should be, or how long the collector should be. Fortunately there are a number of software programs avail-

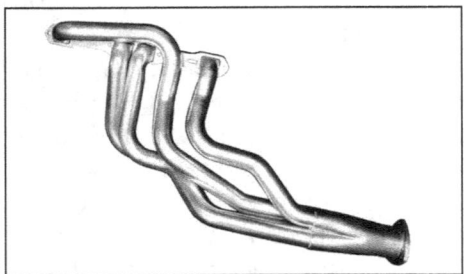

These 2-inch headers from TTi are designed to fit RB engines with stock exhaust ports or B engines with raised port heads such as the Indy SR or Indy 440-1. (Photo courtesy of Tube Technologies)

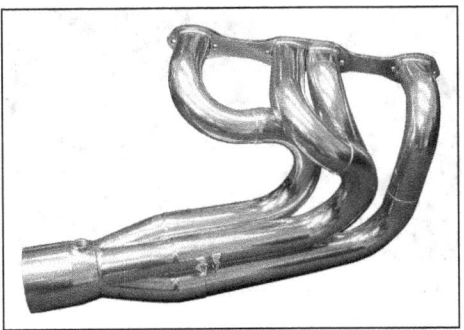

Hedman Hedders has a wide selection of race headers for big-block Mopars. Race headers are designed for specific engine combinations and chassis fitments and are much more expensive than generic headers from the mail-order super stores. (Photo courtesy of Hedman Hedders)

able that can calculate the optimum size for the exhaust system. One SW package that we've used for several motor designs is called PipeMax.

For a typical 500-inch Mopar with Max-Wedge-size ports, we would expect about 700 hp at 6,500 rpm. For this combination, PipeMax tells us that the perfect header will have 2-inch-diameter tubes that are 32 inches long, and a 3.50-inch collector that is 13 inches long. If we have a 540-ci motor making 900 hp and heads that flow 400 cfm at .800 lift, then PipeMax tells us that we want 2.25-diameter main tubes that are 30 inches long with a 4-inch collector that is 12 inches long.

With those two data points, you can start to see the trend and maybe start to correctly guess what headers will work for them. In a very general sense, if you're building an engine with standard port heads, then the common 1⅞-diameter headers should work fine. If you're building an engine with the larger MaxWedge port sizes, then it is probably wise to step up to the larger 2-inch-diameter headers. If you're going all out and expect to be making more than 800 hp, then there is a good chance that you'll need 2.125- or even 2.250-diameter headers and they might need to be custom-built to get the correct tube length and collector size.

Relocated Exhaust Ports

Be aware of the potential effect of using an aftermarket head with a raised exhaust port on the fitment of the exhaust headers. Many of the aftermarket heads have moved the exhaust ports up and out in order to improve the exhaust flow. The Indy heads such as the SR and 440-1 have the exhaust ports moved up about 3/4 inch. The Edelbrock Victor heads have relocated exhaust ports as do the Brodix B1-BS heads.

In some cases, the raised port heads when used on a low-deck block provide the same basic port location as an RB motor with standard heads. In these cases you get lucky because standard RB headers should fit. But the use of raised port heads on an RB block means the exhaust ports have now been moved significantly up in the car and this combination can cause significant issues in getting parts to fit. There are a few header vendors who have released designs that match the raised port heads so if you're working with a popular combination, then there might be an option for you. This is certainly an area to research before your final decision on cylinder heads is made or else you might end up having to pay for expensive custom headers.

When putting a big-block into an A body car, the headers situation gets even more difficult. There are a number of alternatives for big-block A-body headers, but there might not be a set that fits your exact needs. If you need large tube headers to fit a raised port head in an A body you might very well need to dig deep and

EXHAUST SYSTEMS

buy some custom headers. Another option is a fenderwell-type header where the tubes exit the engine compartment by going into the fenderwell area. These types of headers eliminate space issues in the engine compartment, but the problem will just move further downstream. Some fenderwell designs limit the tire size that can be mounted on the front wheels and/or they limit the turning radius of the vehicle.

Many of the larger headers require the use of the late-model "mini-starter" in order to clear. The mini-starter is a good idea for any performance engine anyway because they are much lighter and they tend to work better with high-compression motors. You will also find that many of the large tube headers will not fit a scattershield without some modifications. There can also be a problem when using the larger diameter 143-tooth flywheel with large tube headers, so that is yet another issue to research before making a purchase decision.

The header collector length is somewhat like the situation discussed earlier about intake manifold heights. For reasons of economy and easy fitment, the collector length on most exhaust headers is usually shorter than it should be for maximum torque production. Shorter headers are easier to manufacturer and install. However, most racers know that they need to experiment with the length of the collector if they want to maximize the power output. A little bit of playing around with PipeMax will quickly show that the optimum collector length is usually 12 to 18 inches long while the typical header available over the counter has collectors that are only a few inches long. Next time you visit an NHRA event take a quick stroll through the Stock Eliminator pits and look at the really

Because B1's exhaust ports are raised significantly from the stock location, many production headers will not fit properly. Fortunately, the aftermarket has stepped up with a selection of headers that will fit raised port heads.

long collectors hanging from the headers. Those Stock class racers know how to wring every last bit of power out of their combinations, which makes their cars a good place to look for tips and tricks.

Merged Collectors and 4-2-1 Headers

Racing engines designed to operate at higher engine speeds, such as those used in NASCAR racing or professional drag-racing classes such as Comp Eliminator, often use something other than a simple 4-into-1 collector. Both merge collectors and megaphone collectors have become popular with some builders while others use a 4-into-2-into-1 style of collector. If you're building a high-output motor that operates in a narrow power band, then you might want to explore using a different collector style. It is possible that the shape of the collector as well as the length and diameter of the collector can be used to extract a little more

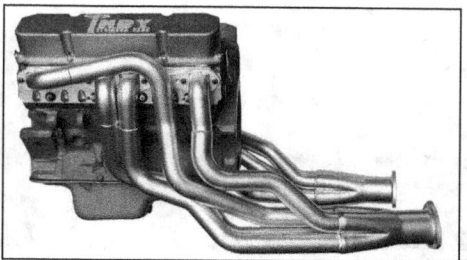

Higher-performance engines fitted with a stepped header, such as these from TTI, will provide more power. These headers are designed to fit RB blocks with raised exhaust ports. (Photo courtesy of Tube Technologies)

power from the engine. There are a few companies that make special collector designs and there are a number of vendors who specialize in custom-built racing headers.

Stepped Tubes

Stepped-tube headers are development for generating even more power. As the theory goes, the exhaust gases cool down and expand as they travel away from the exhaust port, so the size of the exhaust tube should also expand. The velocity of the gas stream is then kept constant, which helps to extract the exhaust from the engine. There are few stepped headers available off the shelf for production Mopar vehicles, but TTI does have a 2- to 2⅜-inch stepped-tube header for B and E body cars with Indy heads on an RB block. Hedman's Web site offers stepped headers as an option on some of their race headers so that might be another possibility. Stepped headers are readily available for roadsters or dragsters because those applications are more universal and much easier to fabricate for. If your performance big-block is going into a dragster, you'll have an easier time obtaining a set of stepped headers for it.

CHAPTER 16

TUNING

Experienced builders will pay close attention to what the motor is telling them while they are tuning. Fouled spark plugs or odd noises are obvious signs that something has gone wrong. If the valve lash is constantly opening up, the root problem should be investigated and solved rather than just continuing to re-set the lash. A burned spot on a spark plug will develop into a failure if it isn't solved. A minor coolant leak might be the first sign of a failed head gasket. Mechanical parts do not fix themselves; but rather small problems tend to turn into big problems. So the closer attention you pay to the operation of the engine, the better you'll be able to find and fix small problems before they develop into budget-busting, project-stalling, big problems.

Reading the Plugs

Reading the spark plugs is one traditional part of tuning up a performance engine. Since the spark plug is actually part of the combustion chamber it is a good window into the operation of the engine. Given a set of eight spark plugs, an experienced plug reader can tell quite quickly if the motor is running lean or rich and if the ignition timing is correct. Reading the plugs is quite valuable on the dyno or at the drag strip where you can shut down the engine after a run and look at plugs. If the engine is driven back to the pits, then the plug reading might not be accurate because the idle circuit of the carb could mask the wide-open-throttle operation. There are many Web sites that can do a good job of teaching you how to properly read spark plugs. Also the spark plug vendors often have plug reading tips in their catalogs or on their Web sites.

Reading the spark plugs is a good way to see what is happening in the engine but pulling the headers off sometimes provides more information. These exhaust ports all show a healthy light grey color after several 800-hp pulls on the dyno.

Wide Band

Given the recent advancements in wide band oxygen tuning equipment, no performance engine should be built without budgeting some money for this invaluable tuning tool. A wide band oxygen sensor located in the exhaust header provides the tuner with a real-time glimpse of the actual air/fuel (AF) ratio as the engine is running. When you have access to real-time AF ratio

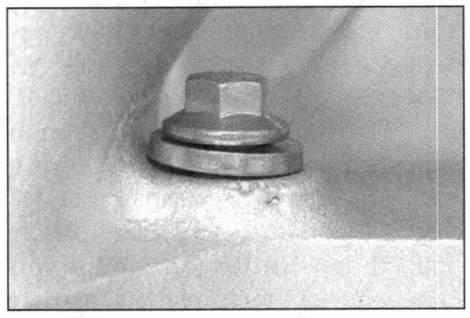

The runner material on this intake prevents the washer under the intake bolt from sitting flat on the manifold rail. A simple mistake like this can cause a vacuum leak, which could result in engine damage. A few moments with a die grinder will remove the interference and allow the intake bolt to be properly installed.

TUNING

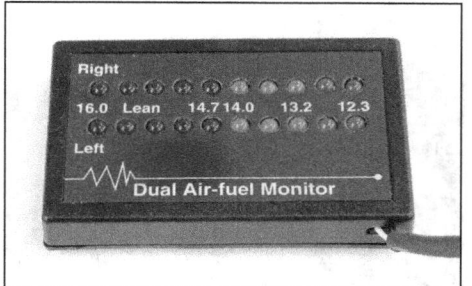

These older-style narrow-band O_2 sensor systems are only useful if your tune-up is nearly spot on.

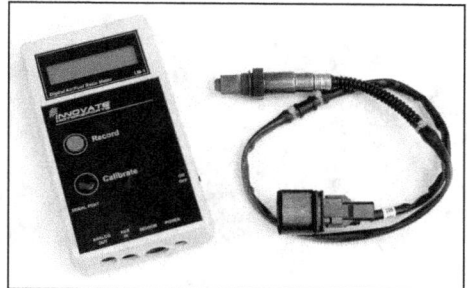

The LM-1 from Innovate Motorsports really set the performance world on its ear when it first came out. After gear heads got the chance to see how the AF ratio was responding during engine operation they were able to take carb tuning to a new level.

information, you can make much better decisions about necessary changes. The display on the wide band controller reacts to changes in the AF ratio quick enough to show you how the various circuits in the carburetor are operating. For example, it is possible to see transient effects from the accelerator pump on the wide band output, which is something that cannot be seen by reading the plugs.

Tuning with a wide band setup is much the same process as with other tools but it is much more precise. The rule is to always work from idle toward WOT. With the engine warmed up and at idle speed, the AF ratio is noted on the wide band controller. The idle mixture screws are adjusted to get an AF ratio of 14:1 or so. If the idle mixture screws cannot obtain this ratio, then the idle feed jets or restriction inside the carburetor need to be adjusted in size. Newer carbs, such as the Holley Ultra HP series, have jets in the idle feed circuit so it is a simple task to change the jet size in order to get the idle-mixture screws back into their proper range.

The main circuit can be calibrated either while driving or while on a chassis dyno. The main circuit is usually adjusted by changing the primary jet size or the metering rod on a Carter-type carburetor. The main circuit should be adjusted to an AF ratio between 13.5 and 14.5 because it typically operates during low power demands.

Monitoring the WOT calibration is difficult while driving the car so most wide band controllers have a data acquisition mode to capture this data. Another possibility is to do the WOT calibration on a chassis dyno because this will provide the operator with a safe environment for observing the instruments. Most gas engines should be tuned for an AF ratio of around 12.5 at full power. The power valve restriction channel is what controls the full power mixture on a Holley carb; while on a Carter-type carb, it would be a combination of the secondary jet size and the small step size on the primary metering rod.

The wide band can also be used to calibrate the transition modes of the carburetor. The main transition mode occurs at off idle, when the throttle blade is in the transition slot. The difficult part of the carb tuning is to keep the AF ratio constant as the metering switches from the idle circuit to the main circuit. This can require some modification to the carb because the size of the air bleeds and the length of the transition slot will control when the various circuits come into action. A wide band controller is about the only way to actually monitor the AF ratio during this time.

The volume and duration of the accelerator pump shot can also be monitored with the wide band system. If the AF ratio goes lean during acceleration, then most likely the accelerator pump needs more volume—if rich, then less volume is required. If the mixture goes rich, and then lean, before it comes back to normal, then the pump shot is probably happening too quickly. Either install a smaller nozzle size or a different shaped pump cam to solve the problem. With the fast reaction time of a wide band controller, you can actually start to see what is happening inside the engine. Knowledge is power, as the saying goes, so when you can see what is happening, you can then start to understand how to fix it.

Dynamometer Testing

The excellent book, *Dyno Testing and Tuning* by Harold Bettes and Bill Hancock, covers this topic in much

Vacuum Ports

Most high-performance carburetors do not come with a vacuum port on them so it can be difficult to monitor the manifold vacuum when tuning the power valve. To further complicate matters, most of the high-performance intake manifolds are also not drilled and tapped for a vacuum port. Drilling and tapping the intake manifold so that a vacuum gauge can be installed fixes this. A functioning vacuum gauge is required in order to monitor and tune the power-enrichment circuit in the carburetor.

Carb tuning is fairly simple on an engine dyno since there is plenty of room to work. Most dyno operators will want to use one of their own carbs for the initial startup since that will give them a known reference point to tune from.

This engine is mounted on a dolly and is ready to go to the dyno. An external oil filter has been mounted on the motor plate for quick inspection. Also notice the lift plate installed on the carb pad, the electric water pump and the vacuum gauge. These items are all pre-installed in order to reduce the time required to install the engine onto the dyno.

It is very important with a new engine to run the valves after the initial warm-up session on the dyno. Not only does the lash need to be double-checked, but this is a good time to perform the first inspection of the valvetrain.

greater detail than I have the room for here, but I do want to make a few important points.

I highly recommend having any new performance engine dyno tested, preferably by the same shop that does the machine work or the assembly of your new engine. There are many reasons to dyno test the engine before installing it in the car, but one compelling reason for doing it with the engine's machinist/assembler/builder is so that everyone witnesses the engine working (or not working) at the same time and sees the same thing. These maximum-performance engines are not cheap to build; with the mildest of the builds costing well over $10,000, the extra $500 or so for the dyno session is good insurance.

Most people consider dyno testing in terms of finding out how much power the engine produces and that is certainly one aspect of the test, but it is also a significant advantage to be able to break in a new engine within a controlled environment. It is much easier to work on the engine and to perform initial operations—lashing the valves, checking for leaks, running compression tests, etc.—with the engine on a dyno than when it is buried between the fenders in a car.

Dyno testing also provides a good opportunity to try some different items, such as headers and carbs, which the car owner might not have access to. Many dyno shops have "dyno queen" carburetors that are very well dialed in and provide excellent results. It can be very beneficial to run your engine with a known good carb before you try your own setup. Sometimes these back-to-back tests are very enlightening, especially for the people who don't have a lot of experience with testing various equipment and might not want to believe that their existing parts do not work as well as they thought.

Most dynamometers have more instrumentation than the average vehicle. This includes data such as: AF ratio, airflow consumed, EGT for all eight cylinders, oil pressure, water temp, oil temp, power output, torque curve, power curve, etc. Access to the

When performing intake manifold testing on the dyno it is a good idea to make sure the ports are aligned properly. Fortunately, on the larger single plane intake manifolds you can often see the port match by shining a light down the runners.

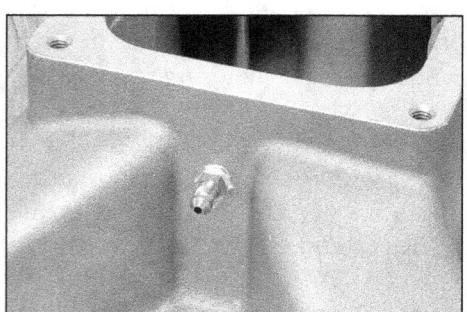

Aftermarket intakes typically do not have a manifold vacuum port so it is necessary to drill and tap for a line fitting. This M1 4500 intake was drilled and tapped for a small AN fitting so a hose could be run to a vacuum gauge during dyno testing.

TUNING

A session on the chassis dyno is a good idea for any performance vehicle. This lets you quickly compare engine performance to vehicle performance so you can isolate any drivetrain issues. The chassis dyno is also a good workout for the car's fuel and cooling systems.

torque and power curves helps tremendously when it comes time to select the proper torque converter, rear end gears, size of the carburetor, headers, etc. If the dyno shows that the engine is only consuming 700 cfm of airflow, this can help you buy a new carb. If the torque peak is at 4,500 rpm, you might want to reconsider those 4.56 gears. If the power peak is at 5,500 rpm, then maybe you don't need a 7,500-rpm shift point. With the dyno printout in your hand, it is easier to tell your buddy that you don't need to change the jets, timing, or whatever else someone wants you to do with your new motor. Remember, knowledge is power.

Chassis Dyno Testing

After the engine is installed in the vehicle, it makes sense to also visit a chassis dyno because the engine will behave differently when all the accessory drives are hooked up and the exhaust system is installed. A chassis dyno test is not as important as the initial engine dyno test, but it can still be a good investment. The chassis dyno session has the advantage of providing a controlled environment, rather than street traffic, in which to read the oil pressure and water temp gauges. Also most chassis dyno shops will have a highly experienced technician to help sort out any tuning issues. Sometimes an extra set of eyes can solve the little problems that often arise with new engine combinations. The less experienced the vehicle owner, the more I'd recommend putting at least one chassis dyno session into the budget.

One issue with chassis dyno testing is that automatic transmission cars, especially ones with high stall converters, tend to produce some odd results on the chassis dyno. Given that, a manual transmission car can get a much better reading on the torque curve of the engine. Also some chassis dyno systems will have a problem with HEI systems because these tend to cause problems with their signal pickups. Another problem you might have at a chassis dyno is installing the wide band sensors because most exhaust systems are not equipped with oxygen bungs.

My car has made numerous trips to the chassis dyno over the years. For a time I strapped the car to the

Loading up the trunk with spare parts is a good idea when visiting the chassis dyno. Remember what the Boy Scouts say and come prepared to test your combination.

chassis dyno every single weekend while doing some extensive cam testing. Through all those test sessions, I developed many tricks that really speeded up the process. These tricks included: built-in hold-downs on the frame of the car for the dyno straps, bungs in the exhaust system so the wide band sensors could be quickly installed and secured, and extra cooling fans for the radiator. I also took a very organized approach by keeping track of the results on spreadsheets, taking photos of each test, and showing up at the dyno facility with spark plugs, plug wires, and other spare parts in the trunk.

If you are operating within a tight budget, it might make more sense to purchase a wide band setup than to pay for a chassis dyno session. The wide band system will provide much of the same tuning information as a chassis dyno session, but it will take more time and probably a second pair of eyes in the passenger seat. A long uphill section of road can be used as a poor man's dyno because it will provide enough load to the engine to stress the carburetor and ignition systems. By watching the AF meter and the vacuum gauge, a passenger should be able to see when the power enrichment circuit begins to operate. If the load on the engine is great enough, then you might also be able to observe the transition from the idle circuit to the main circuit and then when the secondary circuit opens. There isn't any place on public roads where a performance big-block can be safely tested at WOT because that amount of power quickly generates speeds that are unsafe for everyone, but the transition circuit, accelerator pump, and main circuits of the carb can usually be observed while maintaining reasonable speeds.

CHAPTER 17

THE FANTASTIC 451 AND OTHER ENGINE COMBINATIONS

A 400 block with either a 3.750- or a 3.900-stroke crankshaft and a 4.375-bore size makes an excellent street/strip motor. The 3.750-stroke crankshaft makes a 451-ci motor while the slightly longer 3.90 stroke makes a 470-ci combination. With standard port heads, the torque peak will be around 4,200 rpm and the power peak should be around 5,500 rpm. Either the 451 or the 470 can be built to production car specifications and would be capable of long life in a daily driver vehicle. The 451 is nothing more than an overbored 440 in a lower-deck-height block, so it should be capable of lasting as long as any production-type motor when built with high-quality components.

Fantastic 451/470

The low-deck 451/470 is an excellent package that easily fits into most Mopar vehicles. The shorter-stroke crankshafts allow plenty of room for a longer connecting rod in the low-deck block. While a production 440 connecting rod could be used in a budget application, I highly recommend using an aftermarket crankshaft with 2.200 rod journals and a 6.535- or 6.700-long Chevy connecting rod. Pistons should be easy to find for this combination as many vendors offer pistons for the 451/470 combinations.

A cost-effective combination would use either the Performer RPM heads or the Mopar Performance P5153542 heads with the straight spark plugs. A flat-top piston will have compression right at 10:1 in a 451 and about 10.5:1 compression in the larger 470. These compression ratios are about perfect for a daily driver motor using pump gas with aluminum heads.

For street use, a Performer RPM intake manifold is an excellent choice, if it will fit under the hood. If not, then a stock replacement-type of dual plane can be used although it will give up some power when compared to the taller-RPM intake. A low-profile single plane intake such as the Holley Street Dominator can also be used on the 451/470 although it will give up a little low-end torque.

For street/strip-type of use, the 451/470 can be outfitted with higher compression and a high-rise single plane intake such as the Victor 383. A big solid flat-tappet cam or a solid roller cam can be used to make more power, but the use of the standard port heads will limit the power range to 7,000 rpm so there is no reason to go crazy with the cam or the valvetrain.

Any of the low-deck motors can be built with the larger Max-Wedge ports but there are limited intake manifolds for this combination. A 451- or 470-inch short-block with the Max-Wedge heads and the Indy 400-2 intake manifold will make an excellent bracket-race-type of motor. The torque peak will be about 5,000 rpm and the power peak will be around 6,500 rpm. With the higher speed and higher power output that comes with the larger port heads, the short-block should be assembled with a higher-quality level of parts. The early production 400 blocks are strong enough to handle the anticipated 650 to 700 hp that one of these motors will produce, but you will want to keep an eye on the main caps because they might start to walk at these power levels.

THE FANTASTIC 451 AND OTHER ENGINE COMBINATIONS

Two Ways to 512

A 512-inch motor is built by combining a 4.375 bore with a 4.250-stroke crankshaft. The 512 can be built with either a production 400 or 440 block because either will accept the 4.375-bore size and the 4.250-stroke crank. An aftermarket block can also be used if the anticipated power output is going to be more than 700 hp but it isn't required for the more modest builds. There is usually room in the crankcase of a 512 for the stock oil pickup.

The 4.250-stroke crankshaft will typically use the more popular 2.200 rod journals to reduce size, weight, and cost of the rotating assembly. The 4.250-stroke crankshaft will easily fit into the 440 block but will require a little grinding to fit into the tighter confines of the 400 block. The 4.250-stroke crankshaft eats up a bunch of room in the low-deck block so a shorter rod length of 6.535 usually works best. For the taller 440 block, a 6.800- or 7.100-inch long rod can be used without any issues. A flat-top piston in a 512 motor will exceed 11:1 compression with standard 84-cc heads so you might want dish pistons to run pump gas. The 512 is great for race motors because a flat-top piston will make about 12.5:1 compression when combined with the smaller 75-cc combustion chambers that most of the Max-Wedge heads have.

The 512 can be built as a torque monster with standard port heads, or as a higher-RPM racing motor with the Max-Wedge heads. In pump-gas form, the 512 will easily make 600 ft-lbs of torque and 600 hp when using a small street roller-type camshaft and a 850 or 950 carb. For racing, the 512 will come alive when fitted with the larger Max-Wedge heads and this combination will quickly make more than 700 hp with only a big flat-tappet cam and a Dominator carb. If you are going to use large port heads and a roller cam on a 512 motor then you'll want to invest in an aftermarket block because you'll quickly find the limits of a stock casting.

The low-deck 512 has been a very popular combination for many years with the B1 heads. The B1 head package was designed before aftermarket blocks were available so it was designed around the stronger 400 block. The low-deck 512 with B1 heads is capable of making 800 to 900 hp so production blocks need to be modified with aluminum main caps and the water jackets filled with grout. Typically this combination will use the B1 intake manifold with a Dominator carb, a large solid-roller cam, and a fully modified oiling system.

Big Bad 572

The 572 is built by combining a 4.50 cylinder bore with a 4.50-inch-stroke crankshaft. The only way to build a 572 is to start with an aftermarket cylinder block because none of the production blocks are going to allow that size of cylinder bore. There are plenty of choices for the cylinder block including the World Products blocks from Mopar Performance, the KP block, the Indy block, or the Keith Black. The less-expensive street blocks will work very well, as will the more expensive aluminum versions. The 572 can be built from mild to wild depending on the cylinder heads, compression, and camshaft.

The only reason to use a standard-sized cylinder head on a 572 would be if you were building a motor for a tow truck or a tug boat. The Max-Wedge port is going to be the absolute minimum port size for any performance application. With a Max-Wedge, that port size, the torque peak for a 572 motor will be down around 4,500 rpm with a power peak around 6,000 rpm. That doesn't sound like a lot of RPM but with a 4.50-inch stroke the piston speed is 4,500 ft/min at 6,000 rpm and that is approaching the limit for a good-quality rotating assembly.

A pump-gas 572 with Max-Wedge heads, street-roller camshaft, and a Dominator carb would make a very powerful street engine. This combination can be built on a moderate budget if you maintained a strict 6,500-rpm redline. At that redline, you would be able to run one of the budget rotating assemblies in the lower-priced cast-iron aftermarket blocks. If the heads and cam are not too large, this combination would make huge torque down low and would carry it high enough to make 750 to 800 hp up top.

If you have the budget to purchase premium components, then the 572 can certainly use even larger cylinder heads to make even more power. The B1 heads in either original, moved centerline, or PSO versions would work great with the big bore size of this motor. You would need to build the rotating assembly with high-quality parts to withstand the higher piston speed. A motor like this would be capable of making more than 1,000 hp when outfitted with a big roller cam, tunnel ram, and twin Dominator carbs.

With the 4.50-inch stroke, the 572 will most likely require external oil pickups and lines. But with the power capability of a 572 engine combination on hand, you would typically be investing in a premium oiling system that already included a deep oil pan and a high-volume oil pump.

CHAPTER 18

RECIPES FOR POWER

When it comes to building a max-performance Mopar wedge big-block, there's a huge range of equipment and preparation options. The equipment and the engine building procedures are largely determined by the horsepower goals. This chapter provides insight, advice, and prime examples of Mopar big-block engine builds for the 600-, 700-, 800-, and 900-hp output levels.

600 HP

The 600-hp level can be reached the old way with ported cast-iron heads on a stock-stroke 440 block, but it is cheaper and easier these days to use aftermarket heads. At this power level there is no need to use Max-Wedge-sized ports because most any big-block can hit the 600-hp level with well-prepared, standard-port heads. Of course, if there is some money in the budget for a stroker kit, then the odds of hitting the power goal will be increased. At the 600-hp level there is no need to use an aftermarket block. Either the 400 or the 440 block can be used and almost any stroke crankshaft will be able to reach the 600-hp level. The smaller the motor the more highly strung it will need to be to reach 600 hp, while the larger stroker motors can hit this performance mark with ease.

A stock-stroke 400 motor is probably the smallest displacement that would be reasonable to use for a 600-hp build, although if someone was really determined they could use a 383. The 400 can hit the 600-hp mark when fitted with ported standard-size heads, high compression, and a roller camshaft. Since 400 ci is a fairly small displacement, the engine will need to spin up to higher speeds than a larger motor.

Hitting 600 hp with a 400-inch motor will require a solid-roller camshaft with at least 255 degrees of duration at .050 lift. This much duration in a 400 will result in a fairly racy motor with low idle vacuum. This combination will work great in an A body drag car with a high stall converter, but it would be a little hard to live with on the street in a heavier vehicle. A 440-based engine has an easier time to reach 600 hp because the motor will not have to spin as hard. For bracket racing, the old combination of high compression and a big flat-tappet cam is hard to beat. For a street-driven engine with 600 hp the best way to go would be to add some more stroke to the engine. Here are a couple of combinations:

Bracket Racer 451
- 400 or 440 block bored to 4.350 or 4.375
- 3.750-stroke crankshaft
- Stock rods or H beam replacements
- Performer RPM or Mopar P5153542 heads
- 12.5 compression pistons
- Mopar Performance .590 or .620 camshaft
- Victor 440 intake manifold
- Holley 850 double pumper
- 2-inch headers

Pump-Gas Street Driver
- 440 block bored to 4.350 or 4.375
- 4.250-stroke crankshaft
- 6.800 Chevy rods
- 10:1 compression dished pistons
- Performer RPM or Mopar P5153542 heads, CNC ported
- Hyd roller camshaft, 240 duration at .050, .600 lift
- Performer RPM intake
- Holley 950 HP carb
- 2-inch headers

700 HP

Building a 700-hp big-block Mopar takes a little more money and care than a 600-hp motor, but it is still very easy to accomplish these days with the parts that are available. The 700-hp level can be accomplished with standard port heads but it is quite a bit easier to reach the goal with the larger Max-Wedge heads. At the 700-hp level an aftermarket block

RECIPES FOR POWER

is not a requirement but the stock block will be near its limit, so keep an eye on the main caps.

Bracket Racer 512
- 400 or 440 block with 4.375 bore size
- 4.250-stroke crankshaft
- Aftermarket connecting rods
- 13:1 compression
- Head flow of 350 cfm, Indy EZ cylinder heads or Edelbrock Victors
- Large single plane intake
- 1050 Dominator carb
- Large flat-tappet cam such as Comp MM305S-10
- Optional, solid roller camshaft

800 HP

The 800-hp level can be achieved with a 500-ci short-block and a good pair of cylinder heads with Max-Wedge-sized ports. Depending on the cylinder heads, the valve lift will most likely need to be greater than .750 inch in order to generate the amount of air flow needed to produce 800 hp. At higher valve lifts like this, it is almost mandatory to use a roller camshaft and high-quality rocker arms. It is certainly possible to reach this power level with standard shaft-mounted rocker arms, but this power level is at the point where you would want to seriously consider switching over to a multiple shaft system such as Jesel or T&D.

At the 800-hp level, I highly recommend you use an aftermarket cylinder block, such as the KP unit or the World Products block. A production block can be used and will work for some time, especially if it is filled or has a girdle. But as we've discussed elsewhere, the cost of fixing up a production block can be close to the purchase price of an aftermarket block so you should weigh these options before proceeding.

To make 800 hp with a 500-inch short-block, the heads will need to flow at least 350 cfm with more flow being better. Any of the large port heads on the market should be able to support this type of power production including the Indy EZ, SR, and 440-1 heads as well as the Edelbrock Victor head.

Bracket Racer 512
- Aftermarket block with minimum 4.375 bore size
- Good quality crankshaft with 4.250 stroke
- High-quality steel connecting rods, 6.800 or 7.100 long, AL rods an option
- 13:1 compression minimum
- Cylinder head flow of 375 cfm, Indy SR or 440-1, Edelbrock Victors
- Roller cam with .750 lift minimum
- Good oiling system, large sump pan, dual external lines

900 HP

At this power level, you need to start with an aftermarket block and select high-quality or premium-quality components. In order to produce 900 hp, the cylinder heads need to flow at least 400 cfm on the intake ports. The most inexpensive way to make power is to increase the displacement of the short-block up to the limit of the available parts. At this time, the largest short-block that can be built using common components would be a 4.500 by 4.500 arrangement, which produces 572 ci. Any of the aftermarket blocks accept a 4.500-bore size and any of the RB- based blocks should be able to accept a 4.500-inch-stroke crankshaft with only minor clearancing. The combination of a 4.500-stroke crankshaft and 7.100-long connecting rods still leaves 1.375 for the piston height, which is plenty of room for a standard ring package.

The key to making 900 hp in a big-block Mopar is the cylinder heads. The Max-Wedge size is the minimum port size for this power level, with the really big ports also starting to come into play. Cylinder head choices at this level would be the Indy 572-13, B1 original, B1 MC, or the B1 PSO. Most likely, this amount of airflow requires valve lift of at least .800 inch, and this mandates premium valvetrain components and a solid roller cam.

At the 900-hp level the various tricks that were ignored at lower power levels start to come into play. You would seriously consider components such as gas ported pistons, low-tension oil rings, and a dry sump oiling system. These items would not be mandatory at 900 hp but they might be good long-term investments and provide the base for even higher power output in the future.

Bracket Racer 572
- Aftermarket block, 4.500 bore size
- 4.500-stroke crankshaft, premium quality required
- High quality connecting rods, Steel or AL, 6.80 or 7.10 long
- 15:1 compression pistons, gas ports optional
- B1 MC, B1 PSO, Indy 572-13 Cylinder heads
- Multiple shaft rocker arms with 1:70 ratio, Jesel or T&D
- Roller cam with .850 or higher lift, 280 duration at .050
- Large intake such as Indy 440-3X, tunnel ram an option
- Holley Dominator carb
- 2.125- or 2.250-diameter headers
- Excellent oiling system with external pickups, deep sump, and remote filters
- Dry sump oiling system is a recommended option

ENGINE BUILD SHEETS

Engine Blueprint Record
Engine Type	
Build Date	
Displacement	
Special Notes:	

Block
Material	
Manuf./PN	
Bore Size	
Cam Location	
Main Bearing Dia.	
Special Mods:	

Piston Diameter and Bore Clearance
Cylinder #	1	3	5	7
Bore Dia.				
Piston Dia.				
Clearance				

Cylinder #	2	4	6	8
Bore Dia.				
Piston Dia.				
Clearance				
Width				

Piston
Piston Brand/PN	
Compression Height	
Wrist Pin Brand/PN	
Wrist Pin Dia./Length	
Wrist Pin Clearance	
Wrist Pin Retainer	

Piston Ring
Ring Brand/PN	
Top Ring Type	
Width	
Side Clearance	
End Gap	
2nd Ring Type	
Width	
Side Clearance	
End Gap	
Oil Ring Type	
Side Clearance	
Gap	

Piston Deck Height
Cylinder #	1	3	5	7
Deck Height				

Cylinder #	2	4	6	8
Deck Height				

Notes

ENGINE BUILD SHEETS

Rod and Main Bearings

Main Bearing Brand/PN	
Rod Bearing Brand/PN	
Camshaft Bearing Brand/PN	

Crankshaft

Crankshaft Brand/PN					
Stroke					
End Play					
Main	1	2	3	4	5
Main Bore					
Main Bore w/bearing					
Crank Main Journal					
Main Bearing Clearance					

Conn. Rod	1	3	5	7
Big End Dia.				
Big End Dia. w/bearing				
Crank Journal Dia.				
Rod Bearing Clearance				

Conn. Rod	2	4	6	8
Big End Dia.				
Big End Dia. w/bearing				
Crank Journal Dia.				
Rod Bearing Clearance				

Connecting Rods

Rod Brand/PN				
Length (Center to Center)				
Side Clearance	1-2	3-4	5-6	7-8
Wrist Pin/Piston Clearance				
Wrist Pin/Rod Clearance				
Rod Bolt Brand/PN				
Rod Bolt Torque				
Rod Bolt Stretch				

Valvetrain Data

Rocker Arms:	
Make	
PN	
Material	
Offset	
Rocker Arm Ratio:	
Intake	
Exhaust	
Intake Valve Lift	
Exhaust Valve Lift	
Pushrod:	
Length	
Diameter	
Wall Thickness	
Lifter:	
Make/PN	
Diameter	
Offset	
Rev Kit Make	
PN	

Crankshaft

Make of Style/Brand	
Cam PN	
Material	
Intake Duration @.050"	
Exhaust Duration @.050"	
Intake Installed at Centerline	
Lobe Separation Angle	
Intake Lobe Lift	
Exhaust Lobe Lift	
Intake Valve-to-Piston Clearance @ 10° ATDC	
Exhaust Valve-to-Piston Clearance @ 10° BTDC	
Intake Valve Lash	
Exhaust Valve Lash	

HOW TO BUILD MAX-PERFORMANCE MOPAR BIG-BLOCKS

ENGINE BUILD SHEETS

Cylinder Head

Brand/PN	
Chamber Volume	
Intake Port Volume (cc)	
Intake Valve Type/PN	
Intake Valve Size	
Exhaust Valve Type/PN	
Exhaust Valve Size	
Valvespring Brand/PN	
Valvespring	
Inside Diameter	
Outside Diameter	
Installed Height	
Intake/Exhaust	
Valvespring Seat Pressure	
Valvespring Open Pressure	
Coil Bind Height	
Retainer Make/PN	
Keeper Make/PN	
Head Gasket Thickness	

Engine Balancing

Piston Weight (grams)	
Wrist Pin	
Pin Locks	
Ring Set (1 Piston)	
Rod, Small End	
Total Reciprocating Weight	
Rod, Big End	
Rod Bearing (1 Pair)	
Oil	
Total Rotating Weight	
Balance Percent* 0.50 for V-8 90-degree	
Bob Weight = 2 x (Reciprocating Wt. x .50 + Rotating Weight)	

Cylinder Head Flow

Modifications	
Flow Bench	
Test Pressure	
Bore Fixture Dia.	
Intake Valve Dia.	
Exhaust Valve Dia.	

Intake Flow

Lift	CFM
.100	
.200	
.300	
.400	
.500	
.600	
.700	

Exhaust Flow

Lift	CFM	Exh. to Int. %
.100		
.200		
.300		
.400		
.500		
.600		
.700		

Compression Ratio

Swept Volume*	
Dome (-) or Dish (+) Volume	
Ring Land Volume	
Deck Volume	
Head Gasket Volume	
Chamber Volume	
Total Volume	

$$CR = \frac{\text{Total Volume}}{\text{Total} - \text{Swept Volume}}$$

CR = _____ : 1

*Swept Volume (cc) = Bore² x Stroke x 12.87

Source Guide

440 Source
Lancaster, CA 93534
661/951-3700
www.440source.com

Aeroquip Performance Products
800/386-1911
www.aeroquip.com

AR Engineering
Wilsonville, OR 97070
www.ARengineering.com

ARP Inc.
Ventura, CA 93003
800/826-3045
www.arp-bolts.com

Best Machine Racing Engines
Warren, MI 48091
586/759-2673
www.bestmachineracing.com

Brodix, Inc.
Mena, AR 71953
479/394-1075
www.brodix.com

Callies Performance Products
Fostoria, OH 44830
419/435-2711
www.callies.com

Charlie's Oil Pans
Norton, OH 44203
330/825-3586

Cometic Gaskets
Concord, OH 44077
800/752-9850
www.cometic.com

Comp Cams
Memphis, TN 38118
800/999-0853
www.compcams.com

Crane Cams
Daytona Beach, FL 32114
386/252-1151
www.cranecams.com

Crower Cams & Equipment
San Diego, CA 92154
619/661-6477
www.crower.com

Demon Carburetion/Barry Grant
Dahlonega, GA 30533
706/864-8544
www.barrygrant.com

Diamond Racing Products
Clinton Twp, MI 48035
877/552-2112
www.diamondracing.net

Edelbrock Corp
Torrance, CA 90503
310/781-2222
www.edelbrock.com

Fluidampr
Springville, NY 14141
716/592-1000
www.fluidampr.com

Harland Sharp
Strongsville, OH 44149
440/238-3260
www.harlandsharp.com

Holley Performance Products
Bowling Green, KY 42102
270/782-2900
www.holley.com

Hughes Engines
Washington, IL 61571
309/745-9558
www.hughesengines.com

Indy Cylinder Heads
Indianapolis, IN 46239
317/862-3724
www.indyheads.com

Isky Racing Cams
Gardena, CA 90247
323/770-0930
www.iskycams.com

SOURCE GUIDE

Jones Cam Designs
Denver, NC 28037
704/489-2449
www.jonescams.com

Jesel Inc.
Lakewood, NJ 08701
732/901-1800
www.jesel.com

Keith Black Racing Engines
South Gate, CA 90280
562/869-1518
www.keithblack.com

Koffel's Place
Huron, OH 44839
419/433-4410
www.b1heads.com

Mancini Racing
Clinton Twp, MI 48035
586/790-4100
www.manciniracing.com

Manley Performance
Lakewood, NJ 08701
732/905-3366
www.manleyperformance.com

Meziere Enterprises
Escondido, CA 92029
800/208-1755
www.meziere.com

Milodon, Inc.
Chatsworth, CA 91311
818/407-1211
www.milodon.com

Modern Cylinder Head
Clinton Twp, MI 48036
586/468-7914
www.moderncylinderhead.com

Mopar Performance
888/528-HEMI
www.mopar.com

Moroso Performance Products
Gulford, CT 06437
203/453-6571
www.moroso.com

Muscle Motors
Lansing, MI 48906
888/482-4900
www.musclemotorsracing.com

Ohio Crankshaft
Greenville, OH 45331
800/333-7133
www.ohiocrank.com

Oil Filter Service Co.
Portland, OR 97214
888/232-5126
www.oilfilterserviceco.com

Oliver Racing Parts
Grand Rapids, MI 49503
800/253-8108
www.oliver-rods.com

Peterson Fluid Systems
Henderson, CO 80640
800/926-7867
www.petersonfluidsys.com

Porter Racing Heads
S. Burlington, VT 05403
802/951-1955

Pro-Gram Engineering Corp.
Barberton, OH 44203
330/745-1004
www.pro-gram.com

Rocker Arm Specialist
Anderson, CA 96007
530/378-1075
www.rockerarms.com

Ross Racing Pistons
El Segundo, CA 90245
310/536-0100
www.rosspistons.com

SCAT Enterprises, Inc.
Redondo Beach, CA 90278
310/370-5501
www.scatcrankshafts.com

Smith Bros Pushrods
Bend, OR 97701
800/367-1533
www.pushrods.net

T&D Machine Products
Carson City, NV 89706
775/884-2292
www.TDmach.com

Trend Performance, Inc.
Warren, MI 48089
586/447-0400
www.trendperform.com

MORE GREAT TITLES AVAILABLE FROM CARTECH®

CHEVROLET

- How To Rebuild the Small-Block Chevrolet* *(SA26)*
- Chevrolet Big Block Parts Interchange Manual *(SA31P)*
- Chevy TPI Fuel Injection Swapper's Guide *(SA53P)*
- Chevrolet Small-Block Parts Interchange Manual *(SA55)*
- How To Build Max-Performance Chevy Small-Blocks on a Budget *(SA57)*
- How To Build Big-Inch Chevy Small-Blocks *(SA87)*
- How to Build High-Performance Chevy Small-Block Cams/Valvetrains *(SA105P)*
- Rebuilding the Small-Block Chevy: Step-by-Step Videobook *(SA116)*
- How to Build Small-Block Chevy Circle-Track Racing Engines *(SA121P)*
- High-Performance Chevy Small-Block Cylinder Heads *(SA125P)*
- How to Rebuild the Big-Block Chevrolet* *(SA142P)*
- How to Restore Your Camaro 1967–1969 *(SA178)*
- How to Build Killer Big-Block Chevy Engines *(SA190)*
- How to Build Max-Performance Chevy Big-Block on a Budget *(SA198)*
- How to Build Max-Performance Chevy LT1/LT4 Engines *(SA206)*
- How to Rebuild & Modify Chevy 348/409 Engines *(SA210)*
- How to Restore Your Corvette 1963–1967 *(SA223)*
- Chevelle Performance Projects: 1964–1972 *(SA226)*

FORD

- High-Performance Ford Engine Parts Interchange *(SA56)*
- How To Build Max-Performance Ford V-8s on a Budget *(SA69P)*
- Building High-Performance Fox-Body Mustangs on a Budget *(SA75P)*
- How To Build Max-Performance 4.6-Liter Ford Engines *(SA82P)*
- How To Build Big-Inch Ford Small-Blocks *(SA85P)*
- How to Build Ford RestoMod Street Machines *(SA101P)*
- How to Rebuild the Small-Block Ford* *(SA102)*
- How to Rebuild 4.6/5.4-Liter Ford Engines* *(SA155P)*
- How to Rebuild Big-Block Ford Engines* *(SA162P)*
- How to Restore Your Mustang 1964 1/2–1973 *(SA165)*
- How to Build Max-Performance Ford FE Engines *(SA183)*
- How to Rebuild Ford Power Stroke Diesel *(SA213)*
- How to Build Cobra Kit Cars + Buying Used *(SA202)*
- How to Rebuild & Modify Ford C4 & C6 Automatic Transmissions *(SA227)*

GENERAL MOTORS

- How to Build GM Pro-Touring Street Machines *(SA81P)*
- How To Build High-Performance Chevy LS1/LS6 Engines *(SA86)*
- GM Automatic Overdrive Transmission Builder's and Swapper's Guide *(SA140)*
- How to Rebuild GM LS-Series Engines* *(SA147)*
- How to Swap GM LS-Series Engines Into Almost Anything *(SA156)*
- How to Supercharge & Turbocharge GM LS-Series Engines *(SA180)*
- How to Rebuild & Modify GM Turbo 400 Transmissions* *(SA186)*
- How to Build Big-Inch GM LS-Series Engines *(SA203)*
- How to Restore Your Pontiac GTO 1964–1974 *(SA218)*
- High-Performance GM LS-Series Cylinder Head Guide *(SA231)*

MOPAR

- How to Build Big-Inch Mopar Small-Blocks *(SA104P)*
- How to Rebuild the Small-Block Mopar* *(SA143P)*
- How to Build Max-Performance Hemi Engines *(SA164P)*
- How to Build Max-Performance Mopar Big-Blocks *(SA171P)*
- Mopar B-Body Performance Upgrades 1962–1979 *(SA191)*
- How to Rebuild the Big-Block Mopar* *(SA197)*

OLDSMOBILE/ PONTIAC/ BUICK

- How to Build Max-Performance Buick Engines *(SA146P)*
- How to Build Max-Performance Oldsmobile V-8s *(SA172P)*
- How to Rebuild Pontiac V-8s* *(SA200)*
- How to Build Max-Performance Pontiac V-8s *(SA233)*

ENGINE

- Engine Blueprinting *(SA21)*
- Automotive Diagnostic Systems: Understanding OBD-I & OBD II *(SA174)*
- Competition Engine Building *(SA214)*

Workbench® Series books feature step-by-step instruction with hundreds of color photos for stock rebuilds and automotive repair.

SPORT COMPACTS

- High-Performance Honda Builder's Handbook Volume 1 *(SA49P)*
- Honda Engine Swaps *(SA93P)*
- High-Performance Dodge Neon Builder's Handbook *(SA100P)*
- High-Performance Subaru Builder's Guide *(SA141)*
- How to Build Max-Performance Mitsubishi 4G63t Engines *(SA148P)*
- How to Rebuild Honda B-Series Engines* *(SA154)*
- The New Mini Performance Handbook *(SA182P)*

INDUCTION & IGNITION

- Super Tuning & Modifying Holley Carburetors *(SA08)*
- Street Supercharging, A Complete Guide to *(SA17)*
- Demon Carburetion *(SA68P)*
- How To Build High-Performance Ignition Systems *(SA79P)*
- How to Build and Modify Rochester Quadrajet Carburetors *(SA113)*
- Turbo: Real World High-Performance Turbocharger Systems *(SA123)*
- How to Rebuild & Modify Carter/Edelbrock Carbs *(SA130P)*
- Engine Management: Advanced Tuning *(SA135)*
- Designing & Tuning High-Performance Fuel Injection Systems *(SA161)*

DRIVING

- How to Drag Race *(SA136P)*
- How to Hook and Launch *(SA195)*

HIGH-PERFORMANCE & RESTORATION HOW-TO

- David Vizard's How to Build Horsepower *(SA24)*
- How to Rebuild & Modify High-Performance Manual Transmissions* *(SA103)*
- High-Performance Jeep Cherokee XJ Builder's Guide 1984–2001 *(SA109P)*
- How to Paint Your Car on a Budget *(SA117)*
- High-Performance Jeep Wrangler TJ Builder's Guide: 1997–2006 *(SA120P)*
- High-Performance Brake Systems *(SA126P)*
- High-Performance Diesel Builder's Guide *(SA129P)*
- 4x4 Suspension Handbook *(SA137P)*
- Dyno Testing & Tuning *(SA138P)*
- How to Rebuild Any Automotive Engine *(SA151P)*
- Automotive Welding: A Practical Guide* *(SA159)*
- Automotive Wiring and Electrical Systems* *(SA160)*
- Automotive Bodywork & Rust Repair* *(SA166)*
- Muscle Car Interior Restoration Guide *(SA167P)*
- High-Performance Differentials, Axles, & Drivelines *(SA170)*
- How to Make Your Muscle Car Handle *(SA175)*
- Builder's Guide to Hot Rod Chassis & Suspension *(SA185)*
- How to Build Altered Wheelbase Cars *(SA189P)*
- How to Build Period Correct Hot Rods *(SA192)*
- How To Install and Tune Nitrous Oxide Systems *(SA194)*
- Automotive Sheet Metal Forming & Fabrication *(SA196)*
- Performance Automotive Engine Math *(SA204)*
- How to Design, Build & Equip Your Automotive Workshop on a Budget *(SA207)*
- Automotive Electrical Performance Projects *(SA209)*
- How to Port & Flow Test Cylinder Heads *(SA215)*
- Advanced Automotive Welding *(SA235)*
- How to Fabricate Automotive Fiberglass & Carbon Fiber Parts *(SA236)*

HISTORIES & PERSONALITIES

- Yenko *(CT485)*
- Rat Rods: Rodding's Imperfect Stepchildren *(CT486)*
- Lost Hot Rods *(CT487)*
- Lost Hot Rods II *(CT506)*
- Grumpy's Toys *(CT489)*
- Hurst Equipped: More Than 50 Years of High-Performance *(CT490)*
- America's Coolest Station Wagons *(CT493)*
- Super Stock — A paperback version of a classic best seller. *(CT495)*
- Rusty Pickups: American Workhorses Put to Pasture *(CT496)*
- Jerry Heasley's Rare Finds — Great collection of Heasley's best finds. *(CT497)*
- Street Sleepers: The Art of the Deceptively Fast Car *(CT498)*
- East vs. West Showdown: Rods, Customs and Rails *(CT501)*
- Junior Stock: Stock Class Drag Racing 1964–1971 *(CT505)*
- Definitive Shelby Mustang Guide 1965–1970, The *(CT507)*
- Jerry Heasley's Rare Finds: Mustangs & Fords *(CT509)*

---

*Visit us online at **www.cartechbooks.com** for more info!*

CarTech®, Inc. 39966 Grand Ave., North Branch, MN 55056

Ph: 800-551-4754 or 651-277-1200 • Fax: 651-277-1203

More Information for Your Project ...

HOW TO BUILD BIG-INCH MOPAR SMALL BLOCKS The small-block Mopar is one of the easiest engines in which to increase displacement without extensive modifications or specialized machine work – the engine was practically designed for more cubes! This book shows you how to get that big-cube power, and then it shows you how to optimize the small-block's other systems – induction, heads, valvetrain, ignition, exhaust, and more – to make the most of the extra cubic inches. Author Jim Szilagyi is a Performance Specialist for Dodge Motorsports and Mopar Performance Parts. In this book he covers building big-inchers from Mopar 318/340/360 - ci LA or Magnum 5.2-/5.9-liter engines, using both factory and aftermarket parts. Softbound, 8-1/2 x 11 inches, 144 pages, 350 B&W photos. ***Item #SA104P***

SUPER TUNING AND MODIFYING HOLLEY CARBURETORS by David Emanuel. This book covers the super tuning and modifying of Holley carburetors for performance, street, and off-road applications. Shows how to select, install, tune, and modify all popular Holley performance four-barrel models including the 4150/4160, 4165/4175, 4500, and 4360, as well as the 2300 two-barrel. Softbound, 8-1/2 x 11 inches, 144 pages, over 300 B&W photos. ***Item #SA08***

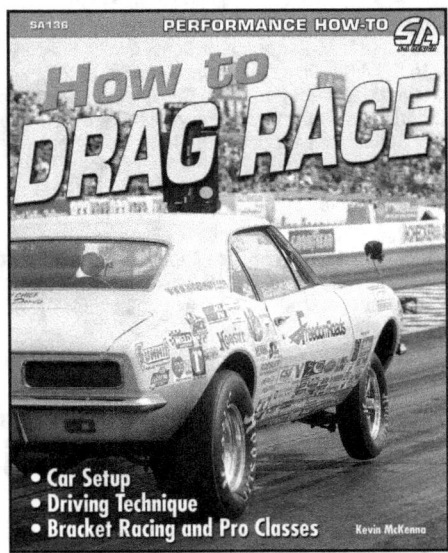

HOW TO DRAG RACE Author Kevin McKenna, senior editor at *National DRAGSTER*, NHRA's weekly news magazine, uses 300 color photos to show you what to expect your first time out, how to set your street car or race car up for consistency and speed, and driving techniques for racers at all levels. He discusses tires, safety equipment, driving aids, such as line-locks and delay boxes, choosing a class, and advanced racer math. Softbound, 8-1/2 x 11 inches, 144 pages, approx. 300 B&W photos. ***Item #SA136P***

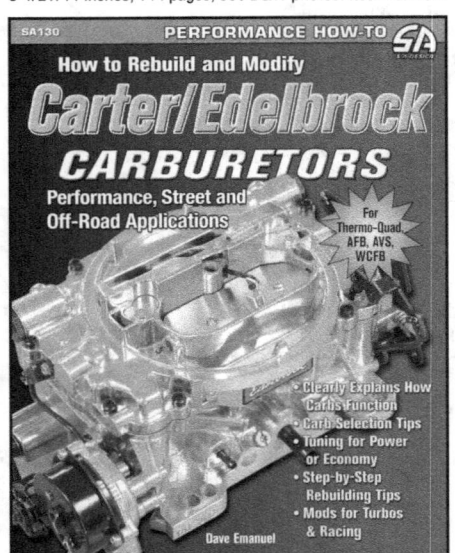

HOW TO BUILD AND MODIFY CARTER/EDELBROCK CARBURETORS There has never before been a book covering the ins and outs of the emerging Edelbrock line of carburetors. This book reflects the emergence of Edelbrock carburetors as the predominant Carter-style carburetors in the market today. It also covers rebuilding, tuning and modifying Carter and Edelbrock carburetors, and features history on Carter as well as the history of the AFB and the AVS since the purchase by Edelbrock. Author David Emanuel outlines carburetor types, gives a thorough look at carb selection and carb function, and offers detailed information on modifications, tuning, and rebuilding Carter/Edelbrock carburetors. Softbound, 8-1/2 x 11 inches, 128 pages, 350 B&W photos. ***Item #SA130P***

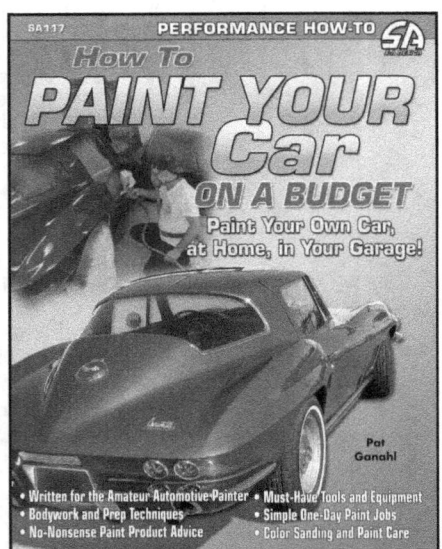

HOW TO PAINT YOUR CAR ON A BUDGET If your car needs new paint, or even just a touch-up, the cost involved in getting a professional job can be more than you bargained for. In this book, author Pat Ganahl unveils dozens of secrets that will help anyone paint their own car. From simple scuff-and-squirt jobs to full-on, door-jambs-and-everything paint jobs, Ganahl covers everything you need to know to get a great-looking coat of paint on your car and save lots of money in the process. Covers painting equipment, the ins and outs of prep, masking, painting and sanding products and techniques, and real-world advice on how to budget wisely when painting your own car. Softbound, 8-1/2 x 11 inches, 128 pages, approx. 400 color photos. ***Item #SA117***

HOW TO BUILD HIGH-PERFORMANCE IGNITION SYSTEMS is the complete guide to understanding automotive ignition systems, from old-school points & condensers to modern distributorless systems. Author Todd Ryden leads you through the various components, systems, & subsystems, explaining the theory behind the operation and how the parts work together to achieve the ultimate goal of efficient combustion. Softbound, 8-1/2 x 11 inches, 128 pages, over 250 B&W photos. ***Item #SA79P***

www.cartechbooks.com or 1-800-551-4754

www.ingramcontent.com/pod-product-compliance
Lightning Source LLC
Chambersburg PA
CBHW051412070526
44584CB00023B/3400